Anglo-Irish Relations
in the Early Troubles

Anglo-Irish Relations in the Early Troubles

1969–1972

Daniel C. Williamson

Bloomsbury Academic
An imprint of Bloomsbury Publishing Plc

B L O O M S B U R Y
LONDON · OXFORD · NEW YORK · NEW DELHI · SYDNEY

Bloomsbury Academic

An imprint of Bloomsbury Publishing Plc

50 Bedford Square	1385 Broadway
London	New York
WC1B 3DP	NY 10018
UK	USA

www.bloomsbury.com

BLOOMSBURY and the Diana logo are trademarks of Bloomsbury Publishing Plc

First published 2017

© Daniel C. Williamson, 2017

British Library Cataloguing-in-Publication Data
A catalogue record for this book is available from the British Library.

ISBN:	HB:	978-1-4742-1696-8
	ePDF:	978-1-4742-1697-5
	ePub:	978-1-4742-1698-2

Library of Congress Cataloging-in-Publication Data
Names: Williamson, Daniel C., 1963- author.
Title: Anglo-Irish relations in the early Troubles : 1969-1972 / Daniel C. Williamson.
Description: London ; New York : Bloomsbury Academic, an imprint of Bloomsbury Publishing Plc, 2017. | Includes bibliographical references and index.
Identifiers: LCCN 2016025238| ISBN 9781474216968 (hardback) | ISBN 9781474216975 (PDF) | ISBN 9781474216982 (ePub)
Subjects: LCSH: Great Britain–Foreign Relations–Ireland. | Ireland–Foreign Relations–Great Britain. | Crisis management in government–Great Britain–History–20th century. | Crisis management in government–Ireland–History–20th century. | Northern Ireland–History–1969-1994. | Northern Ireland–Politics and government–1969-1994. | Social conflict–Northern Ireland–History–20th century. | BISAC: HISTORY / Europe / Great Britain. | HISTORY / Europe / Ireland. | HISTORY / Modern / 20th Century.
Classification: LCC DA47.9.I75 W55 2017 | DDC 941.60824–dc23 LC record available at https://lccn.loc.gov/2016025238

Cover design: Sharon Mah
Cover Image © Hulton-Deutsch Collection/CORBIS

Typeset by Integra Software Services Pvt. Ltd.
Printed and bound in Great Britain

Contents

List of Illustrations

List of Abbreviations and Notes on the Text

CAB	Cabinet Papers (United Kingdom)
CSJ	Campaign for Social Justice
DEA	Department of External Affairs (Ireland)
DFA	Department of Foreign Affairs (Ireland)
DT	Department of the Taoiseach (Ireland)
EEC	European Economic Community
FCO	Foreign and Commonwealth Office (United Kingdom)
HMG	Her Majesty's Government
IRA	Irish Republican Army
MP	Member of Parliament (United Kingdom)
NACP	National Archives at College Park, Maryland (United States)
NAI	National Archives of Ireland
NICRA	Northern Ireland Civil Rights Association
OIRA	Official Irish Republican Army
PIRA	Provisional Irish Republican Army
PREM	Prime Minister's Office (United Kingdom)
PRO	Public Record Office
PRONI	Public Record Office, Northern Ireland
RG	Record Group (United States)
RUC	Royal Ulster Constabulary
SDLP	Social Democratic and Labour Party
TD	Teachta Dála (Member of Dail Eireann)
TNA	The National Archives, Kew (United Kingdom)
UDR	Ulster Defense Regiment
UN	United Nations

Unionist (capitalized)	Refers to a member of the Ulster Unionist Party
unionist (lower case)	Refers to a general supporter of retaining the union between Great Britain and Northern Ireland
US	United States

List of Selected Individuals
Mentioned in the Text

Neil Blaney	Irish Minister for Agriculture, 1966–1970
Kevin Boland	Irish Minster for Local Government, 1966–1970
Ronnie Burroughs	United Kingdom Representative to Northern Ireland, 1970–1971
James Callaghan	British Home Secretary, 1967–1970
Lord Caradon	British Ambassador to the United Nations, 1964–1970
Lord Carrington	British Minister for Defense, 1970–1974
Lord Chalfont	British Minister of State, FCO, 1964–1970
James Chichester-Clark	Prime Minster of Northern Ireland, 1969–1971
Erskine Childers	Irish Tánaiste and Minister for Health, 1969–1973
Liam Cosgrave	Fine Gael Leader in Opposition, 1965–1973
Stewart Crawford	Deputy Under-Secretary of State, FCO, 1970–1973, and Chairman of the Joint Intelligence Committee, 1970–1973
Con Cremin	Irish Ambassador to the United Nations, 1964–1974
Alec Douglas-Home	British Foreign Secretary, 1970–1974
Brian Faulkner	Prime Minister of Northern Ireland, 1971–1972
William Fay	Irish Ambassador to the United States, 1964–1970
Robert Ford	British Commander Land Forces, Northern Ireland, 1971–1973
Ian Freeland	British General Officer Commanding, Northern Ireland, 1969–1971
John Freeman	British Ambassador to the United States, 1969–1971

List of Selected Individuals Mentioned in the Text

Eamonn Gallagher	Official in the Irish Department of External/Foreign Affairs, 1949–1976
Andrew Gilchrist	British Ambassador to Ireland, 1967–1970
Denis Greenhill	Permanent Under-Secretary at FCO, 1969–1973
Charles Haughey	Irish Minister for Finance, 1966–1970
Edward Heath	British Prime Minster, Conservative Party, 1970–1974
Martin Hillenbrand	US Assistant Secretary of State for European Affairs, 1969–1972
Patrick Hillery	Irish Minister for External/Foreign Affairs, 1969–1973
Jack Lynch	Irish Taoiseach, Fianna Fáil Party, 1966–1973
Reginald Maudling	British Home Secretary, 1970–1972
Hugh McCann	Permanent Secretary of the Irish Department of External/Foreign Affairs, 1963–1974
John Molloy	Irish Ambassador to the United Kingdom, 1964–1970
John Moore	US Ambassador to Ireland, 1969–1975
Richard Nixon	US President, 1969–1974
Sean OhEideain	Chargé d'affaires, Irish Embassy, Washington DC
Terence O'Neill	Prime Minster of Northern Ireland, 1963–1969
Donal O'Sullivan	Irish Ambassador to the United Kingdom, 1970–1977
Edward Peck	Permanent Under-Secretary of State, FCO, 1968–1970
John Peck	British Ambassador to Ireland, 1970–1973
William Rogers	US Secretary of State, 1969–1973
Sean Ronan	Irish Assistant Secretary, Department of External/Foreign Affairs, 1964–1972
Kevin Rush	Minister Plenipotentiary at Irish Embassy, London, 1968–1971
Howard Smith	United Kingdom Representative to Northern Ireland, 1971–1972

Michael Stewart	British Foreign Secretary, 1968–1970
Lord Stoneham	British Minister of State, Home Office, 1967–1969
George Thomson	British Chancellor of the Duchy of Lancaster, 1969–1970
Burke Trend	British Cabinet Secretary, 1963–1973
Harry Tuzo	British General Office Commanding, Northern Ireland, 1971–1973
William Warnock	Irish Ambassador to the United States, 1970–1973
Charles Whelan	Charge d'affaires, Irish Embassy, London.
T. Kenneth Whitaker	Irish Secretary of the Department of Finance, 1956–1969, and Governor of the Central Bank of Ireland, 1969–1976
W.K.K. "Kelvin" White	Official in Western European Department, FCO 1969–1971, and Head of the Republic of Ireland Department, FCO, 1971–1974
Harold Wilson	British Prime Minster, Labour Party, 1964–1970, and Leader of Labour Party in Opposition, 1970–1974
Oliver Wright	United Kingdom Representative to Northern Ireland, 1969–1970

Acknowledgments

I am indebted to the professional staff of the National Archives of Ireland, the British National Archives at Kew, the American National Archives at College Park, and Bloomsbury Academic. The University of Hartford and Hillyer College provided me with invaluable grants and course releases in order to facilitate the research and writing of this book.

I would like to express my appreciation to Dr. David Goldenberg, the dean of Hillyer College, and Dr. Anthony Rauche, chair of the Hillyer College Humanities Department, for their support. In addition, I received advice, encouragement, and inspiration from many of my colleagues and friends at the University of Hartford including Professors Robert Churchill, Jonathan Daigle, Mari Firkatian, Richard Koch, William Major, Michael Robinson, and Bryan Sinche. During my numerous research visits to Ireland I was treated with great hospitality by my friends and fellow historians Dr. Michael Kennedy and Dr. Susannah Riordan.

Finally, I would like to thank my wife Cathy and my sons, Conor and Sean, for all the things that they did to help make this book possible.

Introduction: On the Brink of the Troubles

Since the creation of Northern Ireland the Stormont-based provincial government faced repeated threats to its stability and survival. These threats included a number of armed campaigns by the IRA aimed at unifying Ireland, intermittent bouts of sectarian rioting, and the animosity of the Irish State in the South. For more than four decades Stormont survived these threats and maintained the monopoly of power that was enjoyed by the Unionist Party and the privileged position of the Protestant community over the Catholic population. At the beginning of the 1960s this stability seemed secure on the surface, but by the late 1960s Northern Ireland was on the verge of a dramatic breakdown of law and order that would permanently transform the province.

Rejecting the failed violence of the IRA's most recent border campaign, middle-class Catholics in Northern Ireland organized the Campaign for Social Justice (CSJ) in January 1964. The CSJ was inspired by the African-American civil rights movement and focused on equal treatment for the nationalist population of the North. The nonviolent CSJ pointedly ignored the issue of partition and called for an end to specific forms of discrimination against Catholics such as gerrymandering and lack of equality in the allocation of public housing.[1] In January 1967 the Northern Ireland Civil Rights Association (NICRA) was formed to demand equal rights for the Catholic population of the province. It was established by a diverse group of people that included trade union members, radical leftists, moderate supporters of reform, as well as republicans. While the republican movement had been instrumental in giving birth to the NICRA, republicans did not dominate the body and the NICRA, like the CSJ, was dedicated to nonviolent agitation for basic legal equality and made no specific nationalist demands regarding partition. The first major disturbances associated with the civil rights movement occurred in early October 1968 when the Royal Ulster Constabulary (RUC) broke up a banned NICRA march in Derry. Almost 100 people were hospitalized following the violence which had been captured by

Raidió Teilifís Éireann (RTE) cameras. Images of the protestors clashing with the police were shown on television throughout Ireland and the United Kingdom, and the civil rights movement in Northern Ireland became a major international news story and a topic of discussion in the Westminster parliament.[2] As one scholar of the period has noted, the severe rioting showed that the seemingly powerful Stormont government "was in reality desperately unstable and insecure."[3]

Despite efforts by reform-minded Northern Ireland prime minister Terence O'Neill to placate the civil rights movement by meeting some of their demands, the unrest continued. In January 1969 the People's Democracy, a radical left-wing student-led group involved with the civil rights movement, began a protest march from Belfast to Derry. Unionist hardliners, opposed to any accommodation of Catholic demands, repeatedly attacked the marchers. The violence culminated on January 4 in an attack by a unionist mob on the protesters at Burntollet Bridge, near Derry, that resulted in eighty-seven people being hospitalized. The RUC had proven unable, or unwilling, to stop the attacks. Rioting continued in Derry, pitting the RUC against the nationalist community.[4]

The growing unrest in Northern Ireland forced the British government in London to pay much more attention to the province than had traditionally been the case. The parliament in Westminster had, by long tradition, refrained from discussing Northern Ireland unless absolutely necessary. While the Labour Party under Prime Minister Harold Wilson had made some attempts to address issues of civil rights in Northern Ireland, it was not until the rioting in 1968 that London made a serious attempt to force reforms on Stormont. In November 1968 Terence O'Neill met with Wilson in London. Wilson pressed O'Neill on the need to meet many of the demands of the NICRA despite opposition from within the Unionist Party. London hoped that it could remain at arm's-length from the problems in Northern Ireland by simply pushing O'Neill to increase the pace and scope of reforms. Although O'Neill announced a series of reforms later in the month, the situation in Northern Ireland did not calm down. By April 1969 Terence O'Neill was forced to resign as his modest reforms had angered his own party without placating the civil rights movement. He was replaced as Northern Ireland's premier by Major James Chichester-Clark.[5]

In Dublin, the Irish government of Taoiseach Jack Lynch became increasingly concerned about Northern Ireland as the civil rights movement sparked a violent reaction. As the leader of Fianna Fáil, Lynch had inherited his party's traditional condemnation of partition. Rejecting partition had been part of Eamon de Valera's justification for establishing the party. However, Fianna Fáil's anti-partitionism was mainly rhetorical and strictly peaceful in nature and thus rejected the violence of the IRA. Fianna Fáil rejected the legitimacy of partition and the Stormont government but accepted the reality of the existence of Northern Ireland. In general the party's leaders had little understanding of Irish unionists and tended to see Great Britain as the major barrier to reunification.[6] Lynch's predecessor as taoiseach, Sean Lemass, had made some headway in establishing a more practical stance toward Northern Ireland by meeting with Terence O'Neill. Lynch, with the support of the very influential secretary of the Department of Finance, Ken Whitaker, had continued this policy by visiting Belfast in December 1967 and hosting O'Neill in Dublin in January 1968 to discuss cultural exchanges and issues of economic cooperation.[7] However, this period of North–South détente came to an end with the growing violence in Northern Ireland and the resignation of O'Neill.

The Irish government was divided on the proper course of action to take on Northern Ireland and Lynch's position as leader of Fianna Fáil was not secure. Lynch publicly supported the aims of the civil rights movement, and called for an end to partition as the final solution for the problems in the North, but he remained firm in his rejection of the use of violence. However, the taoiseach's moderate stance on Northern Ireland was not universally accepted within the party. Lynch's rivals within the Cabinet included Neil Blaney, the minister for agriculture; Kevin Boland, the minister for local government; and Charles Haughey, the minister for finance. Haughey and Blaney were both interested in replacing Lynch as taoiseach, while all three men were more militant in their views on Northern Ireland and formed the core of internal Fianna Fáil opposition to Lynch.[8]

While challenged by the more militant wing of the party, Lynch was not the only voice of moderation in Dublin. Ken Whitaker, who became the governor of the Central Bank of Ireland in March 1969, advised Lynch behind the scenes to stick to a policy of peaceful support for civil rights reform in the North and to see reunification as a long-term goal that required the consent of the unionist community.[9] Dr. Patrick Hillery, who replaced Frank Aiken as minister for external affairs in July 1969, fully supported Lynch's rejection of violence, but also presented a forceful expression of Irish nationalism in dealing with the emerging crisis in Northern Ireland.[10]

In the years before the crisis began in Northern Ireland, Anglo-Irish relations had been improving. During Sean Lemass's tenure as taoiseach the two nations concluded the Anglo-Irish Free Trade Agreement, and symbolic gestures like the return of Roger Casement's body to Ireland seemed to signal a new era of Anglo-Irish cooperation. Lynch kept up the policy of greater cooperation across the Irish

Sea and in May 1967 the two governments made a joint application to become members of the European Economic Community. Mutually advantageous economic coordination had become the center of Anglo-Irish relations.[11]

However, Northern Ireland increasingly became a focus of Anglo-Irish relations once the civil rights movement sparked violence in the province. Following the first serious rioting in Northern Ireland in early October 1968 Jack Lynch met with Harold Wilson in London. While the meeting on October 30 was officially about economic issues, the two leaders also discussed the situation in the North. Lynch spoke to the press after the meeting, and despite a promise to Wilson to keep the Northern Ireland elements of their discussion in confidence, announced that the prime minister had agreed with his own assessment that partition was the root cause of the problems in the North. This breach of confidentiality obviously upset Wilson who had no choice but to publicly back the Stormont government.[12] Relations between Dublin and Belfast also suffered as O'Neill accused Lynch of rejecting cooperation and returning to the old Fianna Fáil policy of simply condemning Stormont.[13] Further discussions between the Irish and British governments over the next months proved fruitless. When Patrick Hillery met with his British counterpart Michael Stewart on August 1, 1969, he was informed that, as far as London was concerned, Northern Ireland was a strictly internal affair of the United Kingdom and was of no concern to the Irish government.[14] As the unrest sparked by the civil rights movement in Northern Ireland became the more deadly and sustained violence known as the Troubles, Anglo-Irish relations were increasingly tied up with the search for a peaceful solution to the conflict in Northern Ireland.

The purpose of this book is not to provide a general history of the early years of the Troubles but rather to present a detailed analysis of Anglo-Irish relations during the period from the deployment of British troops as peacekeepers in August 1969 until the suspension of Stormont in March 1972. To a lesser extent the trilateral relationship between London, Dublin, and Belfast, as well as the involvement of the US government in the Troubles will also be explored. The period from the summer of 1969 to early 1972 is of particular importance because the general shape that the Troubles would retain until the beginning of the peace process in the 1990s was forged during these years. Some of the major developments that took place during this period that were instrumental in giving shape to the Troubles include the formation of the Provisional Irish Republican Army, the foundation of the Social Democratic and Labour Party, growing divisions in the Unionist Party, an ever increasing role for the British government in Northern Ireland, and the eventual dissolution of the Stormont government.

Figure I.1 British prime minister Harold Wilson and Irish taoiseach Jack Lynch in London. Credit: Popperfoto.

In addition to the establishment of the general pattern of the Troubles, this same period saw the emergence of new levels of Anglo-Irish diplomatic engagement regarding Northern Ireland. Like the wider conflict, Anglo-Irish relations evolved during these years into a recognizable pattern that would persist for decades. The major goal of this work is to examine the development and nature of that relationship. This book attempts to provide insight into the changing pattern of Anglo-Irish relations during the first years of the Troubles and to answer questions about how the conflict in Northern Ireland, as well as other domestic and international political forces, shaped that relationship. Of course, the impact that Anglo-Irish relations had on shaping the Troubles is also examined. As the Irish government sought to internationalize the conflict in Northern Ireland by involving the United Nations (UN) and foreign countries, particularly the United States, these events are also studied in this work.

This book builds on the excellent existing scholarship regarding the Troubles in general and the diplomatic aspects of the conflict in particular, but relies mainly on archival research to provide a fresh outlook on the topic. The national archives of the Irish, British, and US governments as well as online sources constitute the majority of the research for this study. A close examination of the archival sources allows this work to study the evolution of Irish and British policy over this critical period. In addition, the documents in the archives reveal the day-to-day concerns of the government official involved and highlight confidential internal debates over policy that reveal the alternative paths that could have been followed by Dublin and London.

1

The Crisis of August and Confrontation at the UN: August–September 1969

The traditional loyalist Apprentice Boys parade in Derry on August 12, 1969, proved to be the event that pushed Northern Ireland over the edge into a full-blown crisis. The parade itself passed peacefully but as the RUC, accompanied by a crowd of unionists, attempted to confine a nationalist crowd into the Catholic Bogside section of the city, a major street fight, dubbed the Battle of the Bogside, erupted. Nationalists set up barricades and the RUC responded with tear gas. As news of the fighting in Derry spread, nationalists in other parts of Northern Ireland began rioting. In Belfast many Catholic homes were destroyed by loyalist mobs. The growing unrest rapidly stretched the resources of the RUC to the breaking point. Despite the mobilization of the B-Special Reserve Constables the RUC could not contain the violence. On August 14, Northern Ireland Prime Minister Chichester-Clark requested that the British Army be deployed to maintain law and order. The deployment of British troops in Derry and Belfast meant that the prelude was over and that the Northern Ireland Troubles had begun in earnest.[1]

The first weeks of the Troubles were an important period in the development of Anglo-Irish relations regarding Northern Ireland as the simmering unrest caused by the civil rights movement gave way to a widespread breakdown in law and order and more sustained and deadly violence. Both Dublin and London were forced to deal with the new reality of increasing British involvement in the province. The fighting in Derry and the deployment of British troops engendered a public dispute between the Irish and British governments and pushed Lynch's government to appeal to the United Nations to intervene in Northern Ireland. The lack of agreement within Lynch's Cabinet, which was an important factor in shaping Ireland's response to the outbreak of the Troubles, became very clear during the crisis of August 1969. The major concern for both Wilson and Lynch during this period was to avoid a complete break in Anglo-Irish relations.

Figure 1.1 Battle of Bogside, August 1969. Credit: Peter Ferraz.

Dublin's response

Despite having warned Britain that the Apprentice Boys parade might trigger violence, the Irish government was caught off guard by the Battle of the Bogside. The Cabinet members were dispersed on holiday with the taoiseach in Cork and Minister for External Affairs Patrick Hillery in Mayo. Lynch arranged for an initial emergency meeting of the government on August 13, although Hillery was still absent, with additional meetings taking place over the next few days. The divisions within Lynch's Cabinet over Northern Ireland were brought to the surface during these deliberations. Neil Blaney, Kevin Boland, and Charles Haughey called for a tough response. Lynch, who lacked the direct connection to the period of the Irish Revolution that both de Valera and Lemass had possessed, was suspect in the eyes of the more republican leaning elements of the party. During the initial meeting this hardline group argued in favor of an Irish military incursion into the North to create an international incident that would hopefully lead to a United Nations intervention. Lynch rejected military action and he was supported by the tánaiste, Erskine Childers, Minister for Defense Jim Gibbons, Minister for Education Pádraig Faulkner, and Minister for Industry and Commerce George Colley. Feelings ran so high that Kevin

Boland briefly resigned from the government before the unusual intervention of President de Valera, who talked Boland into remaining in the Cabinet. The more republican leaning faction was placated by an unofficial promise by Lynch that if law and order totally collapsed in Northern Ireland, the ill-equipped Irish Army would cross the border to protect the Catholic population and spark UN involvement. The Cabinet agreed that in lieu of military intervention the army would be ordered to set up four field hospitals on the border to treat those injured in the violence. The Irish government also agreed on diplomatic actions that would include an official request to London that the British apply for a UN peacekeeping force for Northern Ireland.[2]

On August 13 Jack Lynch addressed the nation in an aggressive speech that reflected the feelings of the more militant elements of the Cabinet. The belligerent tone helped to mask the fact that no forceful military or economic action would be taken by the Irish government. Despite the bluster of the speech, Lynch announced a series of mainly diplomatic moves that, while confrontational, were designed to avoid violence. After reviewing for his audience the attempts that Dublin had made to warn London of the serious nature of the events in Northern Ireland over the last months Lynch said that in the wake of the outbreak of violence "the situation cannot be allowed to continue" as Stormont and the RUC had clearly lost control in the North. Placing the blame on Unionists, Lynch described the violence as "the inevitable outcome of the policies pursued for decades by successive Stormont Governments." The taoiseach added an even more traditionally nationalist analysis of the Northern crisis by declaring "that the reunification of the national territory can provide the only permanent solution to the problem." This nationalist rhetoric, which surrounded Lynch's statement "that the Irish Government can no longer stand by and see innocent people injured and perhaps worse," made his words sound bellicose but the essential moderation of the government's stance was more clearly represented by Lynch's list of actions that Dublin planned to take, including seeking UN peacekeepers, calling on London to end police violence against civilians, setting up the army field hospitals, and entering into negotiations with the British over the future status of Northern Ireland.[3]

While diplomatic action was highlighted by Lynch's speech it was a domestic address and clearly aimed at the Irish public more than the British government. The US ambassador to Ireland, John Moore, saw the speech as being "politically imperative" given the pressure on Lynch to take a strong stance on Northern Ireland from the members of his own party as well as the other parties and the public at large.[4] The interplay between domestic political concerns and diplomatic action became a hallmark of Ireland's response to the early years of the Troubles.

Lynch's speech has received a good deal of attention from historians. Michael Kennedy has characterized the speech as threatening in its tone and Stephen Kelly's book on Fianna Fáil and partition points out that both Stormont and London saw Lynch's address as adding fuel to the fire. However, other scholars, such as Dermot Keogh and John Walsh, agree that the August 13 speech was a compromise statement that used nationalist language while avoiding any support for violence. Anthony Craig has even suggested that Lynch's address was in fact a veiled call for British intervention in Northern Ireland. Indeed, a British takeover of security in the North might have been inevitable if, as Lynch claimed, Stormont had really lost its legitimacy, and Dublin could offer no alternative except the highly unlikely prospect of a UN intervention.[5] The threatening language of the speech was no accident as Lynch had just faced a near revolt by the more republican leaning section of his Cabinet and needed to placate them without giving into their more extreme demands for military action. Craig's suggestion that Lynch was sending a subtle hint to London that it would need to intervene in Northern Ireland is possible but the taoiseach would certainly not have seen British security involvement as anything but a stopgap solution prior to a permanent new settlement for Northern Ireland that would directly involve the Irish government. While mollifying nationalist sentiment in the Cabinet and the Irish public, the speech put diplomacy front and center in Dublin's reaction to the crisis.

Initial Irish approach to London

The first Irish diplomatic steps were taken even before Lynch spoke publicly on August 13. Kevin Rush, minister plenipotentiary at the Irish Embassy in Dublin, received a call from Hugh McCann, secretary of the Department of External Affairs, who gave Rush instructions from the ongoing emergency Cabinet meeting at 3:30 in the afternoon on August 13. Rush was instructed to deliver a demarche from the Irish government demanding "the immediate cessation of police attacks on the people of Derry." As British foreign secretary Michael Stewart was unavailable, Rush met a few hours later with Minster of State Lord Chalfont. The fluid nature of the situation was highlighted by the fact that Rush received further instruction by telephone after he had arrived at the Foreign and Commonwealth Office (FCO). Dublin instructed the minister plenipotentiary to ask the British to apply to the UN for the dispatch of a peacekeeping force to Northern Ireland as soon as possible and inform them that the Irish were approaching the UN Secretary General to lay the groundwork for the peacekeeping request. Chalfont politely received both the written and oral messages from Rush but pointed out that as Northern Ireland was part of the United Kingdom it was inappropriate for the UN to be involved. Chalfont rejected the Irish characterization that the RUC was "attacking the people of Derry" but promised to pass the message to the Home Office. Informally Chalfont confided to Rush that he hoped the situation in Northern Ireland would improve rapidly as it was looking "very serious at the moment."[6]

The deployment of British troops in Northern Ireland and the response of the Irish government had indeed made the crisis serious. Lynch characterized the use of the British Army as "not acceptable," but also hastened to assure the public that the deployment of Irish Army troops to the border region was solely for the purposes of supporting the establishment of field hospitals to care for those wounded in the fighting in the North.[7] Lynch's words did not reassure everyone that the Irish Army's moves would not make the situation more dangerous. British ambassador to Ireland, Sir Andrew Gilchrist, believed that while Lynch was being truthful, the extensive publicity around the Irish deployment amounted to "monkey business" that was designed to arouse Irish public opinion on the North, deter the British from using troops to maintain law and order, and help any Irish appeal to the United Nations. The ambassador noted in a number of dispatches to the FCO on August 14, 1969, that events in the North were radicalizing the Irish public and the Irish government. Gilchrist reported that "Several Irishmen, generally when in their cups or otherwise excited," had told him that they believed that the IRA should seize a Catholic border town and try to hold it against the British Army in order to spark an international incident that would justify UN intervention. While he dismissed this scenario as unlikely, Gilchrist did warn that Lynch had apparently aligned himself with the hardline nationalist camp in his own party. This development had set the taoiseach on "a slippery slope" that would make it more likely that London, not Stormont, would receive the brunt of Irish public anger and that violent republicanism would be emboldened. Gilchrist suggested that any British official working on Irish affairs should remember a thirty-year-old quote from the *Irish Times* that "The Irish are a dangerously emotional people. They are liable to condone any crime, however horrible, if it can be connected directly or even remotely with a political motive." The ambassador concluded that "All in all, we are in for a fairly difficult time with the Irish. . . . If I were a fire insurance company I would not like to have the British Embassy on my books. (Fortunately, though highly flammable, it isn't ours)."[8]

Hillery visits London

On August 15, 1969, Patrick Hillery, accompanied by the Secretary of the Department of External Affairs Hugh McCann, traveled to London to meet with the British. The Irish were received at the FCO by Lord Chalfont, and Lord Stoneham, minister of state at the Home Office. Chalfont opened the discussion by repeating his earlier rejections of the Irish claim that the RUC was engaged in an attack on the population of Derry or the idea that an international peacekeeping force was an appropriate response to the unrest within the United Kingdom. Hillery countered that events in Northern Ireland could not be considered by London as totally domestic given that Ireland was a single island regardless of partition. As to policing in the North, Hillery described the RUC as "at their best not an impartial force" while the B-Specials were "a partisan armed mob, such as is found only in dictatorships." He argued that the need for an impartial international peacekeeping force was obvious given these facts. Hillery followed up this condemnation of the RUC by calling for talks to be convened between Dublin and London over the constitutional position of Northern Ireland.

Ignoring the wider constitutional point Chalfont refocused on the temporary need for British troops to restore law and order. Stoneham added that many nationalists in Derry were, in fact, happy to see the soldiers deployed. Hillery dismissed the welcoming of the troops as a sign that "people ... were frightened of the police," and predicted that the presence of the army would only "provide extremists from both sides with pretexts for intervention."

The discussion continued to heat up as Chalfont called the setting up of Irish military hospitals needlessly provocative and formally protested a mob attack on the British Embassy in Dublin. Hillery retorted that the stones thrown at the embassy could not be compared to the situation in the North where people were "being shot and terrorized." Hillery then declared that "Northern Ireland is part of Ireland. Our people do not accept that it is part of the UK.... It is Ireland, our island," before returning to the less controversial issue of the need to end the violence.

Lord Stoneham admitted that people were being terrorized by the violence in the North but suggested that the Irish military was exacerbating the situation by giving the appearance that Dublin was contemplating providing military aid to Northern nationalists. The British troops would only stay as long as needed for Stormont to make reforms that would calm the situation. Stoneham and Chalfont agreed that Dublin also needed to be more worried about the possibility of IRA intervention and controlling extremists on their side of the border. Chalfont urged that Dublin needed to be a force for "moderation" not a "reflection of irrational feelings" in order to promote peace in the North and good Anglo-Irish relations.

The two sides disagreed about the wisdom of Anglo-Irish talks about the future of Northern Ireland. The British position was that normal diplomatic channels could handle any concerns that Dublin had regarding the North. Stoneham warned that an Irish obsession with partition would not help the problem. Hillery argued that partition was at the heart of the problem and placed the blame at the feet of the British government which had, in his opinion, "so arranged it that a minority of the people of all Ireland was converted into a local majority (in the Six Counties) which has, ever since, oppressed the local minority."

Chalfont attempted to move the conversation back from a rehash of partition to the safety of the British Embassy in Dublin. Hillery and McCann assured him that the Irish government was doing everything it could to protect the embassy, and then pressed again for an international peacekeeping force. When Chalfont again pointed out that a UN force was inappropriate for an internal UK problem Hillery questioned whether or not the British government "really regarded the Six-Counties as part of the UK." When Chalfont assured the Irish that London did indeed consider Northern Ireland "an integral part of the UK," Hillery and McCann argued that the discrimination faced by Catholics in the province was not at all the norm for the rest of the United Kingdom. Chalfont and Stoneham refused to engage in this particular discussion and asked that the conversation return to the immediate points at hand. However, refocusing the topic did not make Hillery any less antagonistic. The minister for external affairs made the dubious claim that Dublin had assumed that London would agree to a joint Anglo-Irish peacekeeping force for the North and threatened to go to the United Nations since the British refused, a move Chalfont indicated he hoped could be avoided.

Putting the peacekeeping issue aside Hillery presented his major point; "I honestly believe that there is a real danger of a total blowup which would involve us as well," he said. "This could be prevented by cooperation. Abolish the B-Specials. Enter into talks with the Irish Government." Chalfont's reply underlined the major divide between the two countries at this point. While Chalfont stating that "normal diplomatic consultations" would be beneficial, London "could not undertake to consult the Irish Government on how to solve a problem which is essentially a problem for the UK." Britain would not agree to any of the Irish requests regarding peacekeepers, the disbanding of the B-Specials, or further discussions on the future of Northern Ireland. Chalfont made it clear that, in his words, "It would be entirely improper of me to agree with a representative of a foreign Government to take action in our domestic sphere...we cannot be seen to be in negotiation with the Government of Ireland about [Northern Ireland]."[9]

The meeting in London only succeeded in exposing the vast gap between the Irish and British governments. While London wanted to retain good relations with Dublin they were not willing to acknowledge any Irish right to consultation on Northern Ireland. Mirroring the public stance of Lynch's government, Hillery showed no moderation in his rhetoric about Irish claims to sovereignty over the whole island. It was not an auspicious start to relations between the two countries regarding the emerging Troubles.

The Downing Street Declaration

Harold Wilson's government outlined its plan for restoring peace to Northern Ireland on August 19, 1969, following a meeting between Wilson and Northern Ireland premier James Chichester-Clark. The two leaders jointly issued the Downing Street Declaration of principles and goals for dealing with the crisis. The document reaffirmed the Ireland Act, 1949, which pledged London to keep Northern Ireland in the United Kingdom as long as the majority of the population of the province supported the union. London also promised to "take full responsibility for asserting this principle in all international relations." The deployment of British troops was justified by "a breakdown of law and order" and described as "temporary." The declaration asserted that London and Stormont would work together to implement reforms that would guarantee "full equality of treatment" between the nationalist and unionist communities while praising existing reform programs for local franchise rules, public housing allotments, and efforts to make the Northern Ireland government more responsive to nationalist concerns. London and Stormont pledged to continue with the reform program guided by the aim of assuring in Northern Ireland "the same equality of treatment and freedom from

Figure 1.2 Northern Ireland prime minister James Chichester-Clark at 10 Downing Street, August 1969. Credit: Douglas Miller.

discrimination as obtains in the rest of the United Kingdom, irrespective of political views or religion." The two governments hoped to restore "normality" to the North and promote economic development to insure long-term stability in the province.[10]

Ireland and Britain approach the United States

Irish diplomats were active in Washington DC as well as in London. On August 15, 1969, Sean OhEideain, the charge d'affaires at the Irish Embassy met with Acting Secretary of State Alexis Johnson and Mortimer Goldstein who covered Britain and Ireland for the State Department. OhEideain presented a formal note from the Irish government and summarized its contents for the Americans, claiming that Stormont had lost control over Northern Ireland and that British troops were not the solution to this problem. He asked for American support for a UN or joint Anglo-Irish peacekeeping force and for the initiation of talks between the British and Irish over the future of the North that Dublin hoped would lead to reunification. While Johnson had to ask what Stormont was, OhEideain was not surprised and he found Goldstein to be well informed about the topic. Johnson dismissed the need for international peacekeepers as British troops were now in place. From the American perspective Northern Ireland was a part of the United Kingdom and any concerns Ireland had about the province should be handled in a bilateral manner with London. The charge d'affaires explained that Dublin hoped that the United States, as a country friendly to both the Irish and British governments, would use its good offices to push London to accept the Irish proposals to move forward to a long-term solution to the problem of Northern Ireland. Johnson wryly pointed out that Ireland and Britain also had friendly relations with each other and should be able to work out their own problems. OhEideain pointed out that Dublin did not accept the validity of the partition of Ireland and that the outbreak of violence in the North was a threat to international peace. Johnson then raised concerns about the mobilization of Irish Army reserves but OhEideain assured him that they were no threat and that the reservists were only called up to meet the proposed peacekeeping needs. Johnson said the Irish note would be studied by the US government but he closed the meeting by warning that an Irish appeal to the UN might give "an opportunity for some people ... 'to fish in troubled waters.'"[11]

The formal American reply to the Irish note closely followed Johnson's informal response. While Washington expressed deep concern over the "human suffering" in Northern Ireland, it found "no appropriate basis to intervene" in the domestic affairs of the United Kingdom. The State Department advised the Irish government to address Northern Ireland directly with London.[12] Sean OhEideain received the note at a meeting with Deputy Assistant Secretary for European Affairs George Springsteen and Mortimer Goldstein on August 26. OhEideain expressed the hope that the United States would reconsider its response as the situation evolved in Northern Ireland. The Americans acknowledged that Catholics in the North suffered from discrimination that should be addressed but noted that the violence seemed to have calmed down making the situation less of a crisis. OhEideain pressed the Irish case that only reunification would provide a permanent solution to conflict in Northern Ireland. Goldstein asked how soon the Irish believed that reunification could be accomplished given the British guarantee that only Stormont could change the constitutional status of Northern Ireland. The charge d'affaires pointed out that the British Empire had shrunk significantly over the past three decades and "many things that seemed impossible then were late found quite feasible and acceptable by the British and others." In his report to Assistant Secretary

Sean Ronan at the Department of External Affairs, OhEideain advised that the Irish government should continue to focus on lobbying the executive branch of the US government, rather that Congress, as only the White House and State Department would be able to provide the immediate assistance that Dublin needed at the United Nations. He expressed hope that the executive would be open to reconsider its attitude but warned that "there is something like a traditional State Department assumption that Ireland by geography and history belongs within the British sphere of influence, and that unspoken assumption will take a lot of changing."[13]

As Dublin lobbied Washington for support for Ireland's position on the North the British government sought to keep the United States informed about its own plans for Northern Ireland. Home Office officials met with representatives of the American Embassy in London on August 21, 1969, to outline the challenges facing London as well as the proposed British solutions. The British characterized the problem in Northern Ireland as a clash of a small number of extremists who could be separated from the majority of the population through the implementation of the reforms laid out in the Downing Street Declaration. In this private setting the British acknowledged that the B-Specials might well have to be abolished and the entire RUC reorganized. While the Home Office admitted to the Americans that Wilson's government was not at all happy about the level of involvement that London now faced in Northern Ireland, they also promised that they were committed to maintaining law and order until Stormont could be reformed. The possibility of discussions with Dublin on Irish reunification was dismissed by the British who were determined to reestablish a functioning government for the North. The American Embassy staff was positively impressed by the British presentation and advised the State Department that London had a "well-designed" plan that had a good chance of cross-community support if it was not derailed by extremists.[14]

British concerns over the IRA

In Dublin, British Ambassador Sir Andrew Gilchrist remained very concerned about the level of anti-British feelings in the Irish capital. On August 16 Gilchrist reassured the FCO that the Irish Army's movements toward the border and the call up of reserves were not a prelude to any military intervention in Northern Ireland, but he warned that "the political and propaganda intention behind the moves … must cause concern. There was never any belief in any responsible Government quarter that an Anglo-Irish peacekeeping force would take shape and yet the call up [of reserves] took place on that pretext."[15] The ambassador expressed concern that Lynch's government was feeding into extremist nationalist sentiment in the Irish republic. He reported on a large public meeting at the General Post Office on the night of August 16 that issued a call for the Irish Army to enter the North to protect the nationalist community. A smaller section of this crowd marched on the British Embassy smashing windows and overturning cars on route before being disbursed by the Garda. Gilchrist claimed that this demonstration, as well as others in Ireland, was organized by what he termed "the alternative Government of Ireland, the Sinn Fein/IRA complex, IRA for short."[16]

The IRA became an issue in Anglo-Irish relations very early in the Troubles. On August 18 IRA Chief of Staff Cathal Goulding issued a fanciful statement claiming armed and trained IRA units were being dispatched to the North. While in reality the IRA had few members and fewer weapons in the summer of 1969, Goulding's announcement caused concern for both the Irish and British governments. Jack Lynch felt compelled to respond with his own public announcement condemning the IRA. Hugh McCann met with Ambassador Gilchrist to share intelligence on the IRA and call attention to Lynch's statement. Gilchrist expressed appreciation for the cooperation of Dublin but stressed that the British government was concerned about the possibility of IRA infiltration across the border and the large amount of publicity the IRA received from the Irish press. McCann assured the ambassador that the Irish government was doing everything legally possible to curb the IRA.[17]

While his exchange with McCann was polite, Gilchrist had his doubts about the relationship between Lynch's government and the IRA. He told the FCO that the Irish government "had chosen to establish themselves in a menacing position on our flank" rather than really support British efforts in Northern Ireland. The ambassador believed that Dublin sincerely wanted a avoid a cross-border IRA campaign and had moved to stop one from developing, but he also believed that Lynch hoped to use the threat of the IRA, as well as the civil rights groups in Northern Ireland, to put pressure on London. Gilchrist suggested that London consider the use of trade relations and tourism to exert counterpressure on Dublin.[18]

In fact the Irish government did not fully support the British response to the crisis in Northern Ireland even after the Downing Street Declaration. Lynch's government issued a public statement on August 22 mirroring what had been said in private to British and American officials. The Irish claimed that Stormont was a tool of loyalist extremists and had lost the ability to effectively run Northern Ireland. The B-Specials were condemned as sectarian thugs who had abetted the recent violence against Northern Catholics. Dublin's statement made it clear that the responsibility for ending the crisis lay with the British government as the de facto rulers of the province.[19]

Ireland goes to the UN

In addition to meetings with British and American officials the Irish government had made the decision to formally approach the UN regarding the breakdown of order in Northern Ireland. Since Ireland joined the UN it had avoided raising the issue of Northern Ireland as likely to be counterproductive to the goal of reunification. After the crisis of August 1969 began the Irish government revisited the question. A memorandum prepared for Lynch's government suggested that conditions in the North now warranted UN involvement on issues of human rights and as a threat to international peace instead of reunification. The memorandum advised that the General Assembly was a better venue than the Security Council, as the British had a veto in the latter body, but concluded that even a failed approach to the Security Council would help to raise public awareness concerning Northern Ireland.[20]

On August 17, 1969, Con Cremin, Irish Permanent Representative to the UN, wrote to Jaime de Pinies, the Spanish president of the Security Council, to request a meeting of that body concerning an Irish request for peacekeepers for Northern Ireland. Cremin cited both the violence in the North as well as the possibility that the violence might move across the border as reasons for Ireland's request and noted that Britain had refused an earlier Irish suggestion for London to call for UN peacekeepers or participation in a joint Anglo-Irish peacekeeping mission for the North.[21] London did not want the UN involved in Northern Ireland and Lord Hugh Caradon, the British UN representative, launched a lobbying campaign with Security Council member states to counter the Irish efforts. While the British argued that Northern Ireland was a strictly domestic affair that should not be considered at the UN, the Irish position was improved by the fact that the Security Council had traditionally met to at least consider a request from any member state to include an item on its agenda. In order for the Irish request to be formally considered by the Security Council nine of the fifteen member states had to vote to allow for the item to be placed on the agenda.[22] The British were concerned that even if the Irish item did not receive the necessary votes needed to be placed on the agenda, Patrick Hillery might be allowed to address the Security Council to argue in favor of inscription.[23]

Lord Caradon spoke to Hillery and Cremin after encountering the Irish diplomats in the UN building on August 18 and attempted to dissuade them from pursuing their item with the Security Council. Caradon argued that since the Irish were not going to get the votes that they needed for inscription, let alone succeed in having a UN peacekeeping force dispatched to Northern Ireland against the wishes of London, they could avoid embarrassment by withdrawing the request. Hillery replied that he was committed to do everything that he could in order to get Ireland's case heard at the UN including taking the unusual step of speaking in favor of inscribing the Irish request at the Security Council if need be.[24] Foreign Secretary Michael Stewart informed Caradon that while he preferred that Hillery not be allowed to break the precedent that petitioning states were not allowed to speak to the Council regarding the adoption of items on the agenda, it would be better for Britain not to make any move to "muzzle him" as this might actually swing some votes in favor of formal adoption. Additionally, Stewart believed that conceding to the Irish the right to address the Council would give Dublin a moral victory that would bolster moderation in Lynch's government while still allowing the British to publicly claim that the Irish case for UN intervention had been rejected on its merits.[25]

The United States and the UN

Both the British and Irish governments sought the cooperation of the United States at the Security Council. On the evening of August 17 Hillery and Cremin called on Charles Yost, the American permanent representative to the UN to outline Ireland's case for UN intervention. Despite Hillery's claim that the RUC and British Army were not impartial forces, Yost expressed doubt that the UN could do anything meaningful, as a peacekeeping force for Northern Ireland would require the permission of London.[26] In Dublin, Hugh McCann spoke to Ambassador John Moore in an attempt to influence Washington's position. Ambassador Moore, who was sympathetic to the Irish case, agreed to call Secretary of State William Rogers to make the Irish case. Moore made a special trip to London to make the phone call in order to talk on a secure line as he feared that communications from Dublin were being "tapped" by the British.

While Moore was unable to get the secretary of state to support inscription in the Security Council he reported to McCann that Rogers would be willing to meet with Hillery.[27]

The British proved more successful in their lobbying effort with the Americans. On August 17 British Ambassador John Freeman called on the State Department to make London's request for American support. Freeman requested that the United States either vote against inscription of the Irish item on the Security Council agenda or at least abstain on the question. The ambassador requested that the Americans advise the Irish government to abandon its confrontational stance on Northern Ireland to allow time for reform to work in restoring calm in the province. Assistant Secretary of State Samuel De Palma confirmed that the United States agreed with the basic elements of the British position, and would state so in the Security Council, but that it was traditionally American policy to allow a member state to inscribe items on the Council's agenda and that he saw no reason to change that policy in this case.[28]

Unwilling to accept this ambivalent American stance, Foreign Secretary Michael Stewart wrote directly to Secretary of State William Rogers to offer his personal plea for American abstention on the vote. Stewart stressed that London considered Northern Ireland to be a strictly domestic issue and warned against the danger of setting a prescient for UN intervention in the internal affairs of member states. Even a public debate on Northern Ireland, Stewart wrote, "would be most dangerous" and make the task of restoring order "more difficult" as it would increase acrimony in an already volatile situation. Stewart closed by pointing out that the United States had abstained on inscription in the past, including an agenda item regarding Cuba in 1962 when Britain "took the lead at your request in opposing inscription."[29] Stewart's argument proved effective, for on August 18 Rogers informed the American mission to the UN that the United States would abstain on the inscription vote as Northern Ireland was a clearly domestic British concern that could be settled by London. Yost was instructed to inform the Irish about the decision before the Security Council meeting.[30]

At the Security Council

After meeting with the various members of the Security Council seeking their support Ambassador Cremin believed that there was little chance of the Irish winning an inscription vote. A compromise arose from an unlikely source on August 18 when Finnish ambassador Max Jakobson suggested to Cremin that the Council should hear from both the British and Irish representatives and then adjourn without a vote, thus avoiding a certain Irish defeat on inscription while still allowing Patrick Hillery to have a public forum. France advised the Irish to accept the Finnish plan.[31] When the US delegation reported the Finnish proposal to Washington, Secretary of State Rogers approved American participation in this plan.[32]

The Security Council met on August 20, 1969, to formally address the Irish request for inscription on the agenda. Lord Caradon immediately objected to the adoption of the Irish request. Caradon stated that his primary objection was based on the fact that Northern Ireland was a part of the United Kingdom and that the UN should have no role in a purely domestic matter. He went on to make a number of other points to the Council, including stressing the democratic nature of the government in all of the UK, the fact that the British Army now had the violence under control, and his belief that a public debate would only serve to "inflame feelings and reopen old wounds" and undercut ongoing efforts, supported by Dublin, to restore normalcy to Northern Ireland. Following Caradon's objection, Ambassador Jakobson put his plan into motion and suggested that as a matter of courtesy the Council hear from Dr. Hillery. Caradon agreed and the Irish minister for external affairs was invited to speak.

Hillery began by rejecting the idea that the "Six Counties" were an undisputed part of the United Kingdom. "The claim of the Irish nation to control the totality of Ireland has been asserted over centuries by successive generations of Irish men and women" he said, "and it is one which no spokesman for the Irish nation could ever renounce." Even if the UN considered Northern Ireland to be a part of the United Kingdom, Hillery pointed to the precedent of UN discussion of apartheid in South Africa and Britain's own request in 1964 that the UN look into tensions in Cyprus between the Greek and Turkish communities as examples of UN involvement in the internal affairs of sovereign states. Dr. Hillery disputed the British claims that the situation in Northern Ireland was now under control. He cast doubt on British competency in security matters by pointing out that London had ignored Irish warnings about the dangers of allowing the Apprentice Boys parade on August 12 to take place. According to Hillery, the events following that parade had begun the descent into violence and necessitated the deployment of British troops, which the Irish government rejected as a solution. London's refusal to approach the UN for an alternative force, or create a joint Anglo-Irish force, compelled the Irish to request a UN peacekeeping force from the Security Council.

In order to justify this request the Irish minister for external affairs stated that he "must explain that the breakdown of law and order and the plight of the minority in ... the Six Counties have their origins in the partition of Ireland, an act of fundamental injustice." He pointed to Dublin's continual and peaceful rejection of partition since it began. Turning to more recent history, Hillery outlined the discrimination faced by nationalists in the North and the growth of the Catholic civil rights movement as proof of this discrimination. The fact that Stormont had to turn to the British Army demonstrated, according to Hillery, that the government in the North had lost control. From Dublin's point of view British peacekeepers were a poor solution because they represented the continuation of partition while reunification was the only long-term solution to the problems in the North. Hillery closed by pointing out that UN intervention was justified under Article 56 of the United Nations Charter which made the denial of human rights an international rather than domestic issue and that as recently as October 1968 Britain had acknowledged this fact in the General Assembly.

Lord Caradon began his reply by characterizing Hillery's speech as "careful and restrained." While Caradon declined to enter into a debate over the validity of the Irish argument that the UN did have a right to intervene in Northern Ireland he stated that he would respond to certain points made by Hillery, being careful not to further inflame "the intense feelings ... suspicion ... fear and hatred which are at the core of the human problem" in the North. On the issue of sovereignty over Northern Ireland, Caradon pointed out that the Irish government has long accepted the de facto partition of the island. He argued that, contrary to Hillery's claim, the British Army was the best peacekeeping force available. The British ambassador then quoted from the Downing Street Declaration to prove that the United Kingdom was determined "to protect the human rights of all of its citizens" through a program of reform in Northern Ireland. He closed by giving his support to the Finnish plan to adjourn without a vote despite London's preference for a formal vote of inscription. The Security Council then gave unanimous consent to the Zambian ambassador's motion for adjournment without a decision.[33]

The outcome of the UN approach

Ambassador Cremin told Dublin that the outcome of the Security Council meeting "was the 'least bad' which we could have expected, and the general reaction to the Minister's speech was very favourable." Cremin credited Lord Caradon for resisting pressure from London to bring the matter to a vote on inscription (which Cremin believed the Irish were sure to lose) and to stop

Hillery from speaking at all.[34] Patrick Hillery told a press conference on August 22 that the outcome of the Security Council meeting had exceeded the expectation of the Irish government and that while the effort to get a peacekeeping force was over, the issue of human rights in Northern Ireland would be raised again at the United Nations.[35] The official statement issued by the Irish government was less restrained than Cremin's, or even Hillery's, assessment and much more combative. Dublin publicly claimed that "The success of the Irish Mission to the United Nations … in bringing the facts of the present situation in the Six-County area to the attention of the Security Council, is a most satisfactory and welcome development. The facts are now better known than ever before … to the world at large." Despite this claim of victory, the same statement went on to sharply criticize the British government for failing to accept a UN peacekeeping force, moving too slowly on needed reform in the North, and for claiming that Northern Ireland was a strictly domestic issue for the United Kingdom. The statement closed with a denunciation of "Britain's right to exercise jurisdiction over any part of Irish territory."[36]

The outcome of the Security Council meeting pleased the British FCO as much as it had the Irish. In a meeting with officials from the American Embassy in London, Deputy Undersecretary Hayman thanked the United States for its support at the Security Council and said that while there were critics of the decision to follow the Finnish plan, in general the FCO was pleased at the outcome. Mr. Lush of the Western Department further explained that London did not want to injure Anglo-Irish relations with needless confrontation and that the British understood the recent provocations by Dublin (from the mobilization of Irish troops to the UN initiative) as attempts to reduce the appeal of republican extremism within Ireland. The embassy report to the State Department concluded that London had "genuine good will and respect" for the Irish government "and sympathetic understanding of [the] political and public pressures confronting them."[37]

On to the General Assembly

While the Irish visit to the Security Council had passed without causing any lasting damage to Anglo-Irish relations, the Irish government had not finished its approach to the United Nations. As Patrick Hillery had indicated to the press following the Security Council meeting, Dublin planned to approach the General

Assembly regarding Northern Ireland. On August 26, 1969, Hillery wrote to Jack Lynch proposing that Ireland use the upcoming session of the UN General Assembly to raise the issue of human rights in the North. Having publicly declared victory at the Security Council, Hillery argued that the government would "be under very great pressure at home, including from the Dáil, and abroad from Irish societies and individuals to maintain the momentum." In addition to having the Irish delegation speak about the North in the General Assembly, the minister for external affairs suggested that Dublin attempt to include Northern Ireland on the formal agenda. While the focus would be on human rights, Hillery did not believe that the issue of partition needed to be excluded and advised Lynch that Ireland could include a call for Anglo-Irish negotiations on the constitutional status of Northern Ireland.[38]

On September 5, 1969, Con Cremin formally requested that an item entitled "The Situation in Northern Ireland" be included on the agenda of the regular session of the General Assembly. In the memorandum to Secretary General U Thant accompanying the request, Cremin reviewed the history of partition and discrimination in Northern Ireland from its foundation to the ongoing crisis. He presented the Irish case for peaceful reunification as the only plausible long-term solution for Northern Ireland's problems. Cremin argued that Northern Ireland was an issue for the UN because partition and human rights violations by the Stormont government ran counter to the Universal Declaration of Human Rights and that the current situation was a danger to international peace because of its effects on Anglo-Irish relations.[39]

Lord Caradon outlined possible British countermoves in a cable to the FCO. Any item proposed for inscription on the agenda of the General Assembly needed to be approved by the General Committee which was composed of the president and seventeen vice presidents of the General Assembly as well as the chairs of the seven main committees. Caradon explained that a simple majority vote was required by the General Committee and that Ireland would be allowed to make its case before that body. Caradon doubted that he could stop the General Committee from supporting Ireland and warned that even if the Irish lost in committee they could raise the matter in the General Assembly itself where the ambassador believed "the cards will be more heavily stacked against us. The Irish Republic has an outstanding U.N. record and consequently enjoys wide influence." Caradon suggested that Britain's best course of action would be to try to resist the inclusion of the Irish item on the agenda in the General Committee on the grounds of domestic jurisdiction but not make an objection if the Irish then raised the matter in the General Assembly itself. By this tactic,

Caradon argued, London would make its objection known but avoid being on the losing side of a General Assembly vote.[40]

British foreign secretary Michael Stewart instructed Ambassador Gilchrist to privately ask Patrick Hillery what the Irish hoped to gain from this UN gambit and to remind the Irish government that a public dispute in New York would only "exacerbate the situation" in Northern Ireland and might delay needed reforms in the North.[41] Gilchrist reported back that in a brief informal discussion before an official luncheon with Hillery and Hugh McCann he asked about Ireland's main objective at the UN only to have Hillery belligerently reply that national reunification was Dublin's goal. When asked if he had considered the impact that the UN move was having on Anglo-Irish relations Hillery replied that Gilchrist "could scarcely expect him ... to shed tears for the British Empire" while McCann chimed in that human rights in the North "could not be subordinated to other considerations." When Gilchrist countered that London was working to address the issue of civil rights Hillery replied that the current public diplomacy by the Irish could have been avoided if Michael Stewart had heeded Hillery's warning about the Apprentice Boys parade in Derry or if Lord Chalfont had not insisted that Northern Ireland was a strictly domestic concern for the United Kingdom when they had been approached privately in August. Hillery told the ambassador that Dublin had to put public pressure on London to begin high-level talks with the Irish government and that "The Irish desire for such public contacts sprang from their assessment of the minimum that would satisfy their hard-driving public." When the conversation resumed after lunch Gilchrist found that Hillery had calmed down and now predicted that Anglo-Irish relations would not suffer any real damage from "this trivial period of strain" and that he was confident that he could work with Lord Caradon in New York to ensure this end.[42] Gilchrist assessed Hillery's motivations as "national ambition, personal pique and a desire to put on an exhibition of Irish truculence for the benefit of his domestic audience" and agreed with Stewart that a "low key" response to the UN initiative was the best course of action for London to follow.[43]

Michael Stewart suggested to Lord Caradon that Hillery might be willing to make some kind of deal as the Irish had "mixed motives" for approaching the UN. The foreign secretary expressed the hope that Ireland might agree to postpone the item rather than face a confrontation with the British in the General Committee. Stewart dismissed Hillery's claim that London would not talk to Dublin about Northern Ireland and reminded Lord Caradon that while the North was clearly a domestic issue for Britain "we are always willing to discuss with the Irish aspects of the situation which concern them but [Irish] public statements (and troop movements) diminish the chances of fruitful contact."[44] When Caradon spoke to Hillery and McCann in New York on September 16, both reaffirmed to Caradon that British unwillingness to discuss Northern Ireland with Dublin was the major reason for the UN initiative and that Irish domestic opinion demanded that Lynch's government take some public action. However, Hillery agreed with Caradon to limit the length of their remarks to the General Committee and to speak with restraint.[45] At a meeting the same day with Irish press officers from New York, Boston, and Washington, Hillery explained that Irish publicity should be aimed at promoting "official talks on the situation in the North of Ireland" between Dublin, London, and possibly Stormont. The press officers were warned not to be "strongly critical" of the British and "avoid extreme criticism of Stormont at this stage, in view of the objective of getting talks underway."[46]

The promised restraint was put to the test the following day at the meeting of the twenty-five members of the General Committee chaired by Angie Brooks, the president of the General Assembly. Hillery began by claiming "it was now recognized by many, including the United Kingdom Government, that a large part of the population of the North of Ireland was being denied human rights and fundamental freedoms." He argued that this denial of human rights overrode the claim of domestic jurisdiction (Article 2.7 of the UN Charter) that had been put forward by London and pointed to the precedent of UN involvement in the internal affairs of South Africa. Caradon countered that Northern Ireland was indeed covered by Article 2.7 and if the issue were one of human rights then there were standing committees at the UN that could address this without the need for a special debate. He asked that Hillery withdraw the item. The British ambassador argued that London had already taken steps to curb the violence in the North and support political reform and that any public debate at the UN would only inflame the situation. Caradon praised Ireland's contributions to the UN and promised that "if it now rose above the spirit of dispute, it would make an even greater contribution."

Soviet ambassador Malik spoke in favor of the inscription of the Irish item while the American representative said that the vote "confronts many of us with a very unhappy dilemma" and asked if Hillery would withdraw his request as Caradon had suggested. Ambassador Pinera of Chile echoed this sentiment and called for more time to consider the Irish item. Hillery explained that Ireland had no desire to inflame the situation in the North but that Dublin had concerns about the efficacy of reform in Northern Ireland. Hillery called for more time to consider the effect that withdrawing the item would have on the promised reforms. At this juncture the General Committee accepted the proposal of the representative of Nigeria that the discussion should be postponed for an indefinite period.[47]

Hillery provided Jack Lynch with a detailed analysis of the Irish approaches to the United Nations in a message sent from New York on September 23, 1969. The minister for external affairs pointed out that he had been able to focus not only on human rights but also on the fact that partition was the root cause of the problems in Northern Ireland. The lack of support for the Irish arose from the strenuous lobbying of the British who warned other member states that it was dangerous to weaken Article 2.7. Hillery saw the outcome of an indefinite postponement as the best possible outcome for Dublin. The Irish had avoided a sure defeat on the inscription vote while the existence of the item "hangs over the heads of the British" and could be revived if events in Northern Ireland deteriorated in Dublin's opinion. The continued threat of the item "will act as a pressure on the British," he wrote, and might help to move London to talks with the Irish government.

Surveying both the Irish efforts at the Security Council and the General Assembly, Hillery explained to Lynch that Dublin had been successful on a number of fronts. Ireland had brought the crisis in Northern Ireland to the attention of the world and had made its point regarding the need for reunification. "I think that as far as exposing the problem is concerned there is nothing further that we can do by public utterances," Hillery wrote. He believed that the international sympathy raised for support for civil rights in the North has had a real impact on the "speed and sincerity of purpose with which the British approach" reforms.[48]

The British were also pleased by the outcome of the UN encounters. On September 25, 1969, Michael Stewart told a Cabinet meeting that Lord Caradon had convinced Hillery not to pursue inscription of the Irish item on the agenda of the General Assembly.[49] That same day Stewart instructed Lord Caradon to thank Hillery for the Irish government's moderation regarding Northern Ireland and to convey the hopes that such moderation would continue.[50] Hillery's own impression of his talk with Lord Caradon was that while restoring peace in the North was the first goal, "that certainly was not the finish of their thinking, that the British government was planning for the future and obviously from what he said did not exclude us from discussions. He was woolly and at the same time delivered their message that there will be talks from now on."[51]

While in New York, Patrick Hillery had a meeting with Secretary of State William Rogers on September 22. A seemingly relaxed Hillery told Rogers that he had no specific issue to discuss but rather wanted to dispute the British claim that Dublin had no role to play in Northern Ireland. According to Hillery, Dublin believed that the Stormont government had failed and that a new solution needed to be worked out for the North by all the interested parties. Hillery explained that the major goal of the Irish diplomatic moves at the UN was to put international pressure on Britain to address the crisis in the North. Dublin would continue to push for bilateral talks with the British government even though he realized that London would face a political problem if they tried to change the status quo in the North. Rogers expressed American sympathy for the conflict along with Washington's deep reluctance to get involved in a dispute between two friendly governments. Hillery only asked that Rogers might at some point be able to offer "a little encouragement" to the British to seek a solution and then thanked the secretary of state for his time, remarking, "I have got all from you that I could have asked."[52]

In his address to the General Assembly on September 26, 1969, Patrick Hillery covered a wide array of international topics but he reserved the majority of his address for Northern Ireland. Hillery offered no new ideas but reiterated the Irish government's support for reforms in the North and for eventual peaceful reunification. Hillery called for talks with the British government to facilitate these goals. A number of historians, including Michael Kennedy, Anthony Craig, and John Walsh agree that the speech was moderate and conciliatory in nature and designed to avoid a negative backlash from London.[53]

Analysis of the UN initiatives

The Irish initiatives at the UN in August and September 1969 have drawn the attention of a number of scholars. A general consensus exists that going to the UN was helpful for the Lynch government in the domestic political sphere as the high profile nature of the Irish approach helped to placate public demands in general, and from the hardliners within Fianna Fáil in particular, that the Irish government take some action. There is more division as to the effectiveness of the Irish moves at the UN in terms of diplomatic policy. Michael Kennedy described Hillery's trips to New York as "little more than rhetorical drama"[54] that had "no practical value on the international stage," leaving Dublin to return to its policy of seeking talks with London regarding the future of the North.[55]

Anthony Craig agrees with Kennedy's basic points that the UN moves left Ireland back at square one in terms of Anglo-Irish relations and Northern Ireland.[56] In addition, Craig believes that approaching the UN caused Dublin to place too much emphasis on the goal of reunification, which was unrealistic in the face of the growing crisis.[57]

Alternately, some scholars have argued that the domestic political value of the UN missions were sufficient to justify them. J. Bowyer Bell characterized the UN moves as the best option for a weak nation like Ireland which had few alternatives to take any meaningful action regarding the North.[58] Ronan Fanning agrees that the UN moves "at least enabled the Lynch government to appear to be doing something when, in fact, there was very little they could do." Fanning also believes that it was vital for Lynch's government to placate Fianna Fáil hard-liners. Fanning cites an interview in 2001 in which Patrick Hillery told him that the alternative to going to the UN might have been a catastrophic military intervention across the border. This strongly supports a case for calling the UN initiative a practical success.[59] John Walsh concurs with Fanning's overall view and adds the argument that bringing Ireland's case to an international audience was "a notable propaganda victory." In addition Walsh praises both Hillery and Caradon for showing moderation and restraint in their public remarks.[60]

John Walsh argues that that the outcome of the Irish UN initiatives was to promote better Anglo-Irish relations going forward.[61] Dermot Keogh agrees that the compromises that characterized the outcome of the UN initiatives actually helped lay the groundwork for more moderation and cooperation between Dublin and London as Hillery and Lord Caradon had worked together in New York to contain the Anglo-Irish dispute within reasonable boundaries.[62]

The historical record seems to support the idea that the UN initiatives were important in reducing the pressure from within the Cabinet for an Irish military incursion into the North. The most reasonable defense of military intervention by the woefully inadequate Irish Army was that it would spark UN intervention. Once Dublin had publicly, and predictably, failed to secure a peacekeeping force from the UN it would have been impossible to hope that the international community would respond to a cross-border move by the Irish Army as anything other than a cynical attempt at diplomatic blackmail. Shutting down the option of military involvement can therefore be viewed as a diplomatic victory as it avoided a certain catastrophe.

In more general terms, using the UN to bolster Irish public support for Lynch's government helped to keep Dublin moving toward a policy of moderation and nonviolence regarding Northern Ireland. The essential moderation of Lynch and his supporters in the government was instrumental in placing Anglo-Irish relations on firmer ground after the August crisis had passed. The British government understood the political pressure that Lynch was under from republican leaning elements in Ireland for a strong reaction from Dublin. One of the main reasons that London did not attempt to force votes at the Security Council or General Committee was to promote the survival of what was seen in Whitehall as a reasonable Irish government. Diplomacy and domestic politics were too intertwined to be separated at this juncture in Anglo-Irish relations.

While the Irish failed to win a vote at the UN, London clearly did not like Northern Ireland becoming a subject of international debate and wished to avoid more UN involvement. The fact that the Irish item at the General Committee was not decisively voted down in September 1969 and thus survived to possibly be reintroduced did, as Hillery claimed at the time, give Ireland some limited leverage with Britain. Moreover, Anglo-Irish relations were not damaged as a result of the Irish moves at the UN as both Dublin and London expressed satisfaction at the outcome and turned to more bilateral cooperation in the fall of 1969.

Conclusions

The August crisis in Northern Ireland was a great challenge to the Irish and British governments and to their relations with each other. Scholarly analysis of the period is divided as to the efficacy of the response of the two governments. Michael Kennedy has characterized the response of the Irish Cabinet as "reactive" and following "no overall strategy."[63] This view of a poorly planned Irish response is shared by Antony Craig, although Craig places some of the blame with Wilson's government, which was much better prepared for a number of contingencies but failed to share British plans for reform in Northern Ireland with Dublin, a move which may have helped calm the Irish.[64] Ronan Fanning has called the response of both governments "muted" but also stressed the superior preparedness of the British. Fanning also sees evidence that Harold Wilson wanted to promote good Anglo-Irish relations in order to stop any unrest in the North from spreading south of the border.[65]

Jack Lynch's performance during August has been criticized by Catherine O'Donnell who claims that he lost control of Northern policy to the Cabinet hardliners and failed to focus on improving North–South relations and promoting reform in Stormont.[66] Lynch biographer Dermot Keogh takes the opposite view of the taoiseach's performance during the crisis. While admitting that the government's immediate response was "fragmented" and poorly planned, Keogh credits Lynch with "decisiveness in his unwavering commitment to the preservation of democratic institutions" during the crisis period.[67] Rather than losing control of government policy to the republican wing of the Cabinet, Professor Keogh claims that Lynch won a major victory by keeping his fractured Cabinet together, with himself in charge of overall policy, by adopting a rhetorically strong position on Northern Ireland.[68] Similarly, John Walsh praises Lynch and Hillery for working together to avoid the military intervention favored by the Cabinet hawks during August. The diplomatic initiatives undertaken by Hillery under Lynch's direction provided a "viable alternative" to a military incursion into Northern Ireland.[69]

There is no doubt that the descent into violence in Northern Ireland in mid-August 1969 caught the Irish government unprepared. It is equally true that Lynch's government did not take any really constructive actions in the openings days of the crisis. However, it is vital to remember that the Cabinet was sharply divided on the issue of Northern Ireland. This would have made it very difficult for the government to agree on a course of action before they were forced to act by events in the North. This does not excuse the Irish government from having such limited intelligence on the ground in Northern Ireland or for allowing the Irish Defense Forces to have become so obsolete but it helps to explain why no formal contingency plans were in place. The Battle of the Bogside and the subsequent spread of violence were also very emotionally charged events for the people of Ireland. The real achievement of Jack Lynch's government during the August crisis was to prevent the violence that was growing in the North from drawing in the South. By September the Irish government was attempting to put diplomatic confrontation with London behind them and engage the British in constructive talks. The survival of a moderate Fianna Fáil government in power in Dublin after the initial crisis was a major success given that the alternative could have been much worse.

When the violence began in Northern Ireland the British government acted responsibly in attempting to restore a measure of security and to quickly announce plans for reforms that would answer the concerns of the Catholic civil rights movement. In terms of managing Anglo-Irish relations during the period, London did not handle its affairs as well. In the initial meetings between top officials the documents show that the British were tone deaf to Irish sensibilities regarding partition and Dublin's role in the North. While it is true that Harold Wilson's government did not want to damage Anglo-Irish relations, and appreciated the basic moderation of Lynch, they were unwilling to seriously engage with Dublin on Northern issues. Part of the blame can be placed on London's desire to avoid a unionist backlash should it appear that the British were negotiating the fate of the North directly with Dublin, but a meeting between Wilson and Lynch or even some quiet assurances to Lynch's government that the Irish would be able to participate in the reform process would have strengthened Lynch's political standing at home. London seemed to want the Irish to help by remaining quiet regarding Northern Ireland. This was not a realistic possibility for any government in Dublin, no matter how anxious it might have been to cooperate with London. At least the British did not allow the public disputes with the Irish at the UN to have a lasting negative impact on the future of Anglo-Irish cooperation.

During this initial period of the Troubles the American government of President Richard Nixon balanced the wish to remain on friendly terms with Ireland with the stronger desires not to offend Britain, a close NATO ally, or to become involved in the conflict in Northern Ireland. The Americans were willing to meet with Irish diplomats on friendly terms but generally respected London's request that they treat the crisis in Northern Ireland as a matter internal to the United Kingdom.

Search for Cooperation:
September 1969–June 1970

Once the immediate crisis of August had passed, both the British and Irish governments sought ways to move away from confrontation and toward bilateral discussions. Even as the Irish pursued public diplomacy at the United Nations that pitted Dublin against London on the world stage, efforts were being made in private by both governments to open more profitable lines of communication. Following a speech by Jack Lynch at Tralee in late September 1969 the formal policy of the Irish government was to encourage moderation and put an end to violence in the North as an immediate goal with reunification relegated to a long-term aspiration. For the remainder of Wilson's term in office, London and Dublin embraced this moderate stance and focused primarily on promoting the reforms in Northern Ireland that had been promised in the Downing Street Declaration. The two governments exchanged ideas and information through a series of informal discussions between British and Irish officials. However, as the events of the Arms Crisis clearly demonstrated, the Fianna Fáil government was not united in supporting Jack Lynch's strictly peaceful policy nor did the Anglo-Irish talks help to produce a return to peace in Northern Ireland.

The beginning of cooperation

On September 16, 1969, Ambassador Gilchrist had a discussion with Jack Lynch just before the ambassador returned to London for meetings with his own government. Gilchrist described their talk as "remarkably straightforward and friendly" and believed Lynch to be sincere. The taoiseach explained that the ongoing UN effort and the earlier confrontational moves by Dublin were designed primarily to outflank the IRA, placate public opinion, and keep his own Cabinet hawks in check. Lynch claimed that the UN initiative could have been avoided if London had allowed Ireland to have some say in the affairs of Northern Ireland. Hillery's warnings in August about the volatile situation in Derry had proven accurate but he had been rebuffed in London. At Gilchrist's prompting, Lynch implied that once the UN mission was over, Dublin would be willing to wait for the reforms promised by the Downing Street Declaration to take effect. Lynch called his restraining of his more militant colleagues "a remarkable achievement" and promised that his next public speech would be "more mild... and helpful" than any earlier statement, but that Dublin could not accept being told by London or Stormont "to keep its nose out of the affairs of Northern Ireland." The taoiseach claimed that any Irish government would have "to take a close and public interest" in the North if it expected to survive. On the issue of reunification, Lynch downplayed that goal as a long-term aspiration that would require changes in Irish society, but adamantly defended Dublin's right to try to have an immediate impact on the events in the North. "What was needed," Lynch said, "was for some degree of consultation with Britain to be conceded." However, Lynch suggested that Anglo-Irish talks should not directly involve him meeting with Prime Minister Wilson or Home Secretary James Callaghan as this would be fully covered by the press and both sides would end up making unhelpful boilerplate statements. A more quiet conversation using diplomatic channels would be more beneficial. In the meantime Lynch told Gilchrist to assure London that the Irish wanted peace in Northern Ireland, and that while Dublin still fundamentally rejected the deployment of British troops and considered them a target for extremists, the army had so far been acting as an effective peacekeeping body.[1]

Within days Gilchrist had traveled to London to meet with a special Cabinet subcommittee (MISC 244) that Wilson set up to deal with Northern Ireland.[2] The chair of the committee, J.H. Waddell of the Home Office, opened the meeting of September 18, 1969, by relaying a Cabinet directive that ways should be sought to improve relations with the Irish Republic and to make those relations more constructive. This fit neatly with some of the points that Lynch had made in Dublin. Gilchrist informed the subcommittee of the substance of his recent conversation with Lynch stressing the Irish demands for participation in finding a solution to the Northern crisis. The ambassador, who believed that Dublin would never support the status quo at Stormont, supported allowing Ireland to be involved in a reworking of the province's government to fix the problem of the Unionist Party's monopoly on political power. Gilchrist argued that Dublin's involvement would strengthen the Irish government's hand in dealing with the IRA. He assured the members of the committee that Dublin did not seek immediate reunification.

After discussing a number of options the committee agreed to recommend a revival of the idea of a Council of Ireland that had existed in the Government of Ireland Act, 1920, as a method of formally involving Dublin in the North. In the meantime London should seek cooperation with Dublin on improving the civil rights climate in the North and promote low-level cooperation between Dublin and Belfast. The committee also recommended that Home Secretary Callaghan should try to arrange a private meeting with Lynch to hear more of the Irish ideas.[3]

Lynch's Tralee speech

On September 20 Jack Lynch spoke at a dinner in honor of a former Fianna Fáil TD in Tralee, County Kerry. He told his audience that he was going to use this public address to "set out the basis of our thinking and policy." Lynch began with a traditional nationalist analysis of partition as unnatural and unhistorical. He stressed that reunification had to be sought by peaceful means and must be based "on mutual respect and tolerance guaranteed by a form or forms of government authority in Ireland providing for progressive improvement of social, economic and cultural life in a just and peaceful environment." Reunification, Lynch said, was a long-term goal that would require "goodwill, patience, understanding, and at times forbearance." Later in the speech Lynch said that reunification could be achieved by "intermediate stages" such as federation. He argued that Northern unionists need not fear a united Ireland which would respect their civil liberties. "The real barriers," he said, "are those created by fear suspicion and intolerance."

When addressing more recent developments Lynch claimed that the current state of affairs in Northern Ireland demonstrated that partition was not accepted as "fair and just" by the nationalist community in the North. In a passage that had direct relevance to Anglo-Irish relations the taoiseach asserted that Dublin's "views on how peace and justice can be assured in this small island are relevant and entitled to be heard." While accepting the de facto existence and authority of the Belfast government and calling for North–South cooperation, Lynch said that partition would never be formally accepted by Ireland and stressed that the Westminster parliament was the responsible power in the North.[4]

The Tralee speech was hardly revolutionary in its treatment of partition as the cause of political problems in the whole of Ireland. On the other hand, Lynch was trying to move beyond the confrontational rhetoric of the August crisis toward a more constructive policy. He spoke in terms of reunification as a gradual and peaceful process of reconciliation among the people of Ireland. However, Lynch did not follow the advice of Ken Whitaker who drafted the speech, to be even more conciliatory toward Northern unionists.[5] Instead, while he pledged to work to accomplish the long-term goal of peaceful reunification, Lynch placed the emphasis in the immediate future not on North–South talks, but on dialogue between Dublin and London to improve the situation in Northern Ireland.

British response of the Tralee speech

On September 22 Ambassador Sir Andrew Gilchrist sent a memorandum entitled "Options Available: Ireland" to the FCO. He began by underlining the emotional response of the Irish population and Irish political leaders to the Northern Ireland crisis. A great deal of sympathy for Northern nationalists, as well as a feeling that reunification was a real possibility, had gripped Ireland, and, according to the ambassador, could cause unreasonable behavior in the Irish Republic. However, Gilchrist argued that if Britain did not consider Ireland as a partner in seeking a solution to the Northern problem, then a hostile Irish government could cause a great deal of trouble for London if Anglo-Irish relations moved "to the verge of a cold war." In order to foster a positive relationship London would have to allow Dublin "to express its views or have a say on the future of the North." This was particularly important in Gilchrist's opinion because he believed that basic constitutional change that would allow Northern nationalists some role in government, not simple reform, was needed in Northern Ireland. The ambassador envisioned that Dublin would have an advising role in this process of constitution formation through an official Irish representative in Belfast: a move that would force Dublin to recognize the legitimacy of the Northern Irish government but also open the possibility of national reunification "within a foreseeable future." He predicted that this offer could be portrayed as a major victory in Ireland as it fit into Lynch's gradualist views on reunification.[6]

A few days later Gilchrist met with Home Secretary James Callaghan to discuss the state of Anglo-Irish relations. The home secretary called the Tralee address "realistic and conciliatory" and Gilchrist agreed that it marked an important change in Dublin's attitude from the confrontational stance in August. The ambassador told Callaghan that no Irish government could hope to survive politically if it did not take a keen and public interest in the North and that insisting that "affairs north of the Border were no business of the South would provoke an adverse reaction." Callaghan told Gilchrist that he understood that Dublin was under political pressure but that Lynch had to appreciate that there were also political pressures being brought to bear on Stormont and on Wilson's government by unionists. In order to bring relations among London, Dublin, and Belfast to "a different plane," as Callaghan hoped to do, "timing was critical." The first step would have to be reform of Stormont to meet the demands of the civil rights movement. This reform agenda would not be easy to implement and it would be compromised if Dublin were seen to have an increasing role in the North at the same time. Callaghan said that during this first stage Lynch would have to content himself with the use of normal diplomatic channels to express Dublin's views to the British government. Once reform was well underway, Callaghan hoped that London could lead Stormont "down the next path," which might include a tripartite guarantee of civil rights in Northern Ireland. He also expressed the hope that Lynch would try to foster better relations with the Chichester-Clark government once reform was begun. Gilchrist did not press his own view on constitutional reform on Callaghan.[7]

In a note to Prime Minister Wilson on September 23, 1969, Callaghan asserted that the Tralee speech "bore all the marks of the work we have been doing in the last few weeks to establish sensible attitudes on both sides of the border." Callaghan reported that he was upset that Major Chichester-Clark had, just that morning, issued a public statement in which he rebutted some of Lynch's points from the Tralee address. The home secretary had called Chichester-Clark to remind him that London, not Stormont, dealt with all the foreign affairs of the United Kingdom. Callaghan told Wilson that he believed that Chichester-Clark's statement would not seriously harm Anglo-Irish relations and that the Home Office's official statement on the Tralee speech would deem it "a very realistic appraisal of the situation and particularly its references to long term approaches and the need for patience and goodwill."[8]

On September 25 the FCO authorized Ambassador Gilchrist to inform Jack Lynch about the substance of his meeting with Callaghan two days earlier.[9] As it transpired it was not until November that Gilchrist spoke to Lynch. By this time the FCO had changed its tone a little from September, making the communication less official but still of importance. Gilchrist was instructed on

November 10 to speak to Lynch in an informal manner to "avoid giving what you say the dignity of a Government to Government message." However, the ambassador was to make it clear that he was relaying the ideas of Callaghan and that Prime Minister Wilson and Foreign Secretary Stewart had "associated themselves with what follows." The British government wanted Lynch to know that it appreciated his Tralee speech "which had helped set the tone for succeeding weeks." London hoped that Dublin, and Belfast, would join the British in seeking to improve cooperation among the three governments. The rest of the communication remained an unchanged summary of Callaghan's plans as explained to Gilchrist back in September.[10] Gilchrist finally passed the message to Lynch on November 19. The taoiseach accepted the basic points of the message but warned Gilchrist that Stormont was exaggerating the danger of a hardline unionist backlash to frustrate the reform program and that Britain's refusal to abolish the B-Specials and the proposed formation of the Ulster Defense Regiment (UDR) were playing poorly with the Southern public. Lynch also wanted the British Army to disarm loyalist extremists in the Shankill Road neighborhood of Belfast. Gilchrist countered that Ireland had its own extremists to deal with and made reference to the rumors that an Irish Cabinet member (Charles Haughey was named in Gilchrist's record of the meeting but not in the actual conversation) was running some kind of nefarious operation in Monaghan. The ambassador claimed that if these rumors spread to Stormont, this would only reinforce the unionist hardliners. Gilchrist admitted that his information on the Monaghan issue was not reliable, but he considered the rumors plausible enough to be a political problem if they spread to the North. Lynch at first denied any knowledge of this rumor but once Gilchrist confirmed that "a certain member of his Cabinet" was reported to be involved, Lynch agreed to look into the matter.[11]

From public confrontation to low-profile diplomacy

By October 1969 Irish and British officials reassessed the future of Anglo-Irish relations now that the period of public confrontation seemed to have been put behind the two governments. Among the Irish officials who would have a major role in forming Dublin's policy regarding the North and Anglo-Irish relations was Eamonn Gallagher. While Gallagher's assignment at the Department of External Affairs was to work on entry into the European Economic Community, he became an important voice on Northern affairs. Gallagher, who was from

Donegal, formed close friendships with Northern nationalists and spent many of his weekends in Northern Ireland informally collecting intelligence on the province.[12] Hugh McCann, who realized that the Department of External Affairs had very limited knowledge about Northern Ireland, encouraged Gallagher's forays into the North and Gallagher became a key adviser to the Irish government on Northern Ireland.[13] In a memorandum sent to Department of External Affairs assistant secretary Sean Ronan in early October, Gallagher set out his view on relations among Dublin, London, and Belfast. From Gallagher's point of view the Irish government was pursuing a policy of seeking direct talks with London on the major political issues involving the North while relegating relations with Stormont to minor issues of mutual interest. Gallagher approved of this policy and also warned against trilateral talks as this would confer on Stormont "a political credibility which runs counter to our historical attitude." The Unionist regime in Stormont had already been weakened by Dublin's refusal to recognize its legitimacy and there was no reason to change course now. As the British were unlikely to agree to formal bilateral talks with Dublin, Gallagher suggested that the Irish content themselves with the use of existing diplomatic channels with the hopes that these contacts might lead to ministerial level talks and a gradual acceptance by London of the need for direct, even if informal, discussions with Dublin. Even though Gallagher accepted reunification as the long-term goal of Irish policy, he argued that in the short term, Dublin should focus its efforts on pushing Britain to affect reforms in Northern Ireland that would reduce discrimination against nationalists and promote economic growth in Catholic areas. Looking farther into the future he warned against eliminating Stormont altogether as reunification would be best negotiated between the Irish communities.[14]

When the Dáil held its first debate on the Northern Ireland crisis on October 22, 1969, Lynch again showcased his desire to moderate the tone of the Irish response. He began the discussion by acknowledging the "passionate feelings and deep emotion" that were engendered by the issue of the North but he called on all the TDs to avoid any statement which would "tend to further exacerbate an already tragic situation." He called on all parties in the Dáil to work together "calmly and objectively and to act responsibly" so that the Ireland could "contribute … to the easing of present tensions, to the elimination of fear and hate and to the establishment of the free and unrestricted exercise in the northern area of basic human rights and fundamental freedoms." Lynch pointed to his speech at Tralee as an effective outline of his core ideas regarding Northern Ireland. Fine Gael leader Liam Cosgrave pointed out that his party had long advocated the idea of peaceful unification as the key to resolving the last major issue of Anglo-Irish relations. The Fianna Fáil government came under criticism for not recalling the Dáil in August and Hillery's trips to the UN were characterized as useless by the opposition but there were no calls for a more confrontational stance toward Britain. Fine Gael TD Garret FitzGerald warned that the UN moves had in fact undermined Anglo-Irish relations. FitzGerald's opening remarks placed so much of the onus for partition on the unionist and nationalist divisions among the Irish that he felt compelled later in the debate to state that he did not, in fact, place the majority of blame on the Irish but also recognized British responsibility as well.[15]

The conciliatory tone of the Dáil debate did not go unnoticed by the British. Ambassador Gilchrist advised Sir Edward Peck at the Foreign and Commonwealth Office that the Dáil debate, while not indicative of the beliefs of the IRA or even the hardline within Fianna Fáil, had revealed a "sober, cautious, and amicable attitude" by Lynch and the Dáil in general that should be reciprocated by London with "some relatively friendly and mildly and vaguely encouraging response."[16]

Talks on the margins strategy

What emerged from the growing desire of both the British and Irish to cooperate were not official talks on the future of Northern Ireland but a tacit agreement to informally discuss the issue "at the margins" of normal diplomatic encounters. In early November Hugh McCann suggested to Sir Andrew Gilchrist that during Anglo-Irish trade talks scheduled for December it might be a good idea to have a side discussion regarding Northern Ireland and reunification. Informal talks would avoid the need for public statements on these sensitive topics to be issued by either side. McCann told Gilchrist that Patrick Hillery could attend the talks in person to insure that a moderate from the Lynch Cabinet would be the government's voice on Northern Ireland.[17] At a subsequent lunch meeting with Gilchrist and Oliver Wright, the UK representative in Northern Ireland, McCann explained that while public talks would be better for Lynch from a domestic political point of view, private talks could at least be used to show hardliners within the Cabinet that the moderates were at least doing something. An internal FCO memo suggested that the offer from McCann should be accepted. Informal talks would reward the Irish for their recently "helpful attitude" and would represent, for London, a noncommittal method of encouraging further cooperation from Dublin.[18] The informal nature of McCann's original offer had been solidified by the time that Ambassador Gilchrist met with Jack Lynch on November 19. Gilchrist raised the issue of talks "in the margin of the trade meeting" with the taoiseach. Lynch indicated that he and Hillery were planning to consult on the topics to be discussed and expressed a desire to meet with Prime Minister Wilson in the future.[19]

Iveagh House's thinking regarding the possibility of private Anglo-Irish talks was outlined later that month when the Department of External Affairs sent a memo to the Irish government that detailed the department's views on Northern Ireland and Anglo-Irish relations. The document began by making it clear that the Department of External Affairs placed the blame for partition on British policy in the 1920s. Partition was imposed on the Irish people against the will of the majority and the discriminatory nature of Stormont only added to its fundamental illegitimacy. The long-term solution to the problems of the North was reunification. Reunification would have to be achieved through peaceful means and would entail cooperation with Northern unionists. The memo advised the Irish government to continue to publicly renounce the use of violence as a means of securing unity. In the near term, the policy of the Irish should be to support reforms in the North and avoid public clashes with Britain such as the recent UN initiatives. The department also cautioned against pushing too hard for reform to avoid the imposition of direct rule from London which would only serve to more firmly tie Northern Ireland to Britain. On the matter of Anglo-Irish relations it advised the government to "maximize discreet contact with Whitehall…both at the diplomatic level and at the Ministerial level—under cover of other activities if necessary. Dublin's right to be heard on matters affecting the North and Britain's ultimate responsibility should be emphasized." The memo called for discussions that would focus not only on the short-term issue of reforms but also on the long-term future of Northern Ireland. Private bilateral talks would avoid a political backlash in the North and avoid unhelpful public guarantees from London regarding the North's position in the United Kingdom.[20]

In London the Foreign and Commonwealth Office and the Home Office agreed on British strategy for the Anglo-Irish "talks in the margin" in a memo prepared by the Western European Department of the FCO. The British believed that they could not make any real concessions to the Irish "for we are committed to no change in the constitutional status of Northern Ireland except by the will of the majority there." While the document acknowledged that the Irish had a "legitimate concern" with the North, Dublin's need "to show that it was being taken seriously at Westminster" for domestic political reasons was seen as less legitimate. However, as Ireland "could make things difficult for us, both internationally and in Northern Ireland.... It is ... worthwhile paying a small price if we can thereby keep the doves in control in Dublin." The memo went on to argue that the margin talks should not "take the form of a negotiation" but should leave Dr. Hillery with the feeling that he had participated in a friendly and informative exchange of ideas but without any commitments being made. In fact, despite agreeing to talk to the Irish, it was to be made clear to Hillery that Dublin had no "right to be consulted on our political or administrative decisions in Northern Ireland."[21]

Talks on the margins begin

During a formal meeting in London regarding the Anglo-Irish Free Trade Area Agreement the first margin talks were held. Patrick Hillery, accompanied by Hugh McCann and Irish ambassador J.G. Molloy, met with George Thomson, the chancellor of the Duchy of Lancaster, W.K.K. White of the FCO, and Ambassador Gilchrist on December 10 at the FCO. Hillery began by denouncing the recent speech by Irish Cabinet hardliner Neil Blaney at Letterkenny (Blaney had told a Fianna Fáil audience in Donegal that the party had not ruled out violence to achieve reunification even if peaceful means were preferable[22]) and by restating Dublin's commitment to the ideas of Lynch's Tralee speech. Thomson welcomed this, and dismissed Blaney's address as "rather silly." On the broader issue of Anglo-Irish talks, Hillery stressed Dublin's right to be consulted on Northern Ireland. Hillery argued that Dublin had much to contribute including insight into violent republicanism. He acknowledged that formal consultation of Dublin would cause a reaction in Stormont and accepted the need for the type of informal discussion in which they were now engaged. Thomson agreed that for political reasons Dublin, London, and Stormont were best served by informal meetings "under the cover of more general talks" or communication through regular private diplomatic channels. The chancellor also suggested that the two sides agree to ignore the issue of the border as they fundamentally disagreed about partition and focus "on sharing information and ideas, aimed at an improved climate."

The first issue Hillery raised was the formation of the UDR which was to be a locally recruited part-time unit of the British Army for service in Northern

Ireland. The Irish objected to the use of the name Ulster as this province included three counties in the Irish Republic. Hillery characterized recruitment of former B-Specials into the new force as "stupid." Thomson assured Hillery that the name had been carefully considered and that the use of Ulster was better than other alternatives. He warned against the emotionality of even moderate Irish unionists and Irish nationalists when it came to symbolic issues such as the use of Ulster. London needed to keep the moderate unionists on board with reform and, therefore, some compromises had to be made. As far as Dublin's fear that the force would prove sectarian, he told the Irish that the UDR would be controlled by the military and would be "khaki, not orange, in complexion." He assured them that London had no intention of creating a new Black and Tan force.

Thomson turned the conversation to the issue of reform and claimed that a good deal of success had been achieved including the Hunt Committee report on policing, one-man-one-vote legislation, the creation of an Ombudsman, and of a Community Relations Ministry. He claimed that peace was returning to the streets of Northern Ireland and that full equality was the goal of the reforms. Peace and equality were, Thomson said, the first steps toward any long-term changes in the North. He then asked Hillery for his views on the long-term future of the province.

Hillery suggested that there were other areas that needed reform including electoral boundaries and allocation of housing, but that he understood the difficulties of bringing change to the North. He said the reunification would have to be a process not of combining territory but of gradual merging of the "wills and hearts" of the Irish people on both sides of the border. On the issue of North–South relations in a divided Ireland, Hillery suggested that issues of cooperation on "tourism, business and commerce" should increase. He claimed that resistance to cross-border ties was all coming from the North and that, unlike Lynch, Chichester-Clark was not supplying good leadership on the issue. When McCann interjected that leadership in the North now rested with Whitehall, Thomson replied that while James Callaghan was doing a good job, direct rule by London was not the solution. The North's problems could only be solved by placating the fears, "justified or not," of moderate Protestants. According to Thomson, Chichester-Clark was committed to reform and needed the support of London. Hillery agreed but stressed that reforms could not simply be used as a mask to cover a return to the status quo. Thomson concurred that reforms had to be fundamental and not "a mere expedient."

The meeting closed with Hillery asking about the future of the Special Powers Act. Thomson said that there were plans to repeal the Act but then defended certain sections of the legislation as a necessary evil to combat violence and said that Britain and Ireland had similar legislation on the books. McCann denied the comparison of the Northern Ireland statute to British and Irish laws and called Northern laws like the Flags and Emblems Act, which banned the Irish tricolor, "objectionable." Thomson had no direct reply to this but ended the discussion with a wish for future meetings.[23]

Another meeting was arranged within a few months as Hillery again visited London in February 1970. Accompanied by McCann, the new Irish ambassador Donal O'Sullivan, and Kevin Rush, the minister for external affairs called at the Foreign and Commonwealth Office for a discussion with Thomson, Ambassador Gilchrist, and a number of other FCO officials. The Irish and British differed on their views of recent developments in Northern Ireland. Oliver Wright, the UK representative to Northern Ireland appointed in August 1969, claimed that the situation had become much more peaceful due to the implementation of reforms which had partly placated the Northern Ireland Civil Rights Association and divided the moderate civil rights movement from the more extreme elements in the nationalist community. While hardline unionists were putting pressure on Stormont, Wright claimed that Chichester-Clark would be able to keep the Unionist Party on the path to reform. Hillery countered that the Irish government's contacts in the North were growing more afraid of violence and the increasing influence of the right wing of the Unionist Party. He warned that Protestant extremists were well armed and might become more aggressive "under the protection of the British army." Wright expressed the opinion that fear of privately held arms was overblown by both communities in the North and that the army had the situation well in hand. While he admitted that the right wing of the Unionist Party was growing in importance, Wright claimed that London was carefully monitoring the development and there was hope that the trend would not continue. Hillery argued that the situation was worse than the British believed and that Northern Catholics were afraid that the British Army could not adequately protect them. He ominously warned that this left an opening for nationalist extremists to fill, and that a renewal of violence might cause "a situation ... where we could not stand by and leave such unfortunate people defenseless." Thomson claimed that reform was the best way to reduce tensions and fears. Hillery raised, and quickly dismissed, the British idea that Ireland should establish a formal consulate in Belfast.

Putting aside the issue of reform Hillery raised the topic of a "long-term ... political solution" and suggested that the British needed to begin to look at the first steps down that road. Hillery asked Thomson if he had any ideas on how to induce unionists to accept the ultimate need for reconciliation with the South, which to the Irish meant reunification. Thomson argued that the reforms needed time to work and reduce cross-community tensions in the North before any long-term settlement could be considered. Thomson said that any British statement about a long-term political solution would be counterproductive but that they could discuss any ideas in private. Sir Andrew Gilchrist interjected that the Northern crisis had had at least one positive impact in that people in Ireland were beginning "to think deeply and seriously" about new solutions to the issue of partition. McCann added that the British needed to begin that process as well: a sentiment with which Gilchrist agreed.[24]

Talks continue

Following Hillery's two visits to London the Anglo-Irish discussions continued at lower levels. Kelvin White, who was in charge of Anglo-Irish relations at the FCO and was responsible for coordinating Irish policy with the Home Office, visited Dublin for talks with Sean Ronan and Eamonn Gallagher of the Department of External Affairs in early March 1970. White expressed concern that during the last Hillery–Thomson meeting the Irish had been much more pessimistic than the British about the possibility that violence might be expanding in the North. According to White's analysis there was no possibility of widespread violence, reform was making headway, and London accepted that "in due time" it would be possible to address the constitutional status of Northern Ireland. While it seemingly contradicted his initial assurance that law and order were firmly reestablished in the North, White asked a number of questions about the possible Irish response to "widespread disorder" across the border. He wanted to know if the Irish would go to the UN again in that situation. Ronan and Gallagher told White that a complete breakdown was unlikely, that the UN could not handle such a situation, and that it was up to the British government to make sure such a dangerous development never happened. White asked if an Irish Army unit might cross the border under the authority of its own commander if violence escalated or if the Irish government would authorize such an incursion to create an international incident. The Irish assured White that this scenario might have been a danger in August 1969 but was no longer a possibility.

White next asked if Dublin would be content with serious reform in the North. The Irish replied that their government saw reform as a first step on the road to peaceful reunification. When asked if London could "discreetly" help to promote reunification, White gently sidestepped the question and said that Britain hoped to promote good North–South relations. He questioned whether the Catholic population of the North would ever become a majority as they had not gained any demographic ground over the last fifty years. Ronan and Gallagher argued that Catholic emigration from Northern Ireland would be reduced once discrimination in housing and job allocation were ended and that this would lead to a nationalist majority in ten or twenty years and that it was important that this eventuality should be prepared for now. At lunch the next day the conversation returned to North–South relations. Both sides supported the idea in the abstract but could not come to an agreement on how it should be promoted. The idea of an Irish consul in Belfast was rejected by the Irish on constitutional grounds.

In Gallagher's official report of the meetings he expressed his opinion that the "British are quite honest in their determination to reform the North, are quite sincere in their belief that they can contain right-wing unionism and do not rule out *a priori* the view that a new settlement of the Irish question should be reached in due time. In the meantime they are quite obviously anxious that we should keep in touch."[25]

On March 6, 1970, Ambassador O'Sullivan visited James Callaghan to exchange views. Callaghan admitted to being more concerned about the possibility of growing violence in Northern Ireland than other British officials and stated that the Irish government had been right in their warnings about the danger in August 1969, adding "in my personal opinion, you might be right again." However, Callaghan saw a "gleam of hope" in the fact that recent marches had been free of violence due to the calming influence of British troops. He also praised Lynch's "moderation" and called for patience as the security forces worked to "isolate effectively" the extremists from both communities from the bulk of the population who only sought peace and harmony. O'Sullivan said Dublin's main concern was the "build-up of arms" in the hands of the unionist community. Callaghan admitted that the number of weapons stashed "in rafters" of private homes was unknown but probably quite large.

The home secretary expressed pleasure that the UDR had attracted about 25 percent Catholic applicants and that the new force would also keep former

B-Specials from drifting into loyalist militias like the Ulster Volunteer Force. Callaghan did express concern, however, that Catholic applicants would have to be closely screened to keep out IRA infiltrators, as one of the UDR's main jobs would be to stop IRA incursions across the border.

O'Sullivan turned the discussion to the "constitutional problem" and the need to "sooner or later" find a real solution. Callaghan countered that reunification could only take place after peace was firmly established in the North and would require a "change of heart" on the part of unionists. Northern Ireland, O'Sullivan claimed, only existed because of British economic support, meaning London was "financing the maintenance of the Border." While Callaghan agreed, he said there would be no withdrawal of London's financial support. The meeting closed with Callaghan calling for further talks with the ambassador.[26]

Wilson and Childers's informal meeting

Prime Minister Harold Wilson and Tánaiste Erskine Childers held a private conversation in March 1970 after a large diplomatic gathering where both men had given speeches. Childers asked if it was possible that London could publicly support the idea of a reunified or federated Ireland achieved by agreement between moderate nationalists and moderate unionists as a long-term solution for the North. Wilson agreed that the idea was worth discussing but that there was no chance of this type of solution in the near term. Wilson continued the conversation on the understanding that Childers would only share his thoughts directly with Lynch. The prime minister expressed his fear of a "sharp Protestant backlash" in the North. While he believed that Chichester-Clark would remain in control of the Ulster Unionist Party in the immediate future, Wilson said that hardliners were gaining strength and that he expected that moderates would lose seats in Westminster and Stormont. If the hardliners came to control the Unionist Party, Wilson promised that his government would "not flinch from facing" the dire consequences which would likely include the imposition of direct rule from London. Wilson said that any discussions of the long-term future of Northern Ireland might well include Dublin but in the meantime the British saw the North as "a London-Belfast issue." Wilson suggested that a meeting with Lynch regarding Northern Ireland at the moment would not be helpful due to the certainty of a unionist backlash against any such discussion but that informal talks on the margins between government ministers should continue.[27]

More talks on the margin: Agreeing to disagree

Ambassador O'Sullivan, accompanied by Kevin Rush, held a discussion at the FCO on March 23 with FCO deputy undersecretary Sir Edward Peck, Ronnie Burroughs, the newly appointed UK representative in Belfast, and a number of other FCO and Home Office officials. Burroughs presented a favorable view of developments in the North. Chichester-Clark had strengthened his position against the right wing of the Unionist Party by winning a vote of confidence at Stormont. Despite the fact that it seemed that hardline unionist Ian Paisley would win a seat in a coming by-election, Burroughs assured the Irish that the Unionist Party reformers were in a better position than the press believed. O'Sullivan and Burroughs agreed that the most important, and contentious, reform would be to change local government.

Ambassador O'Sullivan warned that the upcoming Easter commemoration would be a source of trouble in the North but Peck and Burroughs assured him that the police and army were well prepared to control the planned marches. O'Sullivan said Dublin remained concerned about the number of weapons in private hands in the North but the British downplayed this fear and Burroughs suggested that nationalists were exaggerating fears of guns in unionist hands as a justification for arming themselves in self-defense. The British dismissed the loyalist Ulster Volunteer Force as more fiction than fact and pointed out that the IRA, on the other hand, was a well-established and widespread organization.

Burroughs pressed O'Sullivan on the need for more North–South cooperation but the ambassador countered that Chichester-Clarke was hardly in a position to be seen to be negotiating closer ties with Dublin as he already had enough trouble from his right wing. From the Irish perspective, Belfast, not Dublin, was the barrier to more cross-border links.

Sir Edward Peck closed the discussion by agreeing to talk again, although he warned against "institutionalizing" the meetings, and requested that the Irish come up with some points of discussion before the next session.[28]

The same basic group met again on April 27 at the FCO and the two sides remained divided in their assessment of the situation in Northern Ireland. Sir Edward Peck began by claiming that the British had been right in predicting that Easter would pass without trouble but when challenged by O'Sullivan he changed that assessment to "fairly right," acknowledging that some violence had in fact broken out. (Serious rioting had indeed taken place in Derry and Belfast with dozens of soldier and civilians being injured and the army using large amounts of CS tear gas against the rioters.[29]) Ronnie Burroughs admitted that the unionists were drifting toward the right (with unionist hardliners Ian Paisley and William Beattie winning election to Stormont on April 16[30]), but he argued that Chichester-Clark and the moderate wing of the Unionist Party were still moving forward on reform and pronounced himself "reasonably optimistic" about the political situation. He pointed to growing Northern nationalist support for the government's policies as one reason to feel hopeful.

Ambassador O'Sullivan said the Irish government disagreed with the optimistic British take on events. Dublin believed that things in the North were "very grave" and as bad as they had been last August. Burroughs injected that the situation was only "potentially grave" at this point. O'Sullivan went on to claim that Irish information on the North seemed superior to that of the British as Dublin had made correct predictions of violence in August 1969 and at Easter and had foreseen the unionist swing to the right. When Burroughs asked what advice Dublin had on the North, O'Sullivan declined to offer any, claiming that it was up to the British to do what they thought was best given the facts on which both sides could agree. The ambassador apologized for being "brutally frank" but asked whether the Labour government simply meant to keep the lid on events in the North until the British general election scheduled for June. To end that line of speculation Burroughs shared the confidential fact that the Conservative Party had already agreed with their Labour counterparts that reform had to continue to have bipartisan support in Westminster regardless of the outcome of the elections.

O'Sullivan continued to badger the British over the scope and pace of reform and complained about the use of CS gas by the army. He also raised the issue of using proportional representation for elections in Northern Ireland but the British told him that Callaghan did not currently support this idea so London would not recommend it to Stormont. Sir Edward Peck closed the meeting by calling for another discussion in a month. O'Sullivan suggested that Hillery might want to come to London himself for the next discussion.[31]

Growing Irish pessimism about reform

Within the Irish government fear that the British-sponsored reform of Stormont was failing was growing stronger. An internal Department of External Affairs memo written by Eamonn Gallagher in early May expressed the opinion that reform of the North through the existing Stormont government was "close to the point of failure." This called into question the basic policy that the department had proposed back in November 1969 that Dublin focus on promoting reform in the North before it turned to the long-term goal of national reunification. Gallagher, while specifically avoiding any particular policy recommendations, argued that the major hurdle to reform and a return to stability in the North was the right wing of unionism exemplified by people like Ian Paisley and William Craig. The British had to be made to see that hardline unionism had to be faced down or the whole structure of reform would be undermined. The note suggested that introducing the issue of the border into the heart of the discussion about Northern Ireland might induce a much needed showdown between unionist extremists and the British government while there was still time. "A failure now to grasp the nettle of unionist reaction," the memo claimed, "could have very grave consequences."[32]

In early May 1970 Hugh McCann, secretary of the Department of External Affairs, paid a call on the newly installed British ambassador, John Peck, to discuss the idea of Hillery meeting again with George Thomson. Peck suspected that the main purpose of the proposed trip by Hillery would be for Lynch's government to demonstrate to a domestic political audience that it was active in trying to resist the growing rightward shift in unionism.[33] As it was, due to the intervening Arms Crisis which involved charges that members of Lynch's Cabinet attempted to smuggle weapons to Northern nationalists, Hillery did not make the trip to London and Ambassador O'Sullivan and Kevin Rush met with George Thomson over lunch at the Irish Embassy in London to convey the minister for external affairs' points. The change of venue and personnel did not change the general dynamic of the conversation. The Irish argued that the situation in Northern Ireland was deteriorating rapidly while Thomson expressed the British view that progress on reform was being made and Dublin should help Chichester-Clark to continue on the path of reform. Thomson argued for "less emotion and more reason." Against the backdrop of the unfolding Arms Crisis in Dublin the question of weapons smuggling into the North to arm unionists was raised by O'Sullivan. The ambassador claimed that communist bloc nations were involved in smuggling arms to extremists on both sides. Thomson suggested that Irish and British intelligence should cooperate on the matter of illegal arms importation.

O'Sullivan told Thomson that Lynch was in a precarious political position and the ambassador said that a public statement by London that it recognized the importance of partition as a root problem "to the present troubles" would help Lynch to survive. Thomson said that a public statement on the border would not help either government and suggested that they could always discuss the matter "privately as between friends." Thomson wrapped up the meeting by again calling for Anglo-Irish intelligence cooperation. He said he understood "the political risks" for the Irish of sharing security information with London but he promised "total discretion" on Britain's part.[34]

Dublin's growing pessimism over the situation in Northern Ireland prompted an appeal to Washington for help. In May, Ambassador William Warnock met twice with State Department officials to discuss Dublin's concerns. Warnock handed the Americans an informal note that the Irish were sharing with a number of friendly governments. It detailed the Irish belief that the British-backed reform effort was on the verge of failure and that Northern Ireland could descend into widespread violence. Warnock claimed that Lynch's government had so far been very conciliatory but that the Irish public was losing faith in this peaceful approach. Dublin wanted the American government to advise its British ally that they should be putting more pressure on Stormont to continue on the path of reform. The Irish public needed to see that Lynch's moderate stance was working and that real change was occurring in the North. Assistant Secretary of State Martin J. Hillenbrand could offer no help to Warnock beyond best wishes for a peaceful solution as he had to reaffirm the American "policy of nonintervention" on Northern Ireland.[35]

The issue of Anglo-Irish cooperation was complicated by the looming UK general elections. On June 9, 1970, a pessimistic Sean Ronan spoke to Ambassador Peck about the situation in the North. He said that Irish government believed that the problem was now mainly a political one rather than an issue of security. Ronan also expressed the Irish government's fear of a Conservative victory at the polls, particularly if the Tories needed the votes of hardline Unionist MPs in Westminster. Ronan said that the current Labour government was the first British government to do anything about the injustices in the North since partition began. Peck tried to reassure Ronan that reforming the North was a priority for both major British parties. Shortly after this meeting the ambassador advised the FCO that "whomever wins the election HMG should firmly restate its support for reform in Northern Ireland."[36]

The Arms Crisis

The divisions within Fianna Fáil came to a head during the so-called Arms Crisis that engulfed the Irish government between the spring and autumn of 1970. The crisis involved charges that members of the Cabinet were involved in a plot to illegally import arms into Ireland for distribution in the North. While many questions remain unanswered about the Arms Crisis the general outline of events is not in doubt. The roots of the crisis can be traced back to August 1969 when the Irish Cabinet agreed to set up a fund of £100,000 to provide aid to victims of the violence in the North. Minister for Finance Charles Haughey was appointed head of the special Northern committee meant to oversee the money. While intended by the Cabinet to provide funds to aid people who had been injured or displaced by the rioting, over the next several months the majority of that fund was used to purchase arms and to attempt to distribute the weapons to Northern nationalists, including the organizers of the Provisional IRA.[37]

The link between the government fund and the Northern nationalists was provided by Captain James Kelly of the Irish Army. When the August crisis broke out the Irish military had very limited intelligence on the situation in the North and Captain Kelly helped to fill this void. Kelly was on holiday in Derry in August and began informal discussions with local nationalists and republicans. When he returned to duty Captain Kelly was formally assigned as an intelligence officer to further develop these contacts. Kelly not only answered to his direct commanders but also made reports to Charles Haughey and Neil Blaney. The extent to which Kelly was following orders from his military superiors is disputed but it is clear that he conceived of a plan to import arms into Ireland for distribution to the various nationalist self-defense committees that were springing up in the North. In early October 1969 Captain Kelly met with Belfast IRA member John Kelly, who was acting as the representative of the Northern self-defense committees, in order to provide arms to Northern nationalists. The Garda Special Branch had Captain Kelly under surveillance and reported the details of the meeting to Peter Berry, the secretary of the Department of Justice. In April 1970, when the weapons were scheduled to be flown into Dublin, Peter Berry ordered the Special Branch to intercept the shipment, causing the arms smuggling plot to collapse.[38]

When Lynch was informed about the plot and the possible involvement of Cabinet members by Peter Berry he confronted Neil Blaney and Charles Haughey and asked them to resign. Both men protested their innocence and refused to step down. Lynch made the Cabinet aware of the situation on May 1, 1970, but took no further action. Captain Kelly was arrested on that same day. While Lynch appeared to be trying to avoid an open split in his government, he was forced to take public action when Fine Gael leader Liam Cosgrave was made aware of the developments by sources in the Garda and confronted Lynch with the information. Lynch was now obliged to make a public move against the accused ministers. The taoiseach induced Mícheál Ó Móráin to resign as minister for justice due to health reasons, although Lynch told the Dáil that Ó Móráin was not involved in the gun running plot. Blaney and Haughey were sacked from the Cabinet on May 5 and both were subsequently arrested. Minister for Local Government Kevin Boland resigned from the Cabinet in solidarity with his two fired colleagues on May 7. In a meeting to brief the Fianna Fáil TDs on May 6 regarding the situation the government received unanimous support for Patrick Hillery's motion that confirmed the taoiseach's right to fire and appoint Cabinet members. The conflict between the moderate and hardline elements within Fianna Fáil had now been played out in public and the Fianna Fáil members in the Dáil, at least for the time being, had chosen to stand by Lynch and the moderates.[39]

The full truth about the Arms Crisis may never be known and certain aspects, such as the extent to which Jack Lynch knew about the plot before the Garda intervened to stop it, are debated by scholars of the period. For instance, Justin O'Brien and Diarmaid Ferriter have argued that Lynch knew more than he claimed and may well have turned a blind eye to the plot.[40] In Catherine O'Donnell's study of Fianna Fáil's relationship to republicanism, she blames Lynch for, at the very least, not firmly controlling the Cabinet and thus allowing the hardliners to believe that they could run guns into the North without interference.[41] Historians such as Dermot Keogh, John Walsh, and Anthony Craig are among those who absolve Lynch of any complicity in the plot. In his biography of Lynch, Keogh accepts the taoiseach's claim that he did not know about the plot before it was officially revealed to him in April 1970. He gives Lynch credit for standing up to his more republican-minded, and politically powerful, Cabinet ministers once the conspiracy became public.[42] John Walsh admits that Lynch could have been more effective in controlling his own Cabinet but ultimately he argues that the plotters were acting without Lynch's knowledge and contrary to his wishes.[43] Anthony Craig places the blame for the gun-running squarely on the shoulders of Charles Haughey. He argues that Haughey was acting without Lynch's knowledge in an attempt to bolster his own republican credibility in order to strengthen his chances of replacing Lynch as the leader of Fianna Fáil.[44] Stephen Kelly concluded that "Haughey and Blaney were ... effectively conducting their own Northern Ireland policy, which was at odds with official government policy."[45] The view that Lynch did not know about or condone the concept of arming Northern nationalists is also supported in the memoir of Pádraig Faulkner, Lynch's minister for education, who categorically

denied the idea that the government ever agreed to "sanction, or involve itself
with the procurement of arms." Faulkner believes that Haughey and Blaney acted
without any authority to funnel money from the relief fund into arms smuggling
and that once Lynch had firm proof that this was the case he promptly sacked
the two men from the Cabinet.[46] Given the number of rumors about Haughey's
activities, including the discussion that Ambassador Gilchrist and Lynch had
back in November 1969, it is hard to image that the taoiseach had no idea that
members of his Cabinet might be involved in arms smuggling before April 1970.
Of course this does not mean that he had detailed and actionable information
nor does it suggest that he in any way supported the plot. In fact his actions after
the Arms Crisis broke out indicate that Lynch, while attempting to limit the
damage to party unity, was sincere in his belief that the Troubles could only be
ended with a peaceful political solution.

Figure 2.1 Charles Haughey.

The Arms Crisis and Anglo-Irish relations

The dramatic events of the Arms Crisis played out during the period of transition from the government of Harold Wilson to that of Edward Heath in London and the diplomatic reaction to the crisis helps to illuminate the state of Anglo-Irish relations during this time. As noted above, rumors of links between Charles Haughey and gun-running were abroad as early as November 1969. On November 10 Ambassador Gilchrist wrote to the FCO regarding the evolution of the civil rights movement in the North. He included unconfirmed reports that Haughey had set up an organization in Monaghan that was collecting intelligence from the North, supplying information to journalists, and making contacts with the various nationalist self-defense committees in Northern Ireland. Gilchrist suggested that Haughey's operation was planning to coordinate military aid to the Northern nationalists and that some weapons may have already been supplied by people associated with Haughey's group. Labour TD Conor Cruise O'Brien reportedly told the ambassador that Lynch had only very recently become "aware of the range of Haughey's activities" and was not pleased about the developments.[47] The British government took no action based on Gilchrist's report which, in any event, portrayed Jack Lynch as an opponent of the actions of the more republican wing of Fianna Fáil.

The public eruption of the Arms Crisis in May 1970 was of concern to London as there was a real fear that Lynch's government would not survive the sacking or resignation of three Cabinet ministers. When Irish ambassador O'Sullivan met with George Thomson on May 6, 1970, in place of Patrick Hillery who had returned to Dublin to help deal with the crisis, he told the chancellor that Lynch's government was under a great deal of political pressure and that it was possible that Neil Blaney would replace Lynch as taoiseach. While O'Sullivan did have some observations and points to make regarding Irish concerns about the deterioration of the situation in Northern Ireland, to his British hosts he appeared more concerned about the political situation in the South. The ambassador asked Thomson for help for Lynch, possibly by way of a public British acknowledgment of the relevance of the border issue with regard to the overall situation in Northern Ireland. Thomson tried to convince O'Sullivan that Northern Ireland was not as unstable as Dublin feared and promised to forward his suggestions to higher levels of the government.[48] On the following day Thomson reported to the British Cabinet that Lynch's "position has [been]... badly shaken" by the firing of Blaney and Haughey and that he feared that the moderates in Dublin would actually be weakened now that the main Fianna Fáil hardliners had no motivation to compromise with Lynch.[49]

On May 6, 1970, Eamonn Gallagher met with David Blatherwick of the British Embassy in Dublin to reinforce the message that O'Sullivan was delivering to Thomson in London. Gallagher stressed once again the Irish fear that the attempt to reform Stormont was failing and that Lynch was paying a political price for his moderate support of British policy. Gallagher said that London needed a new policy for Northern Ireland. While Gallagher would not suggest a specific course of action he did advise Blatherwick that as Lynch had been forced to "grasp the nettle" of militant republicanism within Fianna Fáil and oust Haughey and Blaney, London should now take similar action against the right wing of unionism in the North and accelerate reforms. Blatherwick reported to London that he expected Lynch's government to continue to press the British to take more heed of its advice in order to strengthen the moderate forces in Dublin.[50]

John Peck, the new British ambassador to Dublin, sent his own views on the crisis to Foreign Secretary Michael Stewart in late May 1970. The ambassador believed that it was in London's best interest to cooperate with Lynch to promote moderation in the Irish government. Peck argued that despite Lynch having survived the immediate crisis, Fianna Fáil remained divided into the moderate wing that fully rejected violence and elements that were still sympathetic to the emerging Provisional IRA. The ambassador warned that Lynch would not survive if the North became more violent or if London seemed to be ignoring Dublin's advice. "We have to recognize and be prepared for an element of blackmail in this," Peck wrote, "I submit, however, that it will be necessary to accept this with forbearance as a necessary part of Lynch's domestic fight for survival." Peck concluded that the Irish government would benefit if the British government provided "even the slightest hint that one day they might discuss" the idea of reunification.[51]

Irish Army Intelligence officers in the North

During the Dáil debate on a motion of confidence for Lynch's government following the revelation of the weapons smuggling plot, the taoiseach acknowledged that Irish Army Intelligence officers were active in Northern Ireland.[52] This public admission angered unionist hardliners, like Ian Paisley, who attempted to use the issue to embarrass Chichester-Clark and Wilson.

The Foreign and Commonwealth Office moved to downplay the problem but felt compelled to at least bring the situation to the attention of the Irish government.[53] Sir Edward Peck raised the issue at the end of a meeting with Ambassador O'Sullivan on May 20, 1970, but the FCO made it clear that the British government was not making a formal protest nor did Peck request that Irish military intelligence refrain in the future from being involved in the North.[54]

The issue became more complicated when news of the meeting leaked to the press. The reports of the discussion on RTE placed more emphasis on British concerns about the activities of Irish Army Intelligence in the North than was warranted by the actual exchange between Peck and O'Sullivan. The British Embassy in Dublin called the Department of External Affairs to apologize for the press leak and to explain that the information to the press came not from the FCO but from UK representative Ronnie Burroughs' office in Belfast. Burroughs's hope was to "take the heat off Major Chichester-Clark" who was under pressure from Ian Paisley to protest the presence of Irish intelligence officers in the North.[55] On May 26, 1970, Burroughs wrote to the FCO to report that Chichester-Clark had been able to stonewall Paisley's parliamentary questions in Stormont but that Paisley was now moving to pass a motion of censure against Chichester-Clark that would include reference to Dublin's admission about the intelligence officers in the North. Burroughs recognized the importance to both London and Dublin of avoiding a public dispute over the issue but he advised that unless the British government formally asked Dublin to refrain from sending operatives to the North Paisley would gain a political advantage over Chichester-Clark.[56]

Following Burroughs' advice, and fearful that Paisley would be able to further damage Chichester-Clark, London decided it had to reopen the intelligence issue with Dublin. Ambassador John Peck was instructed to seek assurances from the Department of External Affairs that Irish intelligence officers were no longer operating in the North and that no more would be sent by the Irish.[57] Peck met with Patrick Hillery and Hugh McCann to convey the British request. The Irish argued that given the ongoing Arms Crisis it was politically impossible for Lynch to issue any public statement about withdrawing intelligence officers from Northern Ireland. Hillery contended that bowing to Paisley's pressure only made the right wing of unionism stronger. He suggested that the British government make the most of Lynch's specific words in the Dáil that only spoke of Irish Army officers operating in the North during August 1969 to suggest that it was no longer happening. London could also attempt to focus any public conversation on Lynch's dramatic moves against the arms plotters in his own government and express confidence in British security services. Peck believed that Hillery was trying to be as helpful as he could possibly be given the politically fraught situation for Lynch's government at the time.[58]

The Home Office and the Foreign and Commonwealth Office quickly agreed with Ambassador Peck's assessment of the situation. London had concluded that Chichester-Clark should be advised to play up the fact that the British government had officially made its unhappiness known to Dublin "with sufficient vigour." The Northern premier could also deflect criticism of his administration by pointing out that Westminster was in charge of UK foreign relations and security. Lastly, Chichester-Clark could point to Lynch's actions in stopping arms smuggling.[59]

The controversy surrounding the intelligence officers and the events of the Arms Crisis as a whole provide important insight into the relationship between Ireland and Britain. The public emergence of the weapons smuggling charges in May 1970 brought the threat to Lynch's moderate policies from the more republican-minded elements of Fianna Fáil into stark relief. The taoiseach's struggle against his Cabinet hawks reinforced to London the importance of keeping Lynch in power in Dublin as he had backed up his moderate rhetoric with action by firing Haughey and Blaney. However, while Dublin tried to exploit London's fear of Lynch being replaced by a more radical leader the British were not willing to give any real concessions to the Irish government when it came to policy on Northern Ireland. British assistance to Lynch consisted mostly of keeping as silent as possible on the issue to avoid any appearance that Lynch was a tool of London. The controversy around the Irish intelligence officers in the North shows that the British had their own domestic political concerns to deal with as Wilson's government worked to defend Chichester-Clark from his own hardline opposition. While London felt compelled to formally address the issue of Irish intelligence gathering in the North, the British and Irish governments worked together to keep the dispute as limited as possible.

Conclusions

In the months after the crisis of August 1969, Dublin and London sought to improve their relations with each other by moving away from confrontation and toward cooperation. While public disputes were reduced, real cooperation proved elusive between the Lynch and Wilson governments. Lynch's speech at

Tralee was meant in part as a "reset" of Anglo-Irish relations. While the Irish preference would have been for formal talks and recognition by the British of the right of Dublin to be consulted on Northern Ireland, the Lynch government agreed that low-profile talks "on the margins" were a political necessity given unionist fears. Dublin's aims for the discussions were to facilitate reform of Stormont and lay the groundwork for reunification. The Irish put their faith in the Dublin–London relationship to achieve their goals even as they understood that reunification would require the consent of the unionists. Harold Wilson's government harbored less ambitious aims for the Anglo-Irish relationship. While there were officials, such as Sir Andrew Gilchrist, who argued for real engagement with Dublin over the future of Northern Ireland, London's main goal was to keep the Irish government calm and committed to moderation while the reforms promised by the Downing Street Declaration gradually returned the North to a peaceful state. Sharing information with the Irish was a small price to pay for keeping them on board with the British agenda. London sought to push the Irish into greater cooperation with Belfast as a way of achieving a long-term solution on the basis of cross-border initiatives that would effectively turn the problem of the North over to the divided people of Ireland once peace was restored.

An examination of the numerous Anglo-Irish meetings from late 1969 until June 1970 reveals how little was actually accomplished and how divided the two governments were on Northern Ireland. During the discussions the British generally pointed to successful reforms and argued for more patience to allow Chichester-Clark's government more time to achieve additional reforms. In terms of the security situation, London repeatedly argued that the British Army had been able to stop the widespread violence that had engulfed the North in August 1969 and that law and order were returning to the province. Irish officials painted a different view of the North in their talks with the British. From Dublin's point of view the reforms by Stormont were insufficient and even these limited reforms had promoted a dangerous rightward swing in the unionist community. The Irish were also more pessimistic about the overall security situation. As the months wore on, the Irish became increasingly convinced that Stormont would be unable to achieve meaningful changes in the North and that further violence would result from this failure. However, the Irish offered no specific advice to London on what course of action to pursue in the near future as an alternative to pushing Chichester-Clark toward reform.

As far as a longer range solution to the North's problems, the Irish inevitably moved the Anglo-Irish dialogue beyond the topic of civil rights legislation to the issue of the constitutional status of Northern Ireland. While Dublin realized that reunification was a long-term goal, it was not a goal that the Irish were willing to put aside while more immediate issues were dealt with. Lynch's government hoped that London would publicly promote the concept of peaceful reunification. This would put pressure on the moderate unionists to accept Irish unity as inevitable and work with moderate nationalists to ease the path to national reunification. While Wilson privately acknowledged that consensual reunification was worth pursuing as a topic of Anglo-Irish talks, he rejected the idea that the British government should publicly promote reunification while the unionists were still so adamantly opposed to the concept.

It is not surprising that Anglo-Irish diplomacy did not bring about a major breakthrough in the period from September 1969 to June 1970. The Irish government had unrealistic expectations of how much influence they would be able to have over London, particularly on the issue of reunification. To the British government the low-profile talks with the Irish were not actually meant to achieve anything beyond placating Dublin so that London would have a free hand in pursuing its own strategy of solving the Northern problem through the reform of Stormont. One positive achievement of the "talks on the margins" is that it did allow Lynch and his moderate supporters to demonstrate that the taoiseach was not ignoring the North and that peaceful dialogue with the British was possible if not, at this juncture, very valuable. Lynch's domestic position was secure enough that he was able to win the confrontation with the more extreme elements of his party during the Arms Crisis and maintain his moderate policies. Wilson's government also realized that confrontation with Lynch was not helpful. The British government wanted to reward Lynch's moderation with talks in order to promote a continued helpful stance by Dublin. Unfortunately the talks themselves produced nothing but a venue for disagreement on Northern Ireland.

The Conservatives Come to Power:
June 1970–March 1971

On June 18, 1970, Harold Wilson and the Labour Party were defeated by Edward Heath and the Conservatives in a UK general election. Northern Ireland was not an important issue in the election and the Tories did not initially promise any major change in British government policy on the North.[1] While Edward Heath may have hoped that Northern Ireland would not be a central concern for his government, in fact June saw the beginning of a steady increase in violence. There were 17 deaths from violence related to the Troubles from the summer of 1969 through April 1970. From the point of Heath's election in mid-June 1970 until the end of August there were 19 fatalities.[2] The transition from Labour to Conservative government took place on the cusp of the traditional Orange Order marching season in the North and Heath had to quickly confront the potential violence in the province. Within days of the election Ambassador Peck called the Department of External Affairs to inform the Irish government that additional British troops were being deployed to the North as a precaution against any trouble arising from the parades.[3]

Anglo-Irish relations were strained in the months following Heath's election. The growing violence in the North was increasingly orchestrated by the Provisional IRA and British military attempts to reduce the threat from the Provisionals only tended to increase tensions and violence. In Dublin, Lynch's government had to face the challenge of the militant wing of the party as the Arms Crisis reached its climax. The nine-month period after the Conservative Party came to power saw an increasing divide between Dublin and London over the efficacy of the reform program in the North and the wisdom of Britain's growing focus on the need for Anglo-Irish security cooperation to combat the IRA.

Figure 3.1 British prime minister Edward Heath and some of his Cabinet ministers in Parliament, including, from left, Foreign Secretary Sir Alec Douglas-Home and Home Secretary Reginald Maudling, July 1970. Credit: Peter King.

Irish assessment of Northern crisis

On the very day of the UK general election Patrick Hillery addressed the inaugural meeting of the Irish Inter-Departmental Unit on the North of Ireland that brought together officials from the Department of External Affairs, the Department of the Taoiseach, and the Department of Finance. Hillery began by placing the blame for partition squarely on the shoulders of Irish unionists and by condemning Stormont as having been discriminatory toward Northern nationalists. The minister for external affairs then pronounced that "conditions have changed radically…the days of a separatist regime in the North are numbered." Hillery told his listeners that Stormont would have to accept a more just system in the North that respected the rights of nationalists and that Northern Ireland could not "ultimately…separate itself from the country as a whole. I am not suggesting that we shall see an end to Partition within a very short time. I am suggesting that we shall see an end to Partition within, at most, a generation." Hillery charged the Inter-Departmental Unit with collecting information on economic, social, and cultural factors that might help to bring North and South closer together as they moved toward inevitable reunification. Both Hillery and the Inter-Departmental Unit chair, Sean Ronan, made it clear that the group would not be forming the government's policy on Northern Ireland as this remained the prerogative of the taoiseach and the Cabinet. Ronan went on to explain that the Department of External Affairs had recently developed good channels of communication with the British government regarding the North. According to Ronan, the Irish government was pursuing a three-step strategy on the North. For the next year or two the focus would be on reform of Stormont. The next step would be to promote reconciliation between the North and South that would allay legitimate unionist fears of unification, while the "final stage would hopefully see a constitutional settlement."[4] Ronan's analysis was surprisingly optimistic given that Dublin had been complaining to London for some months that reform was not working.

Ambassador Peck's advice to London

The idea that the situation in Northern Ireland was rapidly changing was not confined to the Irish Department of External Affairs. On June 30, 1970, Ambassador John Peck sent a long message to Sir Alec Douglas-Home, Edward Heath's new foreign secretary, presenting the ambassador's analysis of the state of Anglo-Irish relations as they related to Northern Ireland. Peck began by characterizing the ongoing Arms Crisis as "one of the most momentous events in the fifty year history of the Republic" and one that would have an impact on Britain and Northern Ireland. Launching into an analysis of what republicanism meant in Ireland, the ambassador stated that since the end of the War of Independence the term had come to mean support for Irish unification, and thus every Irish political party claimed to support republicanism while "being divided almost to destruction about what it means." In addition to the mainstream parties the IRA factions considered themselves to be true inheritors of the title. "The gunmen and the gun runners may be the black sheep," Peck wrote, "but we must recognize that they are the black sheep of the family." For the time being, Peck believed, Jack Lynch's moderate and peaceful definition of republicanism had the support of the majority of the Irish public and under his leadership "republicanism has lurched forward 50 years."

In terms of the immediate crisis in the North, Peck reported that Fianna Fáil was divided between an "old guard" that supported arming the nationalist community for self-defense and the Lynch faction that trusted the British to keep order in the province. As for long-term Irish plans for reunification, the "old guard" had no new or even rational strategy while the IRA hoped to use violence to induce London to withdraw from Northern Ireland "and leave the Irish to sort out their own problems." In Peck's opinion, Lynch had the best plan for dealing with the Northern Ireland crisis. Through an analysis of Lynch's public statements, the ambassador concluded that Lynch's government did not recognize Northern Ireland as a legitimate political entity and blamed London for allowing Stormont to discriminate against Catholics for fifty years. However, the taoiseach did accept that the British were responsible for the North, had done a credible job of restoring law and order, and, going forward, Lynch was committed to working with London to find a solution.

Peck believed that partition was a central issue in understanding political life in Ireland and argued that partition was becoming a critical issue for Dublin, Belfast, and London due to the violence in Northern Ireland. The three governments needed to work together to promote stability despite the fact that no Irish government, even one as moderate as that of Jack Lynch, could accept the idea of a permanent division of the island. Furthermore, Peck argued that a permanent border was fueling the violence in the North and creating the danger that violence would "become established as a way of life." In order to break the cycle of violence Peck suggested that London needed to reexamine its commitment to the unionist veto over Irish reunification. The ambassador agreed with the Irish view that, while any discussion of the constitutional status of Northern Ireland was politically difficult, a total lack of discussion of the subject was helping the IRA to attract more and more support among nationalists. Peck was careful to point out that even Dublin saw reunification as a slow multistep process that would involve the consent of the majority of the people of the North but he warned White Hall that there might be no way to end the violence "without taking a new and searching look at the constitutional issues."[5]

Growing violence in the North

Peck's call to look for a long-term solution in cooperation with Dublin took place against the backdrop of a sharp increase in violence in the North. On June 26, 1970, Bernadette Devlin, the youthful and popular independent nationalist MP for Mid-Ulster, was arrested and jailed for six months following the loss of her appeal of her conviction for riotous behavior during the Battle of the Bogside the previous August. Devlin's arrest led to serious unrest in Derry that spread to Belfast. There was a prolonged gun battle in Belfast on June 27 between a loyalist mob attempting to penetrate the Catholic Short Strand neighborhood in east Belfast and a small group of IRA snipers defending the area from the grounds of St. Matthew's Church. Hundreds of Catholic workers at Harland and Wolff shipyard were forced from their job by Protestant coworkers as the rioting continued. The fighting left six dead and 113 wounded, including fifty-two British soldiers. Catholics suffered a very small percentage of the casualties with only one fatality and four injured.[6]

The increase in violence in Northern Ireland was not the direct result of an immediate change in British policies following Heath's election. Thomas Hennessy has argued that blaming Heath's government for the surge in violence "is a myth—an understandable one on the part of the Catholic population but a myth nonetheless." The real cause of the intensification of the conflict was the increase of Provisional IRA attacks on the security forces rather than a British decision to pursue a more aggressive military strategy, although Hennessy admits that heavy-handed British Army tactics in the period resulted in further alienation of nationalists.[7] The Provisional wing of the IRA had split from what became known as the Official wing of the IRA in December 1969. The Provisionals rejected the focus that Chief of Staff Cathal Goulding and his supporters placed on Marxist-inspired politics and the formation of a unionist-nationalist working class alliance. The Provisionals, led by Sean MacStiofain, pledged to maintain a more traditional military stance against partition.[8] Even historians such as John Walsh, who argue that the counterproductive nature of the British Army's tactics in the North helped to increase the level of violence, believe that the Provisional Irish Republican Army (PIRA) was the real driving force in the escalation of the conflict.[9] Even without a change of orders from London, British Army was being dragged into a war with the Provisionals.

On the day of Devlin's arrest Ambassador O'Sullivan, accompanied by Kevin Rush and Eamonn Gallagher, had a meeting at the FCO with Sir Edward Peck and a number of other FCO and Home Office officials. O'Sullivan warned that the traditional 12th of July parades could well be a source of trouble if allowed to go forward and made the correct prediction that imprisoning Bernadette Devlin would provoke a violent reaction from the nationalist community.

Figure 3.2 IRA volunteers in Northern Ireland. Credit: Keystone—France.

The ambassador also complained about a lack of progress on reforms in Northern Ireland, including the failures to create a central housing authority, reform local government, outlaw incitement to religious hatred, and repeal the Special Powers Act. The British officials assured O'Sullivan that the new government meant to carry out the reform plans as outlined by the previous Labour government. Mr. North of the Home Office pointed out that reform of policing and the franchise had already taken place and that the current Northern Ireland parliament was planning to move ahead on the other issues. While North agreed with O'Sullivan that putting Devlin in jail was a foolish mistake, Sir Edward Peck assured the Irish that the British Army was prepared for any trouble with the Orange parades.[10]

On June 27 O'Sullivan telephoned Sir Denis Greenhill, the permanent undersecretary of state for foreign affairs, to request that the British government intervene to release Devlin even on a temporary basis. Greenhill promised to pass the request along to the Northern Ireland government but warned that they were unlikely to release her. O'Sullivan called back later that day to renew the request, adding the warning that Dr. Hillery had been contacted by a number of moderate nationalists in the North who warned of "a general conflagration" if the tensions were not reduced by Devlin's release.

Neil Cairncross, assistant secretary at the Home Office, after consultation with Ronnie Burroughs, and with the approval of the Home Secretary Reginald Maudling, returned O'Sullivan's call that afternoon to report that freeing Devlin would cause the collapse of Chichester-Clark's government: a development that Cairncross argued would not be in the best interest of Lynch's government.[11]

As the situation worsened in the North, Jack Lynch made a public statement about the violence. He characterized the "feelings of Miss Devlin's supporters" as "understandable" but expressed sadness that "the expression of their feelings and the holding of Orange Parades have led to further violence, suffering and even death." The taoiseach bemoaned the fact that the violent nationalist protests and provocative Orange parades only deepened the divisions in the North. Lynch said that Dublin had contacted the British government regarding Irish concerns over the arrest of Devlin and the sanctioning of Orange marches. He claimed that the current violence served as proof that Stormont needed to be reformed as soon as possible. The statement closed with a call for restraint on all sides and urged the citizens of the Irish Republic not to contribute to the trouble "in any way by word or deed."[12]

On June 29 the Irish government dispatched Patrick Hillery to London for an emergency meeting with Sir Alec Douglas-Home. Hillery presented himself as the spokesman for the nationalist minority in Northern Ireland even if the British did not welcome this arrangement. The immediate causes of the current violence, Hillery claimed, were the arrest of Devlin and the Orange parades. Northern nationalists were also concerned about how the new Tory government might act in regard to Northern Ireland. Sir Alec assured Hillery that there was no change in the British policy of maintaining law and order and supporting the reform program of Chichester-Clark. As for Devlin, Home Secretary Maudling and Sir Alec agreed that she would have to remain in jail. Turning to developments in the Irish Republic, Sir Alec questioned Hillery about IRA activity in the South, which Hillery dismissed as negligible. He also enquired about the impact of the Arms Crisis on the Irish government and Lynch's policy of moderation, which London appreciated. Hillery told Douglas-Home that Lynch's government was indeed being tested by the Arms Crisis and that the political fallout was unpredictable, but that the government would not change its policy on peaceful reunification. Douglas-Home promised to pass all of Hillery's comments along to Maudling before the home secretary left for a scheduled visit to Northern Ireland.

When Hillery asked for another meeting to discuss the 12th of July parades Douglas-Home suggested he meet with George Thomson under the cover of EEC discussions.[13]

The Falls Road curfew and Dublin's response

Following the deadly fighting in Belfast on June 27 and 28, British intelligence came to the conclusion that the initial rioting had been orchestrated by the PIRA to draw British units into nationalist areas to facilitate their own attacks on the army.[14] The British Army responded to this escalation of violence by republicans by actively searching for illegal weapons. In Belfast the search led to the military operation known as the Lower Falls Road curfew. The curfew began as a routine search operation that turned violent. On Friday July 3, 1970, British troops searched a house on Balkan Street in the Catholic Falls Road area and seized nineteen firearms that were part of an Official IRA weapons cache. In response to the harassment of the army detachment by rioters, Lt. Gen Sir Ian Freeland, commander of British forces in Northern Ireland, ordered 3,000 troops, supported by helicopters and armored cars, to conduct house-to-house searches of the entire neighborhood of the Lower Falls Road and declared a curfew of the area confining people to their homes. The resulting searches were conducted with great brutality and destruction of property. In addition to heated exchanges between residents and the army, members of both the Official and Provisional wings of the IRA carried out attacks on the troops. Rioters added to the violence and the army responded with tear gas. J. Bower Bell described the violence as a "continuous moving riot." By the time the curfew ended on Sunday July 5 the army had fired over 1,400 live rounds; six civilians were dead and over sixty people had been wounded, including eighteen soldiers. The military seized a total of fifty-two pistols, thirty-five rifles, six automatic weapons, and fourteen shotguns in addition to ammunition and explosives. After the curfew was lifted, the army escorted two ministers from the Unionist government through the area to view "the pacified Falls," an act that further enraged the nationalists of the area. The events added fuel to nationalist fears that under the new Conservative government the British Army had abandoned neutral peacekeeping in order to defend Stormont.[15] The Lower Falls Road curfew was a major event even by the standards of the increasingly troubled province. Numerous scholars have described the events of the curfew as having caused increased alienation between the British Army and Northern nationalists and as a major cause for the increase in support for the Provisional IRA.[16] While Geoffrey Warner's detailed study of the curfew warns that the event was not, in-and-of-itself, a real turning point, but rather part of a more gradual decline in nationalist–army relations, he does acknowledge that the Falls Road curfew was a dramatic event that showcased the growing aggressiveness of the IRA.[17]

In Dublin, Lynch's government felt compelled to take some kind of action to placate public outrage in Ireland or risk seeming weak. Patrick Hillery suggested that he pay a visit to Belfast to assess the situation. The minister, driven in a rented car by Eamonn Gallagher, paid an unannounced visit to the Lower Falls on July 6 where he met with local nationalists and the Catholic Bishop of Down and Connor.[18] Lynch reported to the Dáil the next day that the aim of the visit was to "reduce tension in the area by demonstrating the Government's interest in the welfare of the people of the area and also to obtain confirmation, at first hand, of the information we had already received, and to ascertain the feelings of the people."[19] Although Hillery's visit to Belfast clearly demonstrated Dublin's interest in the North, sending the minister for external affairs on an informal inspection cannot credibly be seen as the best method of gathering intelligence on events in Belfast.

While Hillery's trip was unannounced, he held a press conference as soon as he returned. He reported to the assembled media that "I was in the Falls Road and I met people there and saw what had happened ... and talked to people who are not public representatives—those who survived the week-end." Hillery said that his "impressions of the people were that they had a sudden, unexpected and to them quite unwarranted visitation from the British army and I am afraid that they don't regard the British army any longer their friends and protectors." When questioned about the practical impact of his visit, Hillery replied, "It is hard to answer that. We want to demonstrate to the people there that they are not isolated." When asked about any possible embarrassment he might feel on an upcoming official visit to London due of the unannounced nature of his trip to Belfast, he responded that "it would be an awful thing if we had to regard a visit by me to Northern Ireland as something to be embarrassed about. After all, they come to the [Dublin] Horse Show and we say nothing." He added that he was not concerned about having offended Stormont as it had done nothing effective to stop the violence in Northern Ireland nor did the nationalists of the North see any sign of reform from that quarter.[20]

Figure 3.3 British troops during the Falls Road curfew, July 1970. Credit: Wesley.

Diplomatic impact of Hillery's visit to Belfast

As Lynch's government must have known, neither London nor Belfast equated Hillery's Falls Road visit with a holiday to the Horse Show. Northern premier Chichester-Clark issued a statement claiming that he was "astounded" that Hillery would visit Belfast unannounced and concluded that "I cannot regard such a visit as helpful and I deplore it."[21] In meeting on the morning of July 7, Sir Edward Peck of the Foreign and Commonwealth Office blasted Irish ambassador Donal O'Sullivan, claiming that Hillery has "'made life hellishly difficult' for the British Government and for Major Chichester-Clark." Peck complained that the British had been forced to spend the night trying to ensure that Chichester-Clark did not take any "rash" action. In addition, Peck claimed that Hillery must have seen that the reports from the Falls Road had been exaggerated, although O'Sullivan responded that the opposite was in fact true. Peck compared Hillery's visit to espionage and told O'Sullivan that it was unlikely given the circumstances that Hillery would be able to meet with Sir Alec Douglas-Home as scheduled. O'Sullivan was not cowed and replied that "the impression is rapidly gaining ground, not only among the Minority in the North but also at home, that the one-sided raids which took place over the week-end can only be interpreted as a return to the hardline attitudes of the past." O'Sullivan went on to say that "the resentment which had been generated as a result of the events of the week-end…pose a serious threat to my Government." Following the Irish ambassador's warning about the stability of Lynch's government, Peck changed his tone and expressed appreciation for Lynch's moderate response to the crisis in Northern Ireland as a whole.[22]

The adversarial nature of the meeting between O'Sullivan and Edward Peck did not match the more moderate tone that the British government took in private on the matter later that same day. At a Cabinet meeting on July 7, Foreign Secretary Douglas-Home told his colleagues that Dublin had "in general adopted a responsible and constructive attitude" toward Northern Ireland which made Hillery's visit "all the more surprising." While Douglas-Home characterized the event as a "serious diplomatic discourtesy," the Cabinet agreed with his assessment that Lynch's government faced domestic "political difficulties" and strong resistance even within Fianna Fáil. The Cabinet viewed Hillery's trip as an attempt to take some of the pressure off of Lynch during the ongoing Arms Crisis. However, the Cabinet concluded that Dublin's tactic was counterproductive, and had enraged the Unionist government, so it could not be ignored, but that there was little sense in doing anything "which would aggravate the existing strain and shake more the already precarious position of Mr. Lynch, the continued existence of whose administration was on balance in our interest."[23] Later that day Douglas-Home made a statement in the House of Commons regretting that Dr. Hillery had not "consulted H.M.G. in advance if he wished to make a visit. Not to have done so is a serious diplomatic discourtesy. His visit has magnified the difficulties of those who are working so hard for peace and harmony in Northern Ireland."[24]

Lynch and Hillery clearly understood that the latter's visit to Belfast would roil Anglo-Irish relations. When Ambassador John Peck delivered the text of Douglas-Home's statement to Hillery, the minister for external affairs called the House of Commons statement fair and observed that a British rebuke would actually be politically helpful from Dublin's point of view. Hillery made no apology and characterized the Falls Road curfew as a mistake that had helped to alienate Northern nationalists from the British Army. Peck reported to London that when Hillery met with Douglas-Home as scheduled he was "likely to be extremely frank about his and Mr. Lynch's political problems, and welcome indications that we understand them. Their survival largely depends on being able to show some results for Northern Catholics."[25]

In fact, some British government officials shared Dublin's belief that the Falls Road curfew had had unintended negative consequences. Ronnie Burroughs, the UK representative in Belfast, described the arms searches as having "alienated virtually all Catholic opinion whether moderate or extremist." He urged London to stress that illegal arms would be seized from both nationalists and unionists with equal vigor to reestablish the sense that the British government was impartial and in control in Northern Ireland.[26]

While Sir Edward Peck had earlier warned Ambassador O'Sullivan that a scheduled meeting between the two foreign ministers might be canceled as a result of Hillery's visit to the Falls Road, London thought better of that and Douglas-Home and Hillery did meet on July 8, 1970. The Belfast trip came up immediately but Douglas-Home did not take Hillery to task for his diplomatic bad manners. In fact, Sir Alec opened their meeting with the conciliatory phrase, "I am afraid I could not have said less in Commons yesterday." Hillery remained unapologetic and took an aggressive line by reminding the British foreign secretary that Dublin had closely cooperated with London since the Troubles began "and had done very little indeed that could be regarded as having upset the apple cart." He went on to characterize the Falls Road curfew not only as an error on the part of Britain but one that had demonstrated that cooperation with London had no benefits for Dublin. "We had cooperated all along" Hillery claimed. "We were under condemnation at home for doing nothing. The Irish Government felt that our point of view was not being considered; the prestige of the Taoiseach was being eroded and suddenly last week-end we discovered that the matter was again 'none of our business.'" Hillery pressed the British to control the Orange Order and reroute the traditional 12th of July Orange parades away from Catholic areas or risk growing militancy among Northern nationalists.[27]

After the meeting at the FCO Hillery gave a press conference at the Irish Embassy in London in which he chastised the British government. He condemned the Fall Road raids as having alienated Northern nationalists and dismissed the arms found as "old pathetic weapons" that were strictly for self-defense against the threat of unionist mobs. He exhorted London to assert real authority in Northern Ireland and curb the Orange Order. When asked if he had been "rebuked" by Douglas-Home earlier in the day Hillery said, "I would remind people that I represent a sovereign state not to be rebuked by anyone else." Echoing Irish constitutional claims to sovereignty over the entire island he told the assembled reporters, "I believe that I represent any man living in Ireland and I am entitled to visit any town or hamlet in that Island.... I am an

Irishman. If Ireland is completely free I will obey the rules of the games that other nations laid down but while diplomatic niceties are so used as to prevent a large section of Irish people from getting fair play then I won't play the rules—I will play the main rules but not the niceties." While he initially denied that the trip was designed to placate public opinion in the Irish Republic, he seemed to contradict himself when he answered a later question by saying, "I am not a diplomat. I am a politician. I have some of the best diplomats in the world working in the Department of External Affairs and they obey all the rules [but] the behavior of Irish politicians is something related to the actual reality of our needs at home."[28]

In fact, Hillery's belligerent stance did play well back in Ireland. Northern nationalist leader Eddie McAteer telephoned Hugh McCann, the secretary of the Department of External Affairs, at McCann's home in Dublin with a message that he should tell Patrick Hillery "to stand firm on the right of any Irishman, Minister or not, to walk the streets of any Irish city without prior permission of any Englishman. Do please ignore this arrogant rebuke from the British Government whose studied neglect over 50 years has contributed so much to the present crisis."[29] The American ambassador to Dublin, John Moore, reported to Washington on the popularity of Hillery's trip to Belfast, telling the State Department that it "appealed to [the] Irish sense of nonconformity and was favorably received here." Moore also believed that the Belfast trip helped the political position of Jack Lynch's government and its moderate policies in the struggle against the more republican wing of Fianna Fáil.[30]

British ambassador John Peck confirmed to his government that Hillery's trip to Belfast and his performance in London were well received by the press and general public in Ireland. More importantly from London's point of view, Peck believed that the Falls Road trip provided a benefit to Britain in that Irish domestic support for Hillery was "having an important steadying effect here by rallying support for the Lynch Government. We should not take too seriously the fact that this is being achieved by being highly critical of HMG." Peck urged London to further aid Lynch by agreeing to reroute the Orange parades as Hillery had requested. The ambassador went on to call the Falls Road curfew a significant mistake that might drive nationalists to "launch something as irrational and heroic as the Easter Rising. Allowing for Irish hyperbole, this is a fair description of current anxieties. Having sacked the Ministers in his Government most likely to fan such flames, Lynch feels that his future, and the future of sane relations between the two countries is in our hands."[31]

12th of July parades

Hillery's largely symbolic visit to Belfast came in the midst of a more traditional diplomatic effort by the Irish government to pressure the British government to take action to curb the power of the Orange Order and to restrict or ban the traditional 12th of July parades. Dublin increasingly focused its dissatisfaction with reforms in Northern Ireland on the resistance of the Orange Order to fundamental change. Ambassador O'Sullivan telephoned Sir Edward Peck on Saturday July 4 to complain about the Falls Road curfew, but his main point was that Lynch's government was under a great deal of political pressure to compel the British to ban the 12th of July parades (which were scheduled for July 13, 1970, as they were not normally held on Sundays[32]). O'Sullivan warned Peck that if London did nothing, then Dublin would have to make a forceful public statement condemning British inaction. Peck argued that there were arguments in favor of allowing the parades to go on as scheduled and that the matter was still under consideration. Peck also requested that London be provided a copy of any public statement made by the Irish government ahead of time in order to help retain good Anglo-Irish relations.[33]

An internal memo in the Department of External Affairs expressed the growing fear in Dublin that Northern nationalists believed, regardless of the real motivation, that the British Army was disarming their community "to placate the extreme unionists and in order to enable the Orangemen to parade wherever they wish without hindrance on 13th July." The document concluded that in order to avoid a violent reaction from nationalists the British had to disarm unionist areas in Belfast and cancel or limit the parades.[34]

In an interview on the BBC broadcast on July 6, Patrick Hillery responded to a question about Orange parades by saying that "three times in the past 18 months we have warned the British Government of the effects of having these provocative parades and three times we were right, twice there was death and bloodshed and I think this time the British Government must listen to us."[35] Under public pressure from the Irish, Sir Edward Peck advised Ambassador O'Sullivan on July 7 that Home Secretary Maudling was planning to meet with Orange Order leaders regarding the July 13 parades and that Dublin should refrain from further comment on the matter as it would have no impact on the outcome of the decision.[36]

Jack Lynch sent a letter to Edward Heath on July 7 in response to a general message Heath had sent the taoiseach soon after his election as prime minister.

While the general sentiment of the exchange was that both sides wished to continue to consult on Northern Ireland in the manner that had evolved when Wilson was still in power, Lynch also used his message to press Heath to cancel the Orange parades on July 13 in order to avoid inciting violence. Lynch characterized the routing of these parades through nationalist areas as a clear provocation and not an "exercise of normal civil rights."[37]

During the July 8 meeting between Hillery and Sir Alec Douglas-Home that came on the heels of Hillery's visit to the Falls Road the two men had exchanged views on the impending parades and the Orange Order in general. Hillery claimed that Lynch's government had made a great effort, at a significant political cost, to establish good Anglo-Irish relations but that London was not reciprocating by taking the advice of Dublin on Northern Ireland. Lynch's political problems at home were linked to this perception that Irish cooperation with Britain yielded no rewards for Dublin. According to Hillery, the Orange Order, which had created partition in 1920, was still the major block to peace. He characterized the Orange Order as "a totally outdated sectarian and bigoted organization [that] continues to come between the natural growth of Anglo-Irish friendship." Hillery demanded that the British stop the ritual humiliation of nationalists by the Orangemen. In a direct appeal to the foreign secretary, Hillery said, "you are a sensitive man and I am sure you understand what I am saying; as among civilized people, which we both represent, we must between us arrange to put an end to this problem of the Orange Order."

Sir Alec countered that reform in Northern Ireland, which Dublin favored, was the first step forward. Hillery argued that reform was a gradual solution and would not address the immediate crisis developing in the North. Moderate sentiment among nationalists in the North was in danger of being overtaken by support for more violent extremist elements unless London stood up to the Orange Order on the issue of the July 13 parades. While Hillery did agree that only the most provocative of the parades had to be banned, he again stressed that sectarian bigotry had to be stopped by Britain if it wanted to be seen as the legitimate authority over Northern Ireland. Sir Alec promised to pass Hillery's message along to the home secretary.[38]

Patrick Hillery covered much the same ground in a meeting that same day with George Thomson. He claimed that standing up to Orange bigotry was essential to allow democratic governments to function on both sides of the border in Ireland and to maintain a positive Anglo-Irish relationship. Hillery went as far as comparing the need to stand up to the Orange Order to the need to have stood up to Nazism, a rather ironic analogy coming from the foreign minister of neutral Ireland. When asked about Dublin's ability to influence Northern nationalists to stop attacking Orange parades, Hillery countered that unless that British could show that they could at least reroute Orange parades away from Catholic areas than Dublin's ability to promote moderation would continue to decline.[39] In a press conference that Hillery gave that same day in London he stressed that his mission in the British capital was to press the British government to do what Stormont could not do and stand up to the Orange Order.[40]

From Dublin, Ambassador Peck warned the FCO that the Irish government held London directly responsible for the Orange Order parades and that "Irish hopes are concentrated on a single act—the banning and or rerouting of Orange parades ... and nothing will convince them that this is not reasonable or possible or desirable." Peck's own concern was that efforts to control the Orange parades would lead to a counterproductive escalation of violence in the North.[41]

The Irish government was not content to push its case solely with the British government. Hugh McCann paid a visit to Ambassador John Moore to request American assistance in convincing London to cancel or reroute the parades. McCann indicated that he had also requested the same help from a number of other NATO nations who could speak to the British as friends of both the United Kingdom and Ireland. According to McCann, the Irish government feared that full-scale civil war, which would involve both the North and the South of Ireland, could result from unaltered parades on July 13. Moore advised the State Department that McCann's fears were realistic and that the United States could offer such advice to the British without taking sides in the Northern conflict. The ambassador also believed that it was morally right to try to avert violence and that Anglo-Irish relations would continue to improve if violence was avoided.[42]

The American government quickly agreed to make a limited representation to Britain. On July 7 Deputy Chief of Mission Greene from the US Embassy in London paid a confidential call on Denis Greenhill at the FCO to report McCann's request. Greene took pains to praise British efforts at maintaining peace in Northern Ireland and made it clear that he was merely passing the Irish request along without endorsement. The American government's concern, he said, was based on the facts that relatives of US citizens lived in Northern Ireland and that Washington did not want to see anything damage Anglo-Irish relations.[43] While this was the first time that Washington had agreed to any Irish request for involvement in Northern Ireland, the American government only did the bare minimum that Dublin had requested while being careful not to offend the British. The incident did not mark a change in the American policy of noninvolvement in Northern Ireland.

Prime Minister Heath sent a message to the taoiseach on July 11, 1970, noting the issues raised by Hillery's recent visit to London. Heath characterized this type of personal discussion between Irish and British official as having "great value." He went on to inform Lynch that the threat from the July 13 parades was being taken seriously by both Westminster and Stormont and that Chichester-Clark had already announced a considerable amount of rerouting of the parades. Heath closed by restating his devotion to "ensure that law and order are maintained with complete impartiality" while his government sought a way forward to a peaceful and just Northern Ireland.[44]

The rerouted parades on July 13, 1970, passed without a major outbreak of violence and Heath sent Lynch another message on July 15 to praise the Irish leader for his public calls for calm over the weekend. "I feel sure," the prime minster wrote, "that the close cooperation between our governments has been an important factor in keeping the tension down, and I look forward to maintaining to the full the contacts we have already established."[45] Lynch was pleased with Heath's sentiment about continuing Anglo-Irish dialogue but he told Ambassador Peck that things could not continue in the North as they were. Despite having successfully lobbied for a rerouting of the Orange parades in July, the taoiseach told Peck that Northern Ireland was a powder keg that could be set off at any moment by "one fanatic; I.R.A. or U.V.F." and that such an explosion of violence would destroy the Irish and Northern Irish governments as well as "the whole growing edifice of Anglo-Irish understanding." Lynch expressed hope that the recent election of the Conservative government in Britain would open "new possibilities for constructive discussion." Peck reported that Lynch did not specifically mention partition but the ambassador believed that the taoiseach's hope was that reform in the North and closer Anglo-Irish ties, including joint entry into the EEC, would make the border an anachronism that would then disappear by mutual agreement.[46]

While Lynch may have hoped that the border would disappear in the future it was still very much an issue in the summer of 1970. Incidents of British troops crossing the border were frequent during this period. London was generally apologetic for these incidents and Dublin sought to keep the border incursions from becoming a major problem for Anglo-Irish relations. For instance, in July 1970 the Irish minister of justice expressed Dublin's concern to Ambassador Peck over the frequent reports by the Garda and private citizens of illegal border crossings by British troops but did not characterize the conversation as a "formal protest."[47] On July 14 Patrick Hillery told the Dáil during questions that border violations had been addressed with Ambassador Peck and that the British ambassador had apologized and assured him that any crossings were inadvertent, would be investigated by London, and that steps were being taken to avoid these incidents in the future. Hillery pronounced himself satisfied with London's response.[48]

As July drew to a close the British government believed that its relationship with Dublin was in good shape. In a memorandum sent out on July 29 the FCO's Western European Department expressed the belief that Stormont's decision on July 23 to ban all parades or marches for six months would satisfy Irish fears about the traditional August 12 Apprentice Boys parade in Derry as this event was covered by Chichester-Clark's prohibition. Head of the Western European Department at the FCO, John K. Drinkall, characterized relations with Lynch and Hillery as "excellent" and praised the continuing discussions between Irish and British officials.[49]

When Ambassador O'Sullivan, Kevin Rush, and Eamonn Gallagher met with Deputy Undersecretary of State Sir Thomas Brimelow and other FCO and Home Office officials on July 30 the Irish expressed less satisfaction with the situation in the North and the level of Anglo-Irish cooperation. While O'Sullivan said that Lynch would continue to publicly try to reduce tensions in the North by avoiding any volatile rhetoric, Eamonn Gallagher revisited complaints about the British handling of recent events in Belfast. According to Gallagher the British Army had not taken seriously the loyalist threat to the nationalist Short Strand neighborhood in Belfast and thus left the IRA to defend the area. Gallagher maintained that even if this impression was incorrect, the Falls Road curfew the next weekend had been a completely unjustified response to the fighting around St. Matthew's Church and that the British Army had only succeeded in alienating nationalists in the Falls Road area who had once had good relations with the army. Gallagher wanted the British to inform Dublin when the security forces were planning "unusual action" in the future. He also suggested that the RUC could not effectively police Orange parades as so many constables were also members of the order and called for a ban on RUC personnel from joining the Orange Order or the Ancient Order of Hibernians. The British dismissed the idea of informing Dublin of planned security force action as unworkable for security reasons. Sir Thomas asked that Lynch's government continue its public reticence over Northern Ireland to avoid agitating unionist opinion which was already inflamed by the ongoing reforms.[50]

Lynch and Heath agree to meet

On July 31, 1970, Prime Minister Heath reiterated this call for public silence from Dublin regarding the marching season in a message to Jack Lynch. The prime minister argued that Chichester-Clark would be facing a serious political backlash from the parade ban and that both London and Dublin should keep a low public profile regarding Northern Ireland as this was in the best interest of keeping the peace in the province.[51] The taoiseach did not reply to Heath until August 11, 1970. Lynch began by restating his faith that good Anglo-Irish relations "can help greatly to resolve tensions in the North and bring us closer to a better arrangement of affairs." The issue at the heart of the conflict in the North, Lynch argued, was that the "two major Irish traditions" were becoming increasingly alienated from each other. A continuation of this trend would cause "grave damage to the North, to Ireland and to Anglo-Irish relations." Lynch called for the two governments to work together to find a solution for Northern Ireland. While Lynch realized that London and Dublin could not impose peace "against the will of sizeable numbers of people," he claimed that Northern Ireland was "caught in a historic dilemma which it cannot resolve by itself" and urged the British to work with the Irish government "to open the way to a new kind of future." The main stumbling block to that new future, Lynch argued, were the right-wing unionists who "bedevil Anglo-Irish relations." If their power to disrupt the path to a peaceful and equitable society in the North was destroyed, Lynch hoped that "they might well turn to finding their proper place in the Irish nation." Lynch wrote that he was convinced that a new Ireland could be created that took "account of the personality of the Northern majority" and which would have unprecedentedly close relations with Great Britain. However, Lynch warned Heath that there was no time to delay in moving in this new direction. He closed the letter by commending the ongoing talks between British and Irish officials and called for a meeting between Heath and himself if the opportunity arose.[52]

In crafting a reply to Lynch's letter of August 11 and his invitation to meet with Heath, 10 Downing Street naturally sought the input of the FCO. Ambassador Peck had informed Whitehall that the Irish proposal was for a "meeting in the margin of some other occasion" rather than a formal summit on Northern Ireland and the FCO argued in favor of the meeting provided that "the constitutional status of Northern Ireland within the United Kingdom" not be discussed. The memo argued that "Mr. Lynch is far and away the best Irish Prime Minister we can hope for" and that his domestic political position would be aided by a meeting with Heath. A meeting would, furthermore, enhance Anglo-Irish cooperation and allow London to push for better North–South relations. While the Irish desire for unification was sincere, and they were bound to raise the issue, the FCO believed that Lynch was a pragmatist who saw reunification as a long-term goal and would be willing to focus on the need for cooperation in the near term.[53]

The letter that Heath sent to Lynch on August 31 closely followed this advice. Heath made it clear that London would continue to standby the Ireland Act of 1949 and would not be seen to engage in "a dialogue about the constitutional status of Northern Ireland" as to do otherwise would invite a violent backlash by unionists. "At the same time," he continued, "I agree that there is much that we can usefully discuss… with regard to measures of practical day-to-day cooperation between the Republic and the North of Ireland." Heath closed with an invitation to meet with Lynch while the two men were at the United Nations in late October.[54] As one scholar of the period noted, Heath had been in crisis management mode in Northern Ireland since becoming prime minister and now that the volatile marching season was over he had time to catch his breath and look for a more permanent solution for Northern Ireland.[55]

Formation of the SDLP

While the summer of 1970 was a period of conflict and violence in Northern Ireland there was one major development in the peaceful political life of the province that would also have an impact on Anglo-Irish relations. On August 21 the formation of the Social Democratic and Labour Party (SDLP) was announced in Belfast. The new nationalist party was headed by Gerry Fitt. Other founders included nationalist members of the Northern Ireland parliament such as John Hume, Austin Currie, Paddy Devlin, Paddy O'Hanlon, and Ivan Cooper. The new party pledged itself to work for reunification by strictly peaceful means and supported the maintenance of the Stormont government as long as it worked for reforms of the system in Northern Ireland. While the SDLP was formally committed to nonviolence some members of the party, such as Paddy Devlin, believed that the IRA's defense of nationalist areas was justified. The party was also quick to condemn the excesses of the security forces.[56]

The SDLP was more left of center than Fianna Fáil and they were not natural political allies but John Hume in particular believed that the SDLP would have to cooperate with the Dublin government if they wanted to have a real impact on Northern Ireland. The idea of cooperation with Lynch's government was not as fully embraced by other SDLP leaders such as Gerry Fitt and Paddy Devlin.[57] Despite these divisions the SDLP rapidly replaced the declining Nationalist Party and the more radical Northern Ireland Civil Rights Association as the main nonviolent force in nationalist politics in the North.[58] Lynch embraced the idea of close ties with the SDLP as they were in agreement with his policy of a long-term peaceful push for Irish unity as a solution to the Northern Troubles.[59]

Continuing Anglo-Irish friction

In early September 1970 the Department of External Affairs prepared a memorandum for the Irish government that summarized Irish policy on Northern Ireland. Lynch had outlined the long-term policy of reunification in a series of public statements in July. The taoiseach had concluded that animosity between Irish Catholics and Protestants, not a struggle for territory, was at the heart of the Troubles. Unionism had sought to foster that division in Northern Ireland for the last fifty years in order to create a "British" section of Ireland. The experiment in a separate Northern Ireland had been a failure and once the unionists recognized this failure they would be willing to help to create a new unified Ireland that will protect Protestant identity and political liberty within an all-Ireland state. The document concluded that the British government has no desire to hold onto the North and that it had a responsibility to help the Irish government seek a path forward to reconciliation between the Irish communities and reunification of the island.

In examining the near term, the memorandum focused on how Dublin should react to the weakness of Chichester-Clark's government. The memorandum suggested that Northern nationalists would not accept Brian Faulkner or William Craig if either of them replaced Chichester-Clark. It would be preferable if London imposed direct rule on the North. According to the analysis, Dublin had so far discouraged Northern nationalists from trying to destroy Stormont, but if the British had to abolish the North's government because of right-wing unionist intransigence to reform, than the cause of reunification might be aided as partition itself might be revisited if Stormont fell. In the meantime the Irish government had to keep up the pressure on reforms to local government and housing, if only to maintain "a clear confrontation" with right-wing unionists while attempting to conciliate moderate unionists.[60]

The FCO prepared its own general analysis of Northern Ireland's impact on Anglo-Irish relations in a September steering brief prepared for Sir Alec Douglas-Home. The memorandum acknowledged that Northern Ireland dominated Anglo-Irish relations. Lynch's government was described as "vulnerable to their extremists as is the Northern Ireland Government from theirs, but ... Lynch is probably the best Irish leader we are likely to get and it is in HMG's interests to keep him in the saddle." While the Irish government was pursuing reunification, Lynch and Hillery were both committed to achieve that goal only through agreement with Belfast. Dublin understood that the Troubles were providing traditional militant republicanism with an opportunity to expand its power in Ireland, but the IRA had successfully exploited the perception, even among moderate Irishmen, that Northern nationalists were under attack from the British Army. On the positive side, the analysis concluded that Lynch was secure in power and that even Chichester-Clark might survive. However, there was a real danger that Chichester-Clark's pro-reform government would be undermined by right-wing unionists, a development which could force London to impose direct rule. The FCO believed that direct rule would have serious negative consequences to Anglo-Irish relations. The best hope for a stable Northern Ireland was for London to delicately encourage good North–South relations.[61]

While the two governments were not in full agreement in their analyses of the Northern problem they were in agreement on the need to work together for a solution. However, there were often points of friction between Dublin and London over events in Northern Ireland and British policies in the province. On September 22, 1970, Heath wrote to Lynch to give him a one day advance warning that Sir Arthur Young, the British police official who had been overseeing the reform of the RUC along the lines of the Hunt report, was being recalled to London and a new chief constable would be named by Stormont. Heath portrayed the move as part of the normalization process for the RUC and assured Lynch that there would be no rearming of the RUC or revival of the B-Specials.[62]

Lynch was unhappy with the change in leadership in the RUC. He told the British charge d'affaires that he had a hard time believing that the RUC had been fully reformed during Young's brief tenure. He also expressed concern that newly appointed Chief Constable Graham Shillington was a longtime RUC officer who had commanded the police forces arrayed during the Battle of the Bogside. Lynch called the appointment of Shillington "an extremely risky act" that would seem by the Nationalist community as a "retrograde step." If the appointment had to go ahead Lynch urged the British to make it clear "that there is no question whatever of rearming the RUC, reviving the B-Specials or creating any other armed force under the control of Stormont."[63]

Border incidents also caused problems in Anglo-Irish relations. On September 23 Ambassador Peck phoned the Department of External Affairs to lodge a formal complaint about an incident two days earlier near Crossmaglen in Armagh when a small force of British soldiers were attacked by a group of about forty men who came across the border from the South. Peck asked for a public apology for the incident to insure that right-wing unionist critics of Chichester-Clark could not use the attack to politically damage the Northern premier. The Irish government refused to apologize as according to the Garda, the men involved in the attack had crossed from Northern Ireland to launch their attack from the South, and therefore Dublin was not at fault. British charge d'affaires Piper restated the ambassador's case in person and warned Sean Ronan that if Chichester-Clark was made to seem "weak on law and order" then there would be new calls to rearm the RUC and reinstate the B-Specials. Piper stressed that London wanted the issue resolved as quickly and quietly as possible regardless of the facts.[64] While no apology was issued, Dublin did agree to reinforce the Garda in the area to stop any repetition of the incident.[65]

The periodic low-profile Anglo-Irish meetings continued in early October when Ambassador O'Sullivan and Eamonn Gallagher met with officials from the FCO and the Home Office in London. The two sides agreed that it was important for them to promote calm in Northern Ireland and to continue to work for reforms. O'Sullivan pointed out that a year had passed since the Downing Street Declaration and that Dublin believed that major progress still had to be made before the goals of the Declaration were achieved. The ambassador went on to list the concerns of the Irish government regarding what Dublin saw as a dangerous drift toward the right among the unionists. The list included the appointment of hardline unionist John Taylor to a post in Chichester-Clark's government, the replacement of Sir Arthur Young as head of the RUC, the Falls Road curfew, the lax enforcement on the ban on parades, and the recent deployment of spikes at the border near Crossmaglen. O'Sullivan also called for more direct British involvement in housing and local government reforms in Northern Ireland. UK representative in Northern Ireland Ronnie Burroughs calmly defended Stormont's record on reform and downplayed the threat from the right wing of the Unionist Party. He admitted that the Falls Road curfew had alienated many within the nationalist community but argued that the army was repairing the damage. Burroughs only expressed annoyance at the issue of the Irish complaints about the proposed new RUC Chief Constable since Burroughs had repeatedly asked nationalist political leaders in the North, including John Hume, for a list of "acceptable" candidates only to receive no reply. Eamonn Gallagher promised to press the SDLP to respond to future request by London for input. A number of other issues were discussed but no details were agreed upon. The Irish account of the meeting judged it a success and a sign that London was willing to listen to Dublin regarding its Northern Ireland policies as long as the consultation were private and no public statements emerged that damaged Chichester-Clark's position at Stormont. The British also privately concluded that the meeting was "on the whole" valuable, but pronounced it overly long and marked by an airing of the traditional worries of Dublin; some of which were characterized as "pretty neurotic."[66]

The one major follow-up from the London meeting focused on border issues such as spiking roads and British Army incursions into the Irish Republic. On October 9 officials of the Department of External Affairs met with Ambassador Peck and Ronnie Burroughs at the British Embassy in Dublin. The Irish repeated the complaints made in London regarding the spiking of border roads. Burroughs replied that the spikes at Crossmaglen were being replaced by a roadblock and the entire practice was under review by the British government. Burroughs urged the Irish to increase Garda patrols on the border if they wished to see spiking abandoned while Peck warned that any official or press comments in Ireland would derail the possible change in policy. The ambassador argued that Chichester-Clark would face a political problem if he were seen to be reducing border security. Peck went on to assure the Irish officials that any British Army violations of the Irish border were mistakes and that the army was issuing "stringent instructions" to its troops to avoid a recurrence of the problem.[67] Later in October both Ronnie Burroughs and Ambassador Peck made strong recommendations to London that the British Army and the RUC should be extremely careful about crossing the border and if fired upon from Irish territory should only return fire to save lives.[68]

Nixon visits Ireland

The American government showed very little interest in Northern Ireland during this period. American ambassador to Ireland, John Moore, summarized the state of US-Irish relations to the State Department in September 1970. Moore concluded that the relationship between the two nations was generally fine and that the major American goals were to continue to maintain these good relations, help Ireland and Britain to successfully enter the EEC together, and try to gain more Irish cooperation with the NATO alliance. Moore advised that the United States should "avoid any involvement in the delicate and complex

Figure 3.4 President Richard Nixon with Jack Lynch and Mrs. Lynch at Dublin Castle, October 1970. Credit: Popperfoto.

Partition issue" and should try to maintain "friendly impartiality" when London and Dublin quarreled over the North. The ambassador suggested that "we should avoid giving the impression to the Irish that our relationship with the UK overrides our policy considerations affecting Ireland."[69] The American policy of noninvolvement, and Irish acceptance of that, was displayed when President Richard Nixon and his secretary of state, William Rogers, visited Dublin in early October 1970. Lynch did not raise the issue of Northern Ireland with Nixon in public.[70] Hillery did address Dublin's concern that reform was not working in the North with his American counterpart, but Rogers quickly ended the conversation by downplaying the importance of Northern Ireland in the global picture and expressing a vague American concern regarding Northern Ireland.[71]

Heath and Lynch meet in New York

Jack Lynch and Edward Heath had their first meeting as heads of their respective governments on October 21, 1970, while both men were attending the opening of the United Nations General Assembly. The Irish government hoped the meeting might have an important impact on Northern Ireland while acknowledging that the British government was downplaying the importance of the discussion at New York. From Dublin's point of view, it was hoped that Lynch could use the meeting to continue to press for meaningful reforms in Northern Ireland and to make the case to Heath that London needed to stand up to the right-wing unionists who were blocking change in the North. If the British continued to work toward reform the Irish government planned to meet British demands that Dublin try to act as a force for calm in the North.[72]

Lynch opened the discussion with a brief exchange on the EEC, but the bulk of the conversation centered on Northern Ireland. The taoiseach did not stray from Dublin's existing line on the North but reiterated the need for reforms in Stormont that would allow reconciliation between the nationalist and unionist communities in the North. He warned Heath that delay in reform, or weak legislation such as the recent Housing Bill introduced at Stormont, would cause Northern nationalists to lose faith in the reform process and would also damage the political position of moderates in Dublin and within the Unionist Party in the North. Heath argued that the reform program in the North was in fact moving forward successfully.

Turning to the topic of North–South cooperation in Ireland, Lynch claimed that Dublin was in favor of increasing contacts on tourism and regional economic issues but Stormont had retreated from the détente of the O'Neill era and rejected all proposals for cooperation. Lynch viewed this development as proof of the growing influence of the "hardline" element of the Unionist Party. Britain, Lynch argued, had to stand up to the right wing of unionism. Heath rejected the Irish claim that the Unionist Party was now dominated by its right wing. He said that London's policy was to support Chichester-Clark's government and that the Northern premier's political survival was also in the interest of Dublin. The prime minister told Lynch that Dublin had to acknowledge that Chichester-Clark had to be careful not to give Ian Paisley and his hardline allies any more political ammunition than was necessary but once the situation in the North began to quiet down then Chichester-Clark could embrace the reforming spirit of Terrence O'Neill. Heath stressed that his government wanted to reduce the tensions in the North, "not least" in order to withdraw some of the British troops deployed in the province. Heath argued that the recent violence in the North was less a result of a lack of faith in reform and more the work of extremists and a "small element of young thugs." Lynch did not accept the idea that the violence in the North was a simple security problem and reiterated the need for progress on reforms and perhaps the need for a new approach to the whole problem. The real key to change, Lynch said, was to get the two communities in the North to work together. He called reunification the ultimate goal of Dublin but acknowledged that London stood by the guarantee of 1949. Lynch asked Heath to agree to regular annual Anglo-Irish summits, and while the prime minister indicated that he would be happy for an occasional meeting with Lynch, he did not want to schedule a regular event. The two leaders agreed not to issue a formal communique of their discussion but to provide the press with a brief summary if required.[73]

The prime minister held a press conference following his meeting with the taoiseach and described their exchange as "very useful" and confirmed that he and Lynch had agreed to meet again at least once the following year. Heath claimed that reform in Northern Ireland was nearly complete and once this was accomplished "then there will not be any grounds for complaint on discrimination." Once legal equality was achieved Heath declared that extremists who "were using violence for their own purposes" would be separated from the majority in the North who sought a peaceful solution. While reiterating London's commitment to the 1949 guarantee, Heath also said that if the people of Northern Ireland voted for reunification, "we in Westminster would certainly not stand in their way."[74]

In his address to the UN General Assembly on October 22, 1970, Lynch struck a very conciliatory tone toward both Britain and Stormont while continuing to call for reunification. Lynch called partition "a mistaken attempt" to solve Ireland's problems and called for a peaceful end to partition with the consent of the unionist population. According to Lynch, Britain had properly responded to the crisis in the North by pledging in the Downing Street Declaration to promote equality for all the people of Northern Ireland. "We accepted that declaration," Lynch said, "as the true decision of a country which, despite many unhappy things in the past—and there comes a time to stop feeding on those things—we know to be herself a democratic and freedom-loving country with which Ireland has many ties of friendship and mutual interest." He praised Major Chichester-Clark's government for genuinely seeking to enact reforms in the face of "the petty intrigues and manoeuvres of lesser men." The taoiseach called on Northern nationalists to be patient, citing the words of Irish War of Independence hero Terence MacSwiney that "it is not they who can inflict most but they who can suffer most who will conquer." Lynch predicted that reform would, in fact, come fairly quickly and that this reform would pave the way for Irish unification "in all its diversity and cultural richness." He closed with a plea for understanding from all parties. "Let us all recognize and acknowledge," Lynch said, "that governments, like individuals make mistakes. Virtue lies in refusing to become prisoners of our mistakes."[75]

Acquittal in the arms trial

Even as Lynch and Heath were attempting to foster more Anglo-Irish cooperation there was a stark reminder that cooperation was not universally supported. The Arms Crisis that had begun in May 1970 came to its climax that autumn. While the arms smuggling charges against Neil Blaney were dropped, Charles Haughey, Captain Kelly, Belfast republican John Kelly, and accused fellow conspirator Albert Luykx were placed on trial in September 1970. The first case ended in a mistrial but following the second trial all four men were acquitted on October 23. Haughey made an ill-advised attempt to challenge Lynch for leadership of the party following the verdict but the party leaders rallied around Lynch and Haughey's threat collapsed.[76] During the trial in October 1970 certain facts came to light that were potentially problematic for Anglo-Irish relations including the training of Northern nationalists in Donegal in the autumn of 1969 by the Irish military and the movement of arms by the Irish Army to Dundalk during the Belfast rioting in the spring of 1970. However, Edward Heath's government, like Wilson's before it, chose not to make an issue of these developments and to focus during parliamentary questioning on the fact that Lynch had put a stop to all such activities that ran counter to his stance of a peaceful resolution to the Northern situation. While London felt compelled to make an official comment on the revelations to Dublin in order to placate critics like Ian Paisley, there was no acrimony between Irish and British officials regarding the events and both sides seemed to be more focused on the future of Northern Ireland rather than the past.[77] Ambassador Peck's assessment that the Arms Crisis revealed "an almost unbelievable degree of administrative sloppiness" in the Irish state but that "once Lynch discovered what was going on he quickly put a stop both to irregular practices and also to activities which, though officially sanctioned, were clearly inappropriate in the light of developments in Northern Ireland" was generally accepted by London as accurate.[78]

When Lynch returned to Dublin from New York he was forced to defend his UN speech against charges that it had painted an overly optimistic picture of the situation in the North and showed a naïve degree of trust in Heath and Chichester-Clark. Fine Gael TD Michael O'Leary asked Lynch if Heath had given him as yet unknown information during their meeting in New York that had led the taoiseach to have as much "confidence in Mr. Heath and the Stormont Prime Minister" as he had expressed in his "surprising speech" to the UN. Lynch replied that he had never used the word confidence but had been expressing his belief in the "sincerity of purpose" of Chichester-Clark.[79]

Despite such skepticism in the Dáil, Patrick Hillery told Ambassador Peck on October 30 that he believed that the Lynch–Heath meeting had been a success, although he admitted that he was spending most of his time dealing with the fallout within Fianna Fail from Haughey's acquittal. Hillery expressed his extreme surprise that Haughey had attacked Lynch in public after the trial but was confident that Haughey now realized that he could not successfully challenge Lynch for leadership of the party and that he would support Lynch in the Dáil leaving Blaney and Boland with no real support among the TDs.[80] Hillery arranged for Peck to meet with Lynch a few days later despite the fact that a Dáil debate on a vote of confidence for the government was actually underway. Lynch told the ambassador that his meeting with Heath had been valuable and had, in fact, enhanced Lynch's political standing. The taoiseach and the ambassador "agreed that overall, relations were going pretty well, and reforms were really progressing in the North."[81]

While it is not possible to definitively prove that Lynch's belief that his meeting with Heath had helped him politically was correct, it is clear that it did not damage his reputation. Lynch survived the political challenge of the acquittal of the defendants in the Arms Trail in a strong position. He won a vote of confidence from the Fianna Fáil TDs on October 27 by a vote of seventy to three. Lynch survived a Dáil vote of confidence the next day by a vote of seventy-five to sixty-seven. Lynch's main opponents within his party were, for the time being, defeated.[82]

Royal Navy search of Irish ships

While London may have been fairly happy with the state of Anglo-Irish relations in the autumn of 1970 Stormont did not share that assessment. Major Chichester-Clark believed that the British government should put more pressure on Dublin to stop the IRA from maintaining training bases in the Irish Republic and generally crack down on the IRA. In a meeting with Home Secretary Maudling on October 30, 1970, Chichester-Clark expressed these views and requested a meeting with the foreign secretary to make his case. The Northern premier indicated that such a meeting would help him politically as it would help demonstrate his resolve to fight the IRA. Maudling stuck to the advice that had been offered to him by his own Northern Ireland Department and the FCO and strongly advised Chichester-Clark not to request a meeting with Sir Alec Douglas-Home. He explained to Chichester-Clark that Lynch was "as helpful a Prime Minister of the Republic as one was likely to get" and official pressure from London to have the Irish move more forcefully against the IRA would harm Lynch politically. What Maudling did not share with Chichester-Clark was the FCO's belief that the issue of IRA training bases was serious but that it was best raised in the informal, confidential meetings between the FCO and the Irish Embassy.[83] The FCO differentiated between communication with Dublin that was intended "to get things done" and communication that was designed "to give the appearance of getting things done." Official, public complaints to Lynch's government about the need for Ireland to crack down on IRA activity might help Chichester-Clark's political standing in Northern Ireland but it would not result in the Irish government taking any effective actions and would cause a public row between Dublin and London. The FCO believed that low-profile exchanges of information and intelligence between ministers and ambassadors remained the best method of encouraging Anglo-Irish cooperation on security.[84]

Maudling and the FCO's desire to keep issues of security in Anglo-Irish relations as low key as possible was well founded. Public debates on security matters tended to become highly politicized in both Ireland and Northern Ireland. The contretemps surrounding the search of Irish ships by the Royal Navy in November 1970 demonstrate this fact. On November 8 and November 11, 1970, two Irish ships were stopped and searched for arms by the Royal Navy in what Dublin considered to be the territorial waters of Ireland.[85] There was almost immediate reaction in Dáil Éireann with TDs from both Fine Gael and Labour denouncing the British actions. Speaking for the government, Minister for Transport and Power Brian Lenihan assured the chamber "that the Government have made known, in no uncertain manner, to the British authorities the serious view that is taken by the Government, the Dáil and all the Irish people of the boarding and searching of these two boats."[86] Ambassador O'Sullivan presented a demand to the British government for a written assurance that the searches would not be repeated. O'Sullivan told FCO officials that this type of incident "showed a remarkable lack of sensitivity on the part of the British to the delicate political situation in which my Government has found itself in recent months." While the British apologized for the "political embarrassment" they refused to rule out further searches of Irish ships claiming that the Royal Navy had a responsibility to act on intelligence regarding illegal gun-running. The British placed part of the blame on the weakness of the Irish security forces and Permanent Undersecretary of State Anthony Royle suggested to O'Sullivan that the Irish might want to explore the idea of a joint Anglo-Irish committee on security to coordinate such matters. O'Sullivan promised to pass the suggestion to Dublin but warned that searching Irish ships caused a "strong emotional reaction" in the Irish public and could seriously damage Anglo-Irish relations.[87] O'Sullivan's point seemed to be reinforced in the Dáil on November 17 when Patrick Hillery strongly denounced the ship searches. Describing the effect of the ship boarding on Anglo-Irish relations in general, Hillery claimed that "If it became common practice for other nations of the world to behave as Britain has behaved in this case, civilized relations between Governments would be difficult."[88]

Despite the public row, in private officials of both governments were more conciliatory regarding the naval searches. Ambassador Peck spoke to Patrick Hillery, Hugh McCann, and Fine Gael TD Richie Ryan after a memorial Mass for the recently deceased Charles de Gaulle. Peck described the conversation as "amiable and at times hilarious." Hillery suggested that the planned transfer from the Royal Navy to the Irish Defense Force of the warship HMS *Kellington* be expedited to allow the Irish to conduct their own effective search for maritime gun runners. Ryan told the ambassador that he had raised the issue in the Dáil in an effort to defuse the subject before it became more problematic. Ryan agreed with Peck that it would now be best to try to ignore the incident before the very thorny issue of the maritime border between the Irish Republic and Northern Ireland became a major problem for Anglo-Irish relations. Despite the positive attitude demonstrated by Hillery and Ryan, Peck cautioned the FCO that this Irish goodwill was "firmly based on the assumption that there are no more boardings of Irish ships." Even though London had specifically refused to make this guarantee, Peck warned that further searches would provoke ever stronger reactions from Dublin.[89] London apparently accepted Peck's argument as Sir Alec Douglas-Home, with the support of Prime Minister Heath, suggested to the ministry of defense that the Royal Navy should avoid stopping any Irish ships for a few weeks even when they clearly had the right and authority to do so. Douglas-Home rationalized the request by pointing to the need "to avoid damaging Mr. Lynch's already shaky political position."[90]

In a private late-night conversation between the Department of External Affairs' Eamonn Gallagher and an official of the British Embassy, Gallagher claimed that the strong Irish reaction to the ship searches was planned by the Lynch government, against Gallagher's advice, to allow the taoiseach to burnish his nationalist credentials by publicly standing up to the British without causing any real damage to Anglo-Irish relations. The embassy official told Gallagher that the British government had so far tried to soothe Irish feelings over the ship searches but that illegal importation of weapons was a major issue for security in Northern Ireland and further searches could not be ruled out. According to Gallagher, Lynch agreed that the British needed to stop arms smuggling and that Dublin would also engage in maritime searches once Irish forces had the capacity to undertake those missions. In the meantime it would be helpful if Dublin at least had prior warning of plans to stop Irish ships. However, Gallagher warned that Dublin could not discuss issues of security cooperation with Britain, even in private, as this would be a politically indefensible in Ireland if word leaked to the public.[91]

Return to low-profile talks

The low-profile Anglo-Irish meetings resumed in December 1970 in London. In a memo prepared by the Department of External Affairs as a brief for the talks, the idea of British support for reunification was raised as a general goal. The memo stated, "Ireland would like to see Britain not just promise not to hinder reunification, but gently encourage it as a good policy to foster good Anglo-Irish relations." According to the document the British government should be asked to publicly support the idea of helping to facilitate the peaceful, consensual reunification of Ireland while promising to honor the Ireland Act of 1949 until an agreement was reached by the Irish people on both sides of the border. The memo argued that only British pressure to achieve unification would induce even moderate unionists to support an all-Ireland state. The benefits of reunification would include not only "exceedingly close and friendly" Anglo-Irish relations but also a way to end the violence of the Troubles.[92]

The exact authorship of the memorandum is unclear and the concept of British support for reunification may not have been universally accepted as a reasonable goal by Lynch's government as a whole. When Ambassador O'Sullivan and Eamonn Gallagher met with British officials from the FCO and the Home Office in London on December 4, 1970, the reunification issue does not seem to have been raised. Aside from that one topic O'Sullivan followed the other talking points of the department's memo and brought up a number of concrete Irish concerns about the pace of reforms in Northern Ireland. During the talks the British were generally conciliatory and called for patience on the part of the Irish government. The major complaint that the British had with the Irish was that Dublin was not dealing effectively with IRA activity in the South. Sir Stewart Crawford and Kelvin White of the FCO pointed to the very light penalties in Ireland for possession of illegal weapons or explosives. Being apprehended with a machine gun in Ireland might only result in a small fine, while in the United Kingdom this crime could result in a long prison sentence. The British pointed out that Irish laxity toward the IRA not only helped the militant republicans but also helped extreme unionists like Ian Paisley to paint Dublin as part of the problem in Northern Ireland.[93]

On the same day that British officials were warning O'Sullivan that Dublin had to crack down on the IRA, Lynch's government released a statement to the public announcing that it was considering the introduction of internment in the Irish Republic to deal with credible threats from "a secret armed conspiracy" that went unnamed but was presumed to be planning a campaign of kidnappings and bank robberies.[94] The unnamed organization was the left-wing IRA splinter group Saor Éire, which had launched a series of robberies in the Irish Republic and was responsible for the death of a Garda member.[95]

This unexpected announcement caused a great deal of speculation as to the nature of the threat. The BBC reported that British diplomats were the intended targets of the kidnapping plot and the *Sunday Times* on December 6 printed some stories attributed to the British Embassy in Dublin that were critical of Lynch, although the FCO and Ambassador Peck rejected both reports as inaccurate.[96] Peck met with Hillery to reassure the minister of external affairs that no one in the embassy had spoken to the *Sunday Times*. Hillery told Peck that he had no information about the security threat and that only the taoiseach and minister for justice had seen the Garda intelligence that sparked the internment announcement. In Hillery's opinion the threat of internment was aimed at the Irish public's "attitudes toward violence," which were more fearful of state use of force than of illegal use of force. He attributed this view of violence to Irish historical traditions and said it helped to explain the public's outrage at the boarding of Irish ships by the Royal Navy.[97] The government's threat of internment was very unpopular in Ireland. Lynch told Ambassador Peck that he felt that the government did not have sufficient evidence to prosecute the suspects despite solid evidence of the plot. Public disclosure of the evidence would mean revealing the existence of a government informer in the militant's ranks.[98] Cracking down on armed republicans in Ireland was clearly easier said than done.

A new year and new challenges

The coming of 1971 did not bring any new hope for peace in Northern Ireland. The Provisional IRA, which had been more aggressive since the summer of 1970, had begun a bombing campaign of commercial targets in late 1970 and by the beginning of 1971 the PIRA had started to specifically target British soldiers in Belfast. On February 6, 1971, Gunner Robert Curtis of the Royal Artillery became the first British Army fatality of the Troubles. As the British Army sought to strike back at the Provisionals, it increasingly alienated the population of the nationalist areas where the PIRA were based. As Richard English has observed, "not for the first time in Irish history a British Army deployed to undermine republican subversion in fact helped to solidify the very subversion it was supposed to stem."[99] Major Chichester-Clark declared on television on February 7, 1971, that Northern Ireland was at war with the PIRA.[100] The fact that the British Army was playing into the hands of the PIRA was not lost on observers at the time. For instance, SDLP leader Gerry Fitt warned the British government in February 1971 that the republicans were deliberately goading the British Army into taking actions in nationalist areas that only increased support for the Provisionals.[101]

The intensifying conflict in the North was reflected in dramatic events in Irish domestic politics in early 1971. February 1971 saw the struggle within Fianna Fáil reach its final stage. The party *ard fheis*, which began on February 20, was marked by a volatile confrontation between the moderates led by Jack Lynch and Patrick Hillery and the grassroots supporters of Neil Blaney and Kevin Boland. A defeat for Lynch would have meant that Fianna Fáil had rejected the taoiseach's policy of the unambiguous condemnation of the use of political violence in the North and could have had a dramatic impact on Anglo-Irish relations. To counter the challenge of the more republican wing Lynch vigorously defended his policy toward Northern Ireland and won the support of the majority of the delegates at the *ard fheis*, thus securing his leadership of the party. The threat from the hardline group receded after the *ard fheis* with Kevin Boland leaving the party, Neil Blaney reduced in power and eventually expelled from the party in 1972, and Charles Haughey attempting to return to the good graces of the victorious moderates.[102]

On February 5, 1971, Patrick Hillery, accompanied by Eamonn Gallagher, met with James Callaghan, now an opposition MP, for a general discussion of Northern Ireland. Echoing the government's official line, Hillery said that he believed that partition was the root "cause of the present troubles." He told Callaghan, that the more immediate problems facing the North arose from the fact that the British Army was not acting as a neutral peacekeeper but was "engaged" with the nationalist community. Hillery went on to condemn Stormont as an illegitimate government that "had been created by and was still maintained by force." Despite this, Hillery assured Callaghan that Dublin had no intention of using force to reunify the country and added that he personally supported this stance which traced itself back to the founding of Fianna Fáil by Eamon de Valera. Hillery claimed that there was a real possibility that moderate unionists could be persuaded to support reunification if the British withdrew and left the Irish people to decide their own future relations. In any case, Dublin has no desire to force a large number of hostile unionists into a united Ireland. On the issue of the ongoing reforms to Stormont, Gallagher expressed the opinion that hardline unionism was on the rise and the Unionist Party would never willingly enact any reform that was not directly dictated by London. Callaghan argued that unionism had changed more than Gallagher gave it credit for.[103]

In public Jack Lynch sounded a more optimistic note about the possibility of reform than Eamonn Gallagher had done in his private meeting with Callaghan. Speaking in the Dáil on February 10, 1971, the taoiseach decried the use of political violence and called for "patience on the part of the minority and generosity on the part of the majority." He acknowledged that reform in the North would require "an extraordinary effort of will by the Stormont Government" but stated that these reforms were taking place even if the pace was slow. Lynch reminded the Dáil that his government's goal was "reunification through peace, by promoting friendship, goodwill, cooperation and understanding."[104]

Fine Gael leader Liam Cosgrave, offering his party's view of the Northern Ireland situation during the same Dáil session, called for tripartite talks among the governments of Britain, Ireland, and Northern Ireland to seek a permanent solution to the crisis. Having the two Irish governments talk to each other was vital in Cosgrave's opinion as he believed "British politicians never have, and never will, understand Ireland or the Irish people." He also suggested that a UN force should replace the British Army as the main peacekeepers in the North. Labour's Brendan Corish voiced support for Cosgrave's plan for tripartite discussions.[105]

Growing Anglo-Irish divide over IRA violence

On February 16, 1971, Ambassador O'Sullivan, accompanied by Eamonn Gallagher, met with British officials from the FCO and the Home Office as part of the ongoing low-key discussions between the two governments. O'Sullivan explained that Dublin was less hopeful about the North than they had been in December. The Irish believed, as Gallagher had earlier told James Callaghan, that the right wing of the Unionist Party was growing stronger and that Britain would need to keep a closer eye on Stormont. O'Sullivan and Gallagher listed some of the specific Irish concerns including the large increase in gun licenses issued in Northern Ireland, the heavy-handed and seemingly antinationalist tactics of the British Army, and the slow pace of political reforms. Gallagher was particularly adamant that slow reforms meant that more nationalists were attracted to the republican cause. O'Sullivan made the case that British Army weapons searches in nationalist areas were a major cause of the recent uptick in violence in Northern Ireland.

FCO deputy undersecretary of state Sir Stewart Crawford agreed with the Irish that the situation in the North was deteriorating but placed the blame firmly on the back of an increase in IRA violence. The Home Office's Philip Woodfield admitted that the British Army was not the ideal peacekeeping force but argued that the military could hardly ignore good intelligence about weapons caches in nationalist areas as the IRA was taking the offensive against the military. While the British participants reported that the meeting was amicable, Crawford expressed some frustration to Ambassador John Peck in Dublin regarding what he saw as an Irish double standard on the North. Dublin, Crawford wrote, blamed London for militant unionism but took no responsibility for republican extremism. He believed that one of the reasons that the Irish made general complaints about the pace of reform was that they did not want to get into specifics where they might be confronted with "the one question they cannot answer: 'What are you going to do about the IRA?'"[106]

When Patrick Hillery and Sir Alec Douglas-Home met in London on February 25 the issue of the IRA was directly addressed. In the brief prepared by the FCO in preparation for the meeting the political advantages of an Anglo-Irish discussion at the ministerial level was acknowledged. Having Hillery and Douglas-Home meet helped Lynch to be seen as being actively engaged on the issue of Northern Ireland and London viewed Lynch's political survival as in their own best interest. However, the FCO also saw the meeting as an opportunity to make a number of important points to the Irish government. The memo called the need for action against the IRA "the main issue" of the meeting. According to the FCO's analysis Irish cooperation against the IRA was "an intellectually reasonable proposition but for historical reasons it is politically impossible for them to swallow it whole." Therefore, the best way to proceed was to stick to the facts and ask the Irish for concrete suggestions on how to deal with specific problems.[107]

In Dublin a very different view of the problem of the IRA existed. An Irish memo prepared for Hillery in advance of the meeting placed the blame for increased violence on right-wing unionism. While Dublin rejected violence as much as London or Belfast, the Irish believed that IRA violence was a reaction to the growing influence of extremism in the unionist community and therefore standing up to right-wing unionism was the only way to stop the violence.[108] While Irish officials frequently claimed that Lynch's government was doing all that it could to combat the IRA in the South, Henry Patterson's study of the military and political importance of the border during the Troubles sheds some doubt on these claims. Patterson recognizes that the main areas of conflict were Belfast and Derry, but points out that the IRA made use of the Irish Republic for training, weapons acquisition, and as a staging ground for operations on the border. Despite this, the Garda force deployed at the border only numbered around 400 in 1971 and the Special Branch, which was in charge of antisubversive intelligence, was not expanded to meet the clearly growing threat from the IRA. At the same time, Irish courts showed a real ambiguity toward the IRA by often ignoring good evidence to acquit republican defendants.[109]

Hillery and Douglas-Home met at the House of Commons and Sir Alec opened the discussion by claiming that a major problem in the North was an increase in IRA activity despite reforms. Hillery attempted to sidestep the issue and focus instead on what he saw as backsliding on the part of the Unionist Party. When Douglas-Home asked if Dublin had any ideas on how to deal with this problem Hillery raised a new Irish idea about short-term reforms. While the Irish still supported reunification as the ultimate goal, in the short run Dublin believed that the two communities in the North had to learn to live in peace. Hillery proposed a "new form of administration" for Stormont that would allow for some nationalist participation in government as the normal parliamentary system was a failure in Northern Ireland. The Irish proposal was very light on details at this point and Douglas-Home effectively ignored the suggestion by returning to the topic of the need for Ireland to crack down on the IRA. Hillery stuck to his script and said that the growth of the IRA was directly related to "the opposing threat of extreme unionism." From Dublin's point of view any move by the security forces in the North to increase pressure on the IRA could easily backfire if the nationalist community as a whole did not see a viable political alternative to republicanism or if the British Army were seen to be taking sides with unionists against nationalists. Hillery also pointed out that the Irish government was doing all it could against the IRA south of the border and complained about British Army incursions into the Irish Republic. The British countered that any border crossings by the military were accidental and that the British Army was acting in a fair manner in the North. Troops only went into nationalist areas because the IRA was based in those neighborhoods. Hillery closed the meeting by saying that Dublin's policy of seeking an exclusively peaceful solution to the Troubles was well established. He warned that the British government had to make sure that there was some form of positive political movement in Northern Ireland. Without a political solution the whole idea of friendly and cooperative Anglo-Irish relations regarding the North would fail with disastrous results.[110]

British concern about the need for stronger action by Dublin against the IRA was discussed by Heath's Cabinet on February 9. Ambassador Peck approached Jack Lynch with these concerns on February 11. Douglas-Home and the FCO had allowed Peck to decide whether to make the contact official or more informal as the FCO believed that Peck had a good working relationship with Lynch that allowed the two men to discuss sensitive subjects in a discreet manner. Ambassador Peck was conscious of the need to avoid the appearance that Lynch's government was taking too many suggestions from the British. With this in mind, Peck chose to raise the issue in an informal way but left Lynch with a "personal and informal letter" on the subject that London considered as "in effect, an aide-memoire."[111]

Lynch's Saint Patrick's Day visit to Washington

In March 1971 Jack Lynch planned to travel to the United States in time for Saint Patrick's Day and a meeting between the taoiseach and President Nixon was scheduled during the trip. In preparation for the meeting the Department of External Affairs, which had been recently renamed the Department of Foreign Affairs to avoid a title that was used by members of the British Commonwealth,[112] prepared a memorandum on Northern Ireland and talking points for Lynch. Eamonn Gallagher sent the document to the taoiseach's office with a note indicating that Patrick Hillery had personally approved the memo. The document revealed a great deal of pessimism at the Department of Foreign Affairs regarding developments in the North. The nationalist community was suffering from "considerable malaise" and felt that Stormont remained unresponsive to nationalist concerns. As for the Unionists, Iveagh House believed that they were content to allow the party to slide to the right and hoped that the demands of the civil rights movement could be blunted by "paper reforms" that did not actually change the power structure in the North. If real reform was in fact stopped, the memo warned that the minority community would turn increasingly to the IRA "with consequences that would be very grave indeed." Unionists had learned nothing from the events of the past few years and naively believed that if the IRA could be isolated from the Catholic community than nationalists would accept continued unreformed Unionist Party domination as long as the British supplied military and economic assistance to Stormont.

The memo went on to suggest a line of argument that Lynch should take in his discussion with Nixon. It would be valuable to remind Nixon that Dublin warned the British in August 1969 that the situation in the North was about to turn violent only to have London ignore the advice and suggest that Northern Ireland was not a concern of the Irish Republic. While London was wrong to ignore Dublin's advice, when violence did erupt, the British did the responsible thing and restored order to the streets while promising, in conjunction with Stormont, that full equality for both communities had to be ensured in the North. The Irish government, despite domestic opposition, accepted that reforms based on the Downing Street Declaration were a path forward on Northern Ireland. Recently, however, the Irish government has come to believe that the Unionist Party is "virtually incapable of implementing the Downing Street guarantees." Making matters worse, a section of the nationalist community "have taken to the gun" and embraced republicanism. Many unionists, "with the honorable exception of Major Chichester-Clark" now equate moderate nationalist demands "for fair play" with the radical republican demands for a British withdrawal from Northern Ireland. Despite warnings from Dublin, the British government has not accepted that the impending failure of reform will be a catastrophe for the North.

The document urged Lynch to place the blame for the failure of reform on the unionists and to reinforce in Nixon's mind the fact that the unionist community was a tiny minority within the United Kingdom as well as a minority on the island of Ireland. Moreover, this unionist minority, with the military and economic support of Britain, was refusing to provide legal equality to, or accept the "political and cultural aspirations" of, the nationalist community in Northern Ireland. From Dublin's point of view, "London should recognize the need not to continue to cater to this historic abnormality as the consequences could very well be disastrous." The Irish government was not seeking immediate unification as a solution to Northern Ireland's problems, but rather hoped to informally work with the British to promote "peaceful co-existence of the communities in the North." In the long run Dublin would like to see reunification, but only with the consent of the unionists. Lynch's main goal should be to have Nixon agree to informally promote the idea to Prime Minister Heath that there could be no "return to the status quo ante in the North" and that he should work with the Irish government to find a peaceful path forward.[113]

The US State Department had concluded in early 1971 that the situation in Northern Ireland was deteriorating and that even "British observers have stressed the recent change in the character of the conflict from civil disturbance to something approaching armed insurrection." Despite this dire prediction the State Department was hopeful that the British could muddle through by backing Stormont since most Irish nationalists opposed violence and Jack Lynch's government remained a force for moderation.[114] The State Department anticipated that Lynch would raise the issue of Northern Ireland with President Nixon and advised the president to stick to the American position that Northern Ireland was a domestic matter for the United Kingdom. The State Department had a generally favorable view of Ireland's views on global affairs and active role in the United Nations and supported Irish entry into the EEC but advised Nixon that America's friendship with Ireland should not involve any role for Washington in Northern Ireland. Expressions of sympathy for those seeking a peaceful resolution to the Troubles aside, the memo suggested that the United States should offer no help to Lynch.[115]

When Lynch and Nixon met in Washington on March 16, 1971, it quickly became clear that the Irish were aware that the Nixon administration was not inclined to involve itself in Northern Ireland. Lynch outlined Dublin's view of the Troubles but assured Nixon that the press had exaggerated the idea that the Irish government would seek American support for its policies on the North. The taoiseach told Nixon that Britain was committed to reform in Northern Ireland and that stated that Dublin would "welcome anything" that kept London committed to this path without making any suggestion that the United States take any action in this direction. Nixon restated Washington's reluctance to get involved in Northern Ireland but told Lynch that he was free to tell the press that the US government was "not only interested but concerned" and supported a peaceful resolution. Lynch left the meeting with the impression that Nixon was "not completely well informed about the true facts of Northern Ireland."[116]

If Lynch was disappointed by the American stance on Northern Ireland he gave no hint of this in his public statements but focused instead on Dublin's moderation and dedication to peace. In a Saint Patrick's Day television interview on NBC Lynch set forth Dublin's view that the problems in Northern Ireland could only be solved by reconciliation between the Protestant and Catholic communities in the North. He went on to state that Dublin's ultimate goal was peaceful and consensual reunification and indicated his support for the removal of Article 44 from the Irish constitution to eliminate any special status for the Catholic Church as a practical step that the Irish government could take to "pave the way for reunification."[117]

While the taoiseach was in Washington, Major Chichester-Clark's government in Stormont was reaching the end of the line. When Lynch arrived back at the Irish Embassy from his meeting with Nixon he was presented with a message from Patrick Hillery warning that Chichester-Clark's government was on the verge of collapse and that the British might implement internment without trial as a last ditch effort to save the Unionist leader. Hillery believed that internment would lead to the withdrawal from Stormont of the SDLP and other nationalist MPs and provide the republicans with an opportunity to become the leaders among Northern nationalists. He suggested that Lynch ask Nixon to intercede with Heath and advise the British to rethink their basic policy on Northern Ireland.[118]

The following day Prime Minister Heath sent his own message to Lynch confirming Hillery's warning that Chichester-Clark's government was in real danger of falling but dismissing the idea that internment was in the offing. Heath attributed the loss of support for Chichester-Clark among moderate Unionists to the increased activity of the IRA and the belief that more "extremist" Unionists would be more effective against the IRA. Heath planned to send more troops and take other unspecified measures to improve Chichester-Clark's ability to show some success against the IRA. Heath asked Lynch for his cooperation and requested that Dublin "take early and effective action" against the IRA in the Irish Republic including the harassment of IRA training camps and a public relations campaign to convince the Irish population not to support armed republicanism. The prime minister closed with a warning that if Chichester-Clark fell "we shall have hard decisions to make," but reassured Lynch that London was firmly committed to reform in the North and continued discussions with Dublin.[119]

Conclusions

Anglo-Irish relations over Northern Ireland took a turn for the worse after the election of Edward Heath as the new British prime minister in June 1970. Since the fall of 1969 Jack Lynch's government, despite serious opposition within Fianna Fáil, had pursued a policy of low-key diplomatic engagement with London in support of the reform of Stormont. By the summer of 1970, with violence growing in the North, Lynch's government began to question the efficacy of the reform program being enacted by Belfast. Dublin questioned the commitment of Chichester-Clark's government to implement the Downing Street Declaration and called on London to stand up to Orange Order bigotry if the Unionist Party proved unable to do so. Heath's government argued that reforms were making headway and called for patience on the part of Dublin and Northern nationalists. While Lynch's government was still publicly committed to supporting the reform effort, by early 1971 Patrick Hillery was suggesting to Douglas-Home that the basic structure of the Stormont government might have to be radically changed rather than simply reformed.

The declining security situation in the North was also increasing tensions between Dublin and London. The growing power and aggression of the Provisional IRA was pushing the British Army into increasingly counterproductive measures aimed at reducing the violence. The outcome of these military actions, such as the Falls Road curfew, was to alienate Northern nationalists and anger Dublin. Lynch's government, which was still threatened by the more militant wing of Fianna Fáil, had to publicly criticize the British military's handling of the situation. There were also public quarrels between the two governments over border incidents and the search of Irish shipping by Britain. With no sign of a decline in violence, Heath's government began to press Lynch to be more proactive in fighting the IRA in the South. Dublin saw this British focus on combating the IRA as a misinterpretation of the root causes of the violence in Northern Ireland.

Despite these Anglo-Irish disputes there were some positive developments in the relationship during the second half of 1970 and early 1971. Heath had been willing to meet with Lynch and the British government seemed determined to continue to promote a dialogue between London and Dublin and closer ties between Stormont and Dublin. In addition, Lynch was able to largely put the challenge from the militant wing of Fianna Fáil behind him after the party *ard fheis* in February 1971 and his government did not waver in its commitment to find a peaceful solution to the crisis in Northern Ireland, even if it now had growing doubts that reforming the existing Stormont system was the answer.

Conflict over Security: March–August 1971

The next phase of the Troubles is book-cased by a change of government in Northern Ireland and by the imposition of internment without trail in the province. During this six-month period Anglo-Irish relations grew to be more contentious than at any time since the crisis of August 1969. The issue of security was at the center of the disputes between Dublin and London. However, other major factors causing problems between the two governments included the growing alienation of peaceful Northern nationalists from Stormont and Dublin's own loss of faith in the reform program in the North which led Lynch's government to call for more sweeping changes that included an increased focus on reunification as part of the solution to the Troubles.

By March 1971 the security situation in Northern Ireland had become so bad that James Chichester-Clark could no longer continue as prime minister of the province. The ruthless killing of three off-duty British soldiers by the PIRA on March 10 caused nearly universal condemnation but was particularly abhorrent to the unionist community. On March 12, 4,000 shipyard workers staged a rally calling on the government to introduce internment without trial to combat the IRA. The political pressure on Chichester-Clark to take strong action was immense. The Northern Ireland premier traveled to London for talks with British officials including Heath, Maudling, Minister of Defense Lord Carrington, and General Officer Commanding Northern Ireland, Lt. General Harry Tuzo.[1]

Chichester-Clark first met with Maudling, Carrington, and General Tuzo. After claiming that Northern Ireland was becoming increasingly unstable, the Northern premier called for "substantial reinforcements" to allow the British Army to set up permanent bases in nationalist areas that would allow the RUC to reestablish government control. He argued that the IRA would then be either forced to withdraw from the nationalist ghettos and end the intimidation that sustained their support or to fight it out with the security forces. Chichester-Clark stressed that his government would not last longer than a few days if nothing was done. Reginald Maudling expressed both sympathy for Chichester-Clark's political dilemma and a hope that the army could serve to handle both the military and political demands placed upon it. The army's representatives were much less enthusiastic about either sending reinforcements or taking a more proactive stance against the republicans. Lord Carrington pointed out that the British Army only had a total of 46 battalions and could not continue to pour troops into Northern Ireland. General Tuzo claimed that the troops already deployed in Northern Ireland were sufficient to handle any task and warned that more active patrolling in nationalist strongholds would only further alienate Catholics and increase support for the republicans. Tuzo also warned Chichester-Clark that imposing internment would require a large number to additional troops, not only to make the arrests but to handle the inevitable rioting that would follow. Chichester-Clark raised the possibility of creating an elite, armed, "riot force" for the province, separate from the RUC, to help with security once the army ended its peacekeeping duties but Maudling dismissed the idea of Stormont having control over any armed force for the foreseeable future.[2]

After further meetings, including a discussion with Heath, Chichester-Clark only managed to secure the promise of an additional 1,300 troops. Heath would not commit to any major change in British policy regarding Northern Ireland and warned Chichester-Clark that the British Army could not stop the people of Northern Ireland from engaging in a sectarian civil war if they were determined to pursue such a course. On March 20, 1971, Chichester-Clark resigned the office of prime minister to protest what he saw as the failure of Britain to properly respond to the growing threat from the IRA.[3]

Brian Faulkner comes to power

On March 23, 1971, Brian Faulkner defeated his rival William Craig for leadership of the Unionist Party and thus replaced Chichester-Clark as the new prime minister of Northern Ireland. Faulkner was the more moderate of the two candidates but he also included the more hardline Harry West as a member of his new Cabinet to placate the more extreme wing of the party.[4]

As noted in Chapter 3, the British had kept the Irish government informed that the end of the Chichester-Clark government was in sight and Dublin was understandably concerned. Faulkner's reputation in Dublin and among the SDLP was that of an uncompromising unionist and there was fear among nationalists that reform would take a backseat to security under his leadership.[5] Faulkner's reputation as a staunch foe of republicanism can be traced back to his time as Stormont's minister of home affairs during the last years of the IRA's Border Campaign of 1956–62.[6] Once it was clear that Faulkner would replace Chichester-Clark, important figures in the Irish Department of Foreign Affairs began to look at the change in Stormont government as an important turning point. In a meeting with Ambassador Peck, Hugh McCann expressed the idea that if Faulkner did try to implement the reform program he would only end up being replaced as Chichester-Clark had been. McCann suggested to Peck that some type of power-sharing government should be established to encourage the participation of Northern nationalists and reduce the appeal of the IRA. Peck did not directly comment on this suggestion but he did state that in his opinion the only options were Faulkner or direct rule and that London was not willing to accept full responsibility for Northern Ireland at this point. The ambassador characterized Faulkner's premiership as unionism's last chance.[7]

Eamonn Gallagher agreed with McCann's assessment that the time had come to more radically rethink the government of Northern Ireland. Gallagher wrote a memorandum in which he characterized the Stormont government as nothing more than "a puppet of Westminster" that had lost the authority it once had before the beginning of the Troubles. The document suggested that Dublin should pursue a number of goals relating to the decline of Stormont. London should be pressed to pass new legislation that would reduce Stormont to more of a regional administration that seemed less like a sovereign government. Northern nationalists would be more likely to participate in the revised Stormont if Westminster also made it clear that advocating peaceful Irish reunification was a legitimate political agenda in the province. The new Northern Ireland administration would also need to be tied to Dublin by some type of council of Ireland or tripartite council. If these changes took place, Gallagher suggested that Dublin should not press for reunification in the near term but should wait for moderate unionists to diverge from Orange extremism. With unionism divided, the prospects for Irish unity would increase in the long term and would come to be embraced by the British as the best solution to the whole problem of Northern Ireland.[8]

The American State Department shared the Irish Department of Foreign Affairs' belief that Brian Faulkner was in a difficult position right from the start of his ministry. A State Department intelligence document from early April was bleakly entitled "Northern Ireland: Outlook Not Bright for New Government."

The brief argued that Faulkner, like his immediate predecessor, was caught between hardline unionist demands for vigorous action against the IRA and moderate nationalist demands for real reform in the province. Faulkner was further handicapped by the lack of control he had over the British Army. Exhibiting a keen understanding of the goals of the Provisionals, the document concluded that forcing the British to impose direct rule was the main short-term aim of the IRA and that this outcome was a very real possibility if Faulkner could not improve the overall situation in Northern Ireland.[9]

Faulkner himself telephoned Jack Lynch the night he formed his government to tell the taoiseach that he should not worry about the inclusion of the right-wing Harry West in the Stormont Cabinet, implying that he would be able to control West's more extreme views. The new prime minister told Lynch that he wanted to work for closer ties with Dublin and the two agreed that they should meet at some point in the future. While the phone conversation was not made known to the public, the British government was aware of the exchange and approved of closer North–South cooperation.[10]

Despite the calls by some in the Department of Foreign Affairs for more drastic action, Lynch's government initially gave public support to the idea of continuing to support the reform program in the North. Speaking in the Dáil on March 25, 1971, the taoiseach accepted the assurances of Faulkner and the British that they were still committed to the Downing Street Declaration regarding equal rights for all the people of Northern Ireland. Lynch called on Northern nationalists to have patience and stick to nonviolent political activities.[11]

Lynch had a private message conveyed to Heath via Ambassador Peck the following day that doubled as a response to Heath message of March 17 as well as providing an opportunity for Lynch to express some of his concerns about the change of administration at Stormont. Lynch claimed that he was trying to be as helpful as he could be in his public statements but that he believed that the resignation of Chichester-Clark had created a new situation in the North. Hugh McCann, who delivered the message to Peck, pointed out that Lynch was taking a political risk by publicly calling for Northern nationalists to have faith in the reform program. In regard to Heath suggestion that Dublin crack down hard on IRA activity in the Irish Republic, the taoiseach rejected the idea and pointed to political problems as well as the fact that Ireland had "an independent and not necessarily helpful judiciary" when it came to putting pressure on the IRA. Lynch maintained that support for the IRA would dry up if Northern nationalists came to believe that Stormont was sincerely working for reform.[12]

Growing focus on security by London and Stormont

In a meeting with Prime Minister Heath on April 1, 1971, Brian Faulkner assured Heath that he intended to continue the reform program and attempt to get more Catholics involved in political life, but he also stressed that the restoration of law and order was his first priority. While Faulkner had mentioned the possibility of a meeting with Lynch during his telephone conversation with the taoiseach, he told Heath that the time for that meeting was not at hand. However, Faulkner said that Stormont was interested in forging closer North–South ties on specific economic issues. Heath encouraged Faulkner to pursue those links as London placed a great deal of importance on good cross-border relations.[13] Heath also assured Faulkner that the British Army would be more aggressive in moving into nationalist areas to confront the IRA as the British agreed with Stormont on the need to focus on security. In fact, this more aggressive military stance had already been set in motion by the order of General Tuzo on March 24.[14]

London's growing concern about the IRA was described in detail in a Foreign and Commonwealth Office memorandum of May 3, 1971, that was prepared for Heath regarding the possibility of his meeting with Jack Lynch. The FCO acknowledged that any meeting between the two would be a potential political problem for Faulkner and that Lynch would have to agree ahead of time that the constitutional status of Northern Ireland was not open to discussion. The object of any meeting with Lynch would be to focus on security as Heath had already decided that the real problem in Northern Ireland was now one of fighting terrorism instead of establishing equality of civil rights. The FCO concurred that the reforms promised by the Downing Street Declaration were "for the most part enacted or on the way." The memo argued that the Irish government privately agreed with the basic points of this analysis but that Lynch would be expected to continue to discuss the progress of the reform program in any meeting. On the issue of security, the FCO suggested that Lynch should be pressed to harass IRA training camps in the Irish Republic, extradite suspects to British jurisdiction, increase border patrols by Irish forces, coordinate with the Royal Navy to stop maritime gun-running, and discretely share intelligence about the IRA with London. The document argued that Lynch would have to be rewarded for this type of cooperation in order to defend himself from domestic political critics. Among the suggestions were British support for the introduction of proportional representation for election in Northern Ireland to increase nationalist seats in Stormont, an invitation for Dublin to help to find Northern nationalists politicians who would be willing to serve on committees to advise Faulkner's government on local issues, continued support for cross-border economic cooperation, an offer to train members of the Garda and Irish military, and a suggestion that that Dublin be pushed to "nominate an official who would in effect be an 'Ambassador to Stormont', whatever his formal position."[15]

This document demonstrates that the British FCO did not have a good understanding of Dublin's view of Northern Ireland. Even the so-called rewards that Lynch would be offered for increased cooperation against the IRA included suggestions that would hurt the nationalist credentials of any Irish government that accepted them. British training of Irish security forces and the tacit recognition of the legitimacy of the Stormont government by sending an Irish representative to Belfast would surely inflame the more republican leaning elements of Fianna Fáil.

Problems on the border

Events on the border in the spring and summer of 1971 contributed to the problems in Anglo-Irish relations. On May 10 Ambassador Peck advised London that there had been a series of incidents in recent days in which British troops had crossed into the Irish Republic. Peck warned the FCO that violations of Irish territory were taken very seriously by the Irish government and were, at best, "politically embarrassing" for Jack Lynch. He advised London that more had to be done to stop border incursions in order to convince Dublin that the British were taking the problem seriously.[16]

Of course, problems at the border ran both ways and Heath's government was very concerned about the apparent weakness of security on the Irish side of the frontier. Peck believed that the political price to the Irish government of being seen as tools of the British was too high for Lynch to openly cooperate on security matters with London.[17] While the British Foreign Secretary Sir Alec Douglas-Home acknowledged that Dublin would face some political problems from increased border security, he believed that the benefits would outweigh the negative reaction. Sir Alec suggested to Peck that he approach Lynch to informally suggest that the Irish Army, Garda border patrols, and Irish naval patrols should discretely cooperate with the security forces north of the border. London also hoped that the Irish would continue to harass IRA training camps.[18] When Peck spoke to Jack Lynch a few days later he presented the less detailed message that London hoped the Irish government would agree to secretly cooperate on security in general. Peck reported that Lynch seemed open to the idea as long as it was on an *ad hoc* basis and was kept very discreet.[19]

On July 17 Sir Alec Douglas-Home instructed Ambassador Peck to make a formal complaint to the Irish government regarding an incident that transpired earlier that day in which British troops on patrol in the North were fired on from Irish territory. In addition to protesting the shooting, London also believed that an ambulance that sped through a check point at Killeen and entered the Irish Republic was carrying a prisoner who had escaped from a hospital in Belfast. Peck duly informed the Department of Foreign Affairs about London's concern regarding the shooting incident and expressed the hope that "the Irish authorities [not] turn a blind eye to such incidents." He also requested that the Garda find and return the ambulance while arresting those who stole it. In reality Peck had little confidence that Dublin would pursue a more active campaign against the IRA unless it became a serious threat to the security of the Irish state.[20]

British Army behavior in the North and Dublin's growing lack of faith in reform

Conflict between the British Army and the nationalist population of Northern Ireland also caused trouble in Anglo-Irish relations. In late May 1971 a nationalist protest against workplace harassment of Catholics at the Gallaher Company in Belfast resulted in a violent clash between the demonstrators and troops from the Royal Highland Fusiliers. Northern nationalist leaders condemned the army for excessive use of force during the protest. Dublin saw this incident as further evidence that the British Army was unwittingly alienating moderate nationalists and furthering the appeal of republicanism among the Catholic community.[21] Hugh McCann paid a call on Ambassador Peck on May 21 to express the Irish government's concern regarding the incident. McCann pointed out that both the Dáil and moderate Northern nationalists were putting pressure on Jack Lynch to publicly denounce the army's actions. The ambassador countered that the protesters had been vocal in their support of the IRA and that the regiment in question had recently lost three members to IRA action. However, Ambassador Peck promised to raise the issue with the UK representative in Belfast to see what could be done to defuse the situation.[22]

While the British and Irish governments were seeking to de-escalate the situation, a public comment by Brian Faulkner only made matters worse. On May 25 Faulkner told the Stormont parliament that "any soldier seeing any person with a weapon or seeing any person acting suspiciously" was free to fire at that person.[23] When Hugh McCann met again with Ambassador Peck on May 26 the ambassador had to assure McCann that Faulkner had been mistaken and that official rules of engagement limited troops to firing at people who were both armed *and* acting suspiciously.[24]

The growing divide between Dublin and London was clearly on display at a meeting between British and Irish officials at the FCO in London on May 24, 1971. Irish ambassador Donal O'Sullivan, accompanied by Eamonn Gallagher met with Sir Stewart Crawford from the FCO, Philip Woodfield of the Home Office, and a number of other FCO officers. Sir Stewart began the meeting by complaining about a statement that Lynch had issued on May 21 in which the taoiseach had condemned recent actions by British troops in Belfast for using excessive use of force against the demonstrators at the Gallaher Company protest. Crawford described Lynch's words as an "unhelpful" mischaracterization of the events that would promote hostility toward the British Army among Northern nationalists. The Irish responded that Lynch was forced to make a statement to placate concerns raised in the Dáil and that the real problem was the excessive force used by the British military against the protestors. The ambassador stressed that the desire to avoid public spats between London and Dublin could not outweigh the need for Lynch to publicly denounce violence perpetrated by the security forces.

Crawford tried to steer the conversation back to a more positive tone and asked Howard Smith, the UK representative in Belfast, to give the Irish a general view of events in the North since Faulkner had assumed office. Smith assured O'Sullivan and Gallagher that Faulkner was moving forward with reforms in areas like housing and local government and was seeking out consultation with leaders of both the Catholic Church and the SDLP. O'Sullivan dismissed any progress on reform in the North as a mirage that hid the reality that the Unionist Party had no intention of making any real changes to the underlying political situation. The ambassador also warned that the British Army was being manipulated into acting as an armed guarantor of unionist political domination. O'Sullivan, stressing that he was conveying the concerns of Patrick Hillery, called for a "radical change" in Northern Ireland. The Irish government wanted to see the monopoly of real political power by the Unionist Party ended. O'Sullivan argued that a traditional parliamentary democracy was unfitted to a divided society like Northern Ireland and that London had "to impose new structures" on the province. Dublin did not have a specific plan to suggest to the British but O'Sullivan suggested that nationalist membership on various public boards, nominated by the opposition in Stormont, was a first step in the right direction.

Turning to more immediate concerns about the approaching summer marching season, O'Sullivan expressed Dublin's view that "sectarian parades in areas where they were not wanted [are] an intolerable affront to the people of such areas." He urged that British government not to use the military to protect these parades "in order to placate the bigots who control the Orange Order." Howard Smith assured O'Sullivan that Faulkner was working on finding a solution to the parades issue.[25]

When Ambassador O'Sullivan met Sir Stewart Crawford informally at a dinner at the home of the Norwegian ambassador a week after their meeting at the FCO, the two men returned to the topic of Lynch's statement condemning army violence during the Gallaher riot. Sir Stewart apologized for the hardline that the FCO had taken during the formal meeting and explained that Heath's government was under political pressure from Faulkner to reject Lynch's view of the incident. He told the ambassador that the British government did not want to create any political difficulties for Lynch and that London appreciated the generally moderate stance of the taoiseach. Sir Stewart went on to say that London would soon be asking for a meeting between Heath and Lynch. In response to O'Sullivan's suggestion that the two heads of government should focus on a long-term solution that the Irish hoped would lead to reunification, Sir Stewart said that Heath was also looking for a permanent settlement. He told O'Sullivan that Heath "is nothing if not a realist and this long drawn out trouble in the North is not doing the reputation of either of our countries any good abroad."[26]

Another security-related issue that caused disagreement between the Irish and British governments was the proposal to form a full-time battalion of the Ulster Defense Regiment. The Irish Embassy outlined Dublin's objections to the plan to the FCO on June 15, 1971. The main Irish concern was that the UDR would become a sectarian force that would only further alienate the nationalist community. Dublin also believed that increasing the number of full-time security forces was symbolic of London's failure to address the underlying political issues that were driving the violence in the first place. Whitehall responded that the proposed new unit was simply designed to relieve some of the pressure on the British military to maintain its many global commitments and that the UDR was firmly under army control so that it could not be used as a political force by Stormont. The FCO pointed out that the British Army commanders were themselves adamant that the crisis in the North called for a political rather than military solution but that basic security was necessary to achieve a political settlement.[27]

The two governments even argued about the frequency of their official disagreements. In June 1971 a spokesman for the Heath government told parliament that since the Conservatives had replaced Labour in power the Irish government had only made one official diplomatic representation to London regarding Northern Ireland. This statement caused a great deal of concern for Lynch's government as Dublin feared it would give the impression that it was not actively involved in Northern Ireland and therefore strengthen the hand of nationalist extremists. When the Irish Embassy made a complaint to the FCO the British replied that the parliamentary statement was very narrowly legalistic and did not count a large number of less formal discussions between the two governments but that they needed to play down the amount of contact that the two governments had with each other to placate unionist extremists. The British also pointed out that while they were very happy to have frequent low-key consultation with Dublin and, despite recognizing the natural concern that Dublin had for the North, it was still their official stance that Northern Ireland was a strictly domestic affair for the United Kingdom.[28]

Dublin's evolving view of the North

In late June 1971 the Irish Department of Foreign Affairs prepared a memorandum for Patrick Hillery that surveyed the status of the situation in Northern Ireland and made some suggestions of future policies that Dublin should pursue. The document began by stating that Stormont had to rely on the British military for all security needs. This involved London in the day-to-day affairs in the North to an unprecedented degree from which "quite unprecedented consequences must flow." Iveagh House believed that the current policies of the Irish government were broadly acceptable to the British government and people, the international community, the Irish public, and moderate opinion in Northern Ireland, even if Irish policy was sometimes misunderstood. The question that the memo then attempted to answer was what Dublin should do going forward to capitalize on the high regard for Irish policy and the focus that London had on Northern Ireland.

The document advised dividing short-term and long-term goals. In the short term, Dublin should continue to push for political changes in the North that would end "de facto and permanently the Unionist hegemony." If that level of reform proved unattainable, then Dublin should make sure that the onus for failure rested on the Unionist government. The long-term goal was, of course, reunification. In achieving the first goal, the memo suggested that civil disobedience and protest marches were useful tools for Northern nationalists to put pressure on Stormont while the full-scale violence of the republicans should continue to be condemned. Unfortunately, the current trend was one of growing support in the North for the IRA. The Irish government was advised to continue to try to move the British government away from its unconditional support of unionism to a more balanced view of Anglo-Irish relations. The fiftieth anniversary of the 1921 truce was suggested as an occasion for Jack Lynch to give a major speech promoting the idea that Irish unification should be supported by the British government as the best method to secure "harmonious relations between the two islands," even though London currently had no interest in unification.

The memo acknowledged that the Unionist government was, of course, dead set against discussing reunification. In addition, moderate Northern nationalist leaders had recently told the Department of Foreign Affairs that they did not believe that Faulkner's government had any intention of enacting any reforms that would move beyond window dressing and actually give nationalists some voice in governing the province. Dublin and the Northern moderates would benefit from demonstrating to London that the real problem in the North was "the intransigence of the Orange Order." Changing London's attitude toward active support for Irish unity, coupled with Dublin's own efforts to pave the way for reunification by encouraging cross-border economic cooperation and preparing the Irish public for the necessary constitutional changes, were policies that were slow moving by their very nature. The memo suggested that, with the situation on the ground in the North becoming more violent, there might not be time to stick to such a policy of gradual change. Dublin might have to attempt to accelerate the pace of change with new initiatives or move the long-term objective of reunification "nearer to the top of the agenda."

The document then went on to weigh the pros and cons of a shift in Dublin's short-term goals. The negatives included the fact that London was not ready to support unification and the unionists would be united in opposition of the idea. In addition, a focus on Irish unity might only make the situation in the North worse and harm the Irish economy without achieving any result. The arguments in favor of a new policy included the facts that the British were growing tired of the costs of protecting the status quo in the North, and that the reform program that London counted on as the center piece of its policy seemed to be on the verge of collapse. These factors should open London up to a radical reappraisal of their current plans for Northern Ireland. In addition, public opinion in the Irish Republic, as well as among Northern Catholics, was running in favor of a change in Dublin's policy on the North.

If Dublin did refocus on reunification as a more immediate goal there were a wide range of possible consequences. The memo suggested that reunification could be best achieved in a step-by-step process that would include the end of Stormont as it currently existed and the creation of an interim government that would include representatives from both communities overseen by a British official. This would promote peaceful cooperation between the divided Northern communities and allow unionists time to "reconsider their position in an Irish society."[29]

The department's proposal that Dublin should call on the British government to support reunification was acted upon on July 11, 1971, when Jack Lynch marked the fiftieth anniversary of the signing of the Anglo-Irish truce with a speech at the Garden of Remembrance. He pointed with pride to the economic and political gains that the Irish state had achieved since winning its independence but mourned the fact that partition divided the people of Ireland and reduced the potential of the whole island. Lynch called on both nationalists and unionists to reexamine their ideas and turn away from intolerance and prejudice to arrive at a mutually agreeable reunification. He acknowledged that it was foolish to consider partition to be "a paper wall, to be unmade by a stroke of legislation." Rather, Irish unification would be a gradual process that would involve changing the mindset of both Irish communities. None of these sentiments were new as Lynch had been calling for peaceful reunification by mutual consent since at least September 1969. However, the taoiseach did include the new idea that the British government should play a role in encouraging Irish unity. Lynch condemned the Ireland Act of 1949 as a mistaken policy that "pledges British support, financial and military, as well as British prestige" to the survival of a unionist dominated government at Stormont. The Ireland Act's "principal result, in its present form is to encourage infamous conduct…again and again…throughout the North." Lynch urged London to abandon its de facto unconditional guarantee of partition. "It would take nothing away from the honour of Britain or the rights of the majority in the North," he declared, "if the British government were to declare their interest in encouraging the unity of Ireland, by agreement, in independence and in a harmonious relationship between the two islands." Lynch concluded that the settlement of the War of Independence had been a failure and that the Ireland Act of 1949 only helped to perpetuate that failure. The time had come to look for a new solution based on Irish reconciliation.[30]

The British Embassy in Dublin took notice of Lynch's speech and reported to the FCO that the main goal seemed to be to urge London to "make the Unionists in the North feel less secure in their position." This would presumably encourage the unionists to make a deal with Irish nationalists that would lead to real change in Northern Ireland. The embassy dismissed the idea that Lynch's address reflected a growing support for republicanism in Ireland and concluded that it was meant as a public call for the British government to seriously consider Dublin's ideas regarding reunification.[31] A subsequent conversation between the British chargé d'affaires, John Williams, and Eamonn Gallagher of the Department of Foreign Affairs confirmed that Lynch had meant his comments for Heath's government. Gallagher added some details and informed Williams that Dublin did not expect a repeal of the Ireland Act of 1949 or even an immediate British declaration in favor of reunification. Rather, the Irish hoped that a slow process would begin at this point and that, if Heath avoided denouncing the idea out of hand, the two governments could begin a dialogue that would eventually lead to London expressing its support for reunification as a solution to the crisis in Northern Ireland. Williams reported that the Irish did not see the need to include Stormont in these discussions.[32]

Patrick Hillery gave additional context to Lynch's address of July 11 when he spoke to Ambassador Peck on July 21. Hillery pointed out that Lynch's government "was in a very difficult position" as the Irish public and moderate Northern nationalists had lost faith that Brian Faulkner intended to institute meaningful reform in Northern Ireland. Lynch remained committed to peaceful and gradual reunification but this policy was being undermined by Dublin's inability to show any tangible results for this moderate stance. Since London seemed to back up Faulkner's position that reunification was impossible, Lynch had to publicly reassure Irish nationalists that his government was working toward Irish unity.[33]

The SDLP boycott

At the same time that Jack Lynch was calling for Anglo-Irish cooperation to promote eventual Irish reunification, the two communities in Northern Ireland were becoming even more divided by the Troubles. On July 8, 1971, during a riot in Derry, a British soldier fatally shot Seamus Cusack. News of Cusack's death set off a fresh round of disturbances that led to another deadly incident in which nineteen-year-old Desmond Beattie was also killed by the British Army. More rioting followed as outraged nationalists in Derry took to the streets. While military authorities claimed that both men were armed, local eyewitnesses disputed this assertion.[34] The two shootings dramatically increased support for the Provisionals in Derry. The SDLP, fearful that it would lose support among the nationalist community to the republicans if it did nothing, demanded an official inquest into the deaths and threatened to withdraw from the Stormont parliament if this demand was not met.[35] John Hume, a leading member of the SDLP, informally expressed his concern over the shootings to Dublin which prompted Lynch's government to approach both the British Embassy in Dublin and the FCO in London to express doubts over the British Army's version of the events. Sir Stewart Crawford told Ambassador O'Sullivan that he did not believe an official inquiry was warranted. On July 10 Eamonn Gallagher, the Department of Foreign Affairs' unofficial point man on Northern issues, told John Hume that he believed there was no prospect of an official inquest. Gallagher's prediction proved correct. The SDLP withdrew from Stormont in protest on July 16, 1971, and formed an alternate Assembly of the Northern Irish People.[36]

Eamonn Gallagher, speaking to the Inter-Departmental Unit on the North of Ireland, expressed his support for the withdrawal of the SDLP the day before the action became official. Gallagher claimed that "Britain might ignore the withdrawal for a while but eventually would realize that the opting out had roots which ran deeper than an unrequited demand for an inquiry into two deaths." The underlying issue, he argued, was the total failure of unionism despite the attempts at reform. The British understood this reality, Gallagher claimed, but had so far been unwilling to accept the failure of Stormont. The boycott of Stormont by the SDLP would force London to accept the alienation of the nationalist community, the failure of the reform movement, and the need to seek a new solution. "The obduracy of the Northern Protestants may have been increased in the short-term," Gallagher said, "but the boil had to be lanced sooner or later."[37]

A few days after the SDLP staged its withdrawal from Stormont, Ambassador O'Sullivan spoke to Sir Stewart Crawford at the FCO. The ambassador had been instructed to lodge a formal complaint about a public statement made by Stormont Cabinet minister John Taylor that the security forces in Northern Ireland should be more willing to fire on demonstrators. O'Sullivan asked for London to repudiate this statement. He also issued a request from Dublin that the Scottish regiments, which had particularly bad relations with Catholics, be withdrawn from Belfast and Derry. Lastly, the ambassador requested that the Apprentice Boys parade in Derry be canceled. Sir Stewart assured O'Sullivan that the British Army did not take its orders from John Taylor and were fully controlled by London. However, when passing the ambassador's request to the Home Office he argued that the Irish had a "fair point" regarding Taylor's statement. Sir Stewart rejected as unfounded the Irish charge that Scottish regiments had poor relationships with the nationalist community and pointed out to O'Sullivan that London did not have an endless supply of troops to deploy as they wished. As for the parade in Derry, even if London agreed, that decision to cancel rested with Brian Faulkner. He also asked O'Sullivan if Dublin had encouraged the SDLP boycott of Stormont. O'Sullivan replied that it was "unthinkable" that the SDLP was advised to take that step by any official of the Irish government.[38] The ambassador's point regarding the SDLP was confirmed by Patrick Hillery in a meeting with Ambassador Peck on July 21. Peck reported that Hillery "said that the Irish Government were horrified by the action of the S.D.L.P. in withdrawing from Stormont, and that move had taken them wholly by surprise: He was despondent about the chances of getting them to reconsider their position before Stormont reassembles."[39]

The taoiseach further enumerated the concerns that Hillery had expressed to Peck in a message he sent to Edward Heath on July 23, 1971. Lynch explained that the withdrawal of the SDLP was prompted by the controversial shootings in Derry but that the underlying cause was a belief among Northern nationalists that the reformation of Stormont was failing and that there were "increasing signs of a restoration of old-style Unionist authority." Lynch pointed to a number of factors that were encouraging this despondency including the "hardline" and "sectarian-minded" nature of Brian Faulkner's Cabinet and the "refusal of the Unionist Party to break their continued association with the Orange Order." While Lynch acknowledged that Dublin and London had differing opinions on some of the details of the supposed drift to the right by Faulkner, he argued that there was no debating the fact that the SDLP had left Stormont and that the moderate leadership of Northern nationalists "would not have given up easily

Figure 4.1 Stormont SDLP MPs Austin Currie and John Hume in London, 1971. Credit: Bentley Archive/Popperfoto.

and have acted as they have done out of something close to despair." Lynch closed by explaining that he wanted Heath to discuss these developments with his government with an eye to "the future administration of the North."[40]

Britain considers internment

While Lynch was looking for a different political future for Northern Ireland, albeit with no specific suggestions offered as to what that future might be, London remained focused on the deterioration of the security situation in the North. Sir Alec Douglas-Home cabled Ambassador Peck on July 27 with instructions to informally approach Lynch about the possibility of internment being imposed on both sides of the border. The foreign secretary described the increase in IRA activity in the North as a campaign "to disturb society ... destroy economic life and discredit the Stormont Government." In the face of this threat, internment in the North was being considered. Douglas-Home pointed out that if internment were limited to Northern Ireland it would not take the IRA long to regroup in the Irish Republic and resume its violent campaign. In order for internment to work it had to be introduced on both sides of the border simultaneously. If Dublin would not cooperate on internment Douglas-Home predicted that Faulkner's reform program would fail and London might have to impose direct rule on the North. The cable advised Peck to argue to Lynch that defeating the IRA was as much a concern for the security of the South as for the North. Douglas-Home instructed Peck that he was to treat the entire conversation with Lynch as a hypothetical question and that Dublin had to keep the discussion in strict confidence. The foreign secretary acknowledged that the chances of Dublin agreeing to joint internment were small. He advised Peck that the best argument that the ambassador could make was based on the security situation and that he should downplay the role that political pressure on Faulkner to act against the IRA had on the decision to consider internment.[41]

Peck reported back to the FCO that he believed that Lynch would only impose internment for "domestic reasons" and that he was unlikely to give any answer to "a hypothetical question." The ambassador suggested that he inform Lynch that interment in the North was possible in the coming weeks and to ask what the official response would be from Dublin in that eventuality. Peck also argued that Dublin was already doing what it could to harass the IRA in the South even if convictions were hard to come by in court. Internment in the Republic, while not ruled out by Dublin, would be "an extremely contentious political issue," according to Peck and coordination between North and South on internment was most unlikely.[42]

When Peck confidentially spoke to Lynch on July 30 the taoiseach left no doubt about his attitude toward internment. "He said," Peck reported to the FCO, "that he could state categorically that he could not possibly contemplate internment at the present time, there were no immediate grounds for doing so, and if he tried to introduce it in consequence of our doing so, neither his nor any Irish Government could survive such a measure." In fact, Lynch strongly advised the British to give up any idea of internment lest it "produce an explosion which would be impossible to contain." Lynch warned that anyone who was not a republican before they were interned would surely embrace the IRA afterward. Furthermore, the moderate nationalists "would identify with the internees," causing even more alienation between the Catholic community and the security forces. Peck considered Lynch's reaction as indicative of his overall belief "that the only solution to the security situation is political."[43]

In a separate cable Ambassador Peck provided the FCO with a more detailed analysis of Lynch's reaction to the idea of internment. He stressed that Lynch's response showed that any Irish government had to take account of the fact that domestic political opinion in Ireland did not support the "status quo in the

North." According to Peck, the taoiseach had reunification as his long-term goal but was more focused on the immediate goals of "peace, security, and justice now for the Catholic minority," which Lynch believed was the path to defeating the IRA. "Moreover," Peck wrote, "he is convinced that our difficulties could be largely overcome if we somehow reformulate our attitude on the long-term constitutional question so as to give a glimmer of light at the end of a long tunnel to the increasingly despondent and consequently blood-minded minority."[44]

The American Embassy in Dublin held a view similar to Peck's analysis that Lynch's government had to take domestic political concerns seriously when forming Dublin's policies toward the North. The embassy warned the State Department in July 1971 that Lynch, despite his rejection of political violence, would have to limit the steps he took against the IRA due to its popularity with the Southern electorate. Perhaps more troubling, American officials also believed, "By Irish standards, the 'Provisionals' now constitute a formidable fighting force."[45]

By the time Peck approached Lynch regarding internment, the idea had already been discussed at length by British and Northern Irish officials. London and Stormont had begun to talk about how to implement internment if the step became necessary as early as February 1971.[46] By the summer pressure was building toward internment. On July 19, 1971, Brian Faulkner told Reginald Maudling, UK representative to Belfast Howard Smith, and General Tuzo that the time had come to implement internment unless the British had another idea. Tuzo suggested a more limited army action to arrest top IRA leaders and hold them for at least 48 hours. The targeted arrest actions were executed on July 23 and 27 but failed to quiet the situation in the North. In fact, the army's actions were condemned by moderate nationalist leaders like John Hume and Paddy Devlin who called for demonstrations to protest what they saw as antinationalist bias in the raids which were carried out exclusively in Catholic neighborhoods.[47] Faulkner informed Maudling on July 28 that his government was convinced that the time for internment had come as the army raids had failed. While Maudling argued that the recent army arrests should be given time to work, and General Tuzo remained opposed, London was by this point seriously considering implementing internment.[48] In the opinion of historian Anthony Craig, Heath's government had decided that it would allow Faulkner to go ahead with internment not because London believed that internment itself would defeat the IRA, but rather that internment might be a useful intelligence gathering tool, would prop-up Faulkner's government for a while, and would be valuable to have in place if London had to resort to direct rule. According to Craig's analysis, London, without whose permission Faulkner could not start internment, naively saw the step as "a 'win-win' situation, for even if it backfired they would not be blamed." The formal decision was taken on August 4, 1971, in a meeting at Downing Street attended by Heath, Faulkner, Maudling, Carrington, Douglas-Home, General Tuzo, the RUC Chief-Constable, and the British Chief of the General Staff, Field Marshal Sir Michael Carver. The British gave permission for Faulkner to declare internment as long as he agreed to ban all parades in Northern Ireland for six months.[49]

Internment begins

On August 9, 1971, internment without trial was formally introduced by Faulkner's government. The security forces detained 342 men from a list of 450 targets. Despite the advice of Reginald Maudling, the list included no unionists. Many of the men seized were not republicans and many IRA leaders had already gone into hiding as the threat of internment had been openly discussed for months.[50] Of the detainees, an estimated 100 were members of the Official or Provisional wings of the IRA while 116 were quickly released. The reaction in the nationalist community was violent. Rioting over the next three days led to twenty-one deaths, and as many as 7,000 people, mainly Catholics, fled their homes.[51]

The imposition of internment caused a major stir in Anglo-Irish relations. Edward Heath sent a message to Jack Lynch shortly before the formal announcement of internment, but after the round-up had already begun, putting as positive a spin on the policy as he could and pleading for Lynch's forbearance. The prime minister placed the onus for the decision on Stormont. He told Lynch that Faulkner believed that this was the only way to combat the increasing levels of IRA violence and stressed that the British had extracted from Faulkner a promise to ban all parades and marches for at least six months, if not more, and a guarantee that there would be no discrimination between unionist and nationalist extremists "except as the facts of the situation made inevitable," in return for British acquiescence to internment. Heath claimed that both he and Faulkner were aware of the potential downside to internment and the "implications and dangers" to Lynch's government. He bemoaned the fact that Lynch had ruled out cooperation with his own announcement of interment in the Republic. "I regret no less than you," Heath wrote, "that these new measures have been found necessary. I hope that, in the light of what I have said, you will be able to react to them with understanding, even if regret.... I also hope that, however you may feel obliged to react in public, you will in practice keep up the pressure of harassment of the IRA south of the border." The prime minster closed with a hope that internment would not harm Anglo-Irish relations or stop cooperation on issues of mutual concern such as entry into the European Economic Community.[52]

Lynch's public statement on internment later that day left no doubt as to Dublin's unhappiness with the policy and desire for a new political agenda to be set for the North. "The introduction of internment without trial in the North this morning," the statement read, "is deplorable evidence of the political poverty of the policies which have been pursued there for some time and which I condemned publically last week." Lynch predicted that any reduction in violence would be temporary and derided internment as a policy that did nothing to achieve "the necessary long term solutions." He condemned the move as an unjust "attempt to maintain a regime which has long since shown itself incapable of just Government and contemptuous of the norms of the British democracy to which they pretend allegiance." Lynch announced that the Irish Army had been instructed to prepare refugee centers for "any dependents of internees who seek accommodation." Lastly, he suggested "a conference of all the interested parties take place in order to obtain a new form of administration for Northern Ireland. There is no other way to avoid further deaths and injuries."[53]

Lynch was just as adamant in his condemnation of internment when he spoke by phone with Heath on August 10. He repeated his main points that the Stormont government, under the sway of the Orange Order, had lost legitimacy by imposing internment in the North and that a new political system had to be devised for the province. "We believe," he told Heath, "that in this present set-up it [Stormont] will never produce peace, it will never produce a stable democracy or the kind of democracy the British people would want in their territory."[54]

On August 10 the Irish government announced that Patrick Hillery would be dispatched to London for talks with the British government to further Dublin's "main objective" of ending "the appalling carnage and violence in the North."[55] Hillery met with Home Secretary Maudling as well as some officials from the FCO at the Home Office on August 11. The Irish foreign minister was even more pessimistic than Lynch had been in his communication with Heath. He predicted that current British policy "would lead to war in Ireland, not only in the North." The reemergence of the IRA was due to the fact that the British government was "preserving the dominance of the Orange Order" by propping up Stormont. Hillery warned the British that they did not "appreciate the urgency of the situation" and the fact that London's more aggressive military policy regarding the North was destroying Anglo-Irish relations. The army's relationship with the nationalist community in the North had also degenerated to the point where "Catholics now saw the army as having taken the place of the B-Specials." Hillery pointed out that no Protestants had been interned and claimed that few of the internees were really members of the IRA. Maudling presented the British counterpoints, arguing that Stormont was "lawfully and democratically elected," and committed to further reform. He claimed that internment was made necessary by "terrorism on an intolerable scale." The British Army, the home secretary argued, was acting with restraint but had come under fierce attack by the IRA which was sheltered in the nationalist neighborhoods. The connection between the IRA and the Catholic population also explained why the internees were drawn from that community. Maudling told Hillery that Dublin should be more active in fighting the IRA itself as the republicans were a threat to the Irish state as much as to Northern Ireland. The Irish foreign minister reminded the home secretary that it was politically impossible for Lynch to be seen to crack down on the IRA if the only result would be that Stormont was made more secure.

After both sides laid out their well-known disagreements, Hillery offered a suggestion for a replacement for the current, failing, Stormont system. A "commission in which both communities could be represented equally" could take over the responsibility of provincial government or act as a body to seek a permanent solution. He argued that a traditional parliamentary system would never work in the North because it simply cemented unionist control over the nationalist minority. Giving moderate nationalist leaders a real role in government would strengthen their hand, prompt a return of the SDLP to participation in government, and weaken the IRA's appeal.

Maudling said that while he privately agreed that the Stormont system "had not been a great success," he could only discuss the constitutional status of Northern Ireland with Hillery if their conversation was kept from the public. In private, Maudling said, he was willing to hear any suggestion for a long-term solution to the Northern crisis. However, he was concerned that Hillery's commission proposal would spark a unionist backlash if it was actually meant to replace Stormont. Hillery responded that the British had to make it clear that a return to government exclusively controlled by the Unionist Party was unacceptable and that the commission idea had to be attempted soon if it was to have any chance of success. The home secretary demurred, arguing that the way forward to a political solution was through the ongoing reform program. That reform program could only make progress if the violence in Northern Ireland was reduced. Internment was designed to reduce violence and thus serve reform and Irish Republic should "do everything it could to assist in dealing with gunmen in its own territory."[56]

The FCO's take on Hillery's visit, cabled that same day to Ambassador Peck, was that Dublin saw internment "as a deliberate choice of the use of force" rather than political means, to control the situation in Northern Ireland and that both Hillery and Lynch were "really alarmed at the prospect" of the Irish government being replaced by "more militant political forces." Peck was also informed about Hillery's "vague" proposal for an intercommunity commission and London's decision to refrain from telling Brian Faulkner about the idea.[57] Peck confirmed that Hillery's presentation to Maudling accurately reflected the views of Lynch's government. The ambassador believed that the major flaw with the Irish position was that it underestimated the fact that a powerful unionist backlash might cause political problems at Westminster, spark a declaration of direct rule, or even cause an armed unionist revolt.[58]

The day after Hillery raised the issue of a new commission in the North in private at the FCO, Lynch gave a public statement supporting the concept. Rather than relying on private diplomacy the Irish government meant to introduce the commission idea directly to the general public and the British voters in particular. Lynch began his statement by condemning internment as an attempt to suppress the rights of the minority in the North. He called the violent reaction to internment "not surprising" even while denouncing the use of political violence by anyone. "We hope the British people," Lynch wrote, "will come to realize that the administration of Northern Ireland is now and has been since it was created directed at the suppression of the civil and human rights of the more than a third of the population. We know that the British public, if fully aware of the facts, would turn away in horror from what they have been asked to support … all these years in Northern Ireland." Since the current Stormont regime was unwilling, or unable, to fully implement the promises of the Downing Street Declaration of August 1969, Lynch called for the Stormont government to be "replaced by an administration in which power and decision-making will be equally shared between unionist and non-unionist. The Stormont regime, which … bears responsibility for recurring violence … must be brought to an end…. This is a surer road to peace and justice than self-destructive violence."[59]

Lynch took some questions from the press following his statement. He added a few details on the concept of the commission, including clarifying that he proposed an equal number of representatives from each of the two communities and that the commission would only be a temporary administration. The taoiseach tried to downplay the extent of discord in Anglo-Irish relations with regard to the North, characterizing the British government as well-intentioned but ill-informed about Northern Ireland. While he refused to discuss the details of Hillery's talks with Maudling, Lynch told the assembled reporters that Anglo-Irish relations "were good during the Wilson Government's term of Office. They have been good since Mr. Heath came to power. They are now exactly the same."[60]

Ambassador Peck's analysis of Lynch's statement concluded that it was shaped by a need to placate the more extreme elements within Fianna Fáil. On the other hand, Peck pointed out that there was really nothing new in the statement, except that the ideas were expressed in public instead of in private with British officials. He also believed that Lynch "can have no illusions about the likely response from Westminster and Stormont" to the commission proposal. The practical results of the proposal, Peck believed, would be to forge closer ties between the SDLP and Dublin and create more public calls to peacefully abolish Stormont. This would place Lynch's government firmly behind the wishes of the majority of the Irish public with regard to the North.[61]

While Dublin was pushing for a new arrangement for shared government in Northern Ireland, the SDLP's reaction to internment had been to declare that their boycott of Stormont would not end until internment was lifted.

Figure 4.2 Patrick Hillery outside the Home Office in London amid internment protestors, August 1971. Credit: Central Press.

Additional measures taken by moderate nationalists in a broader campaign of civil disobedience and disengagement from the state included the beginning of a rent and rate strike, a large number of resignations of Catholics from the UDR, and the general withdrawal of nationalist participation from local government.[62]

A public dispute

Brian Faulkner traveled to Chequers, the official country retreat of the British prime minister, to meet with Edward Heath on August 19 to discuss the situation in Northern Ireland. In the wake of Lynch's public call for the end of the existing government at Stormont, Heath reassured Faulkner that London was not considering any constitutional change in the North that was not approved by Stormont and pledged his continued support in attempting to "eradicate terrorism." Heath also indicated that the British government would put more pressure on Dublin to cooperate against the IRA. Heath told the Northern premier that while he would probably need to meet with Jack Lynch in the near future, the British government would defend the existing Stormont system and attempt to focus the Irish government on harassing the IRA in the South. Having reassured Faulkner of London's support and commitment to fighting the IRA, Heath raised the possibility that Reginald Maudling might attempt to start talks with moderate nationalists in the North before "the terrorist campaign was totally crushed" in order to coax the SDLP back into Stormont and assuage the British public's desire for a peaceful resolution to the violence. Faulkner agreed as long as Maudling did not promise the nationalists any more concessions that would undermine "the basic concept of majority rule" in Northern Ireland.[63]

Lynch inserted himself into the meeting between Heath and Faulkner by sending a telegram, the text of which the Irish government released to the public, to Chequers. He characterized internment and the resulting upsurge in violence in the North as proof of both "the failure of internment and of current military operations as a solution to the current problems in Northern Ireland." The taoiseach called for a political solution based on "full equality of treatment for everyone in Northern Ireland." Lynch warned that if the British continued to pursue a military solution, Dublin would "support the policy of passive resistance" being implemented by the SDLP and other moderate nationalists. On the other hand, if London sought a political solution, then Lynch announced that he would be willing to meet with all the interested parties to look for ways "of promoting the economic, social and political wellbeing of all the Irish people, North and South, without prejudice to the aspiration of the great majority of the Irish people to the reunification of Ireland."[64]

Heath promptly responded to Lynch's message that same day. The prime minister called Lynch's cable "unjustifiable in its content, unacceptable in its attempt to interfere in the affairs of the United Kingdom" and unhelpful in the search for a "solution to the problems of Northern Ireland." Heath reminded Lynch that London and Stormont were already committed to equal treatment for all the people of the North and defended internment and other military actions as being aimed "against armed terrorists" whose actions often "originate in or are supported from the Republic." Heath urged Lynch to "join me in suppressing" the gunmen.[65]

On the off chance that Heath's anger wasn't clear from the text of the message, Ambassador Peck was instructed by the FCO to deliver the cable in person to Lynch and make it clear that the prime minister was "personally appalled that Mr. Lynch should take this public position when the Prime Minister and he have been trying so hard to deal sensibly and amicably ... with the whole range of matters of common interest. Particularly when the Prime Minister had agreed with Mr. Lynch that, if Mr. Lynch should want to bring forward the date of his meeting with the Prime Minister [tentatively scheduled for October], he had only to ask."[66]

Peck delivered Heath's message to Lynch at his home that night. The ambassador reported that after reading the cable Lynch commented, "Well, fair enough, I suppose I had to expect it." The taoiseach then proceeded to lay out for Peck the reasons behind his message to Chequers. He said that he had a responsibility as taoiseach to represent the Irish people on both sides of the border and that he was overcome by "despair" regarding the present situation in the North. Lynch complained that he had been correct about the dangers of implementing internment but that London only listened to the advice of "the Protestant management" when it came to the North. Lynch pointed out that the nationalist community in general was now alienated from the British Army and were increasingly drawn to the IRA. The taoiseach admitted to Peck that he was also under a great deal of pressure from within his own party and that the "Blaney–Boland–Haughey factions" of Fianna Fáil were still a real threat to his leadership.

The ambassador tried to lower the temperature of the discussion by telling Lynch that Heath still had every intention of meeting him in October as they had planned and suggesting that public "polemics" should be avoided in the run-up to the meeting. Peck reported that as their talk continued Lynch relaxed and engaged in a more friendly conversation over drinks with the ambassador during which the taoiseach acknowledged the fruitless nature of a public quarrel with London. However, Peck also warned that the threat to Lynch from the more republican wing of Fianna Fáil was real and that the taoiseach might not be "master of his own house."[67]

Peck's discussion with the taoiseach did not end the exchange as Lynch issued a public rebuttal to Heath's message the next day. He termed Heath's interpretation of his cable to Chequers as "regrettable." Lynch rejected Heath's claims that the violence in the North was largely fueled by republicans acting from the Irish Republic. As for the prime minister's assertions that the recent actions of the British Army were aimed squarely at terrorist and were designed to lead to greater harmony between the nationalist and unionist communities, Lynch pointed out that Northern nationalists leaders, and the large number of Catholic refugees entering Irish territory, did not share that view. Lynch went on to say that he doubted that London and Stormont were serious about equal treatment for all the people of the North as internment had been aimed exclusively at nationalists. Lynch ended his message by rejecting partition as unacceptable to "the great majority of the Irish people" and calling for talks among all parties interested in "a peaceful solution" to the crisis in Northern Ireland.[68]

Despite the fact that Lynch did not back down from his initial statement in any meaningful way, and completely rejected Heath's interpretation of events in Northern Ireland, the taoiseach's second pronouncement was met with a very different response from London. Douglas-Home cabled Peck that he should let the Irish government know that "The Prime Minister remains keen that we should cease these public exchanges and get back to serious and sensible discussion of a whole range of matters of common interest." The foreign secretary added that if Peck believed it was "appropriate" he should let Lynch know that Whitehall thought that his latest statement "was carefully designed so as not to exacerbate matters any further."[69] After Peck spoke to the taoiseach he reported that Lynch agreed that public disputes were not helpful. Lynch also expressed gratitude for Heath's desire to discuss a "whole range of matters of common interest" which Lynch interpreted as meaning that no "aspect of the Northern question were ruled out." However, the taoiseach added that he did not "expect, or indeed welcome, any kid of negotiation" when he met with Heath.[70]

The reaffirmation from London that Lynch and Heath would meet soon may have been a major aim of the Irish government in starting a public argument with the British. In an interview which Eamonn Gallagher gave to historian Anthony Craig, Gallagher reported that he had drafted Lynch's intentionally provocative message of August 19. Gallagher claimed that the British response was anticipated by Dublin and that the British offer to move up the date of a Lynch–Heath meeting was one of the intended goals of sending the cable to the Heath–Faulkner meeting as Dublin also wanted to be involved in talks with London.[71]

Washington and internment

The American government was also very concerned about the imposition of internment without trial in Northern Ireland and Dublin attempted to draw Washington into the situation. Ambassador John Moore reported from Dublin that following internment the situation in the North was seen in Ireland as the worst it had been "in many years, perhaps decades." Moore believed that internment was causing increased sympathy for the IRA on both sides of the border. Many people in Ireland saw the move as an insult to Lynch and Moore believed that the public outcry would "further undermine" the "heretofore dominant moderate position" of the Irish government.[72]

William Warnock, Irish ambassador to the United States, met with Assistant Secretary of State Martin Hillenbrand to present Lynch's August 12 public statement and ask for American assistance on Northern Ireland. Hillenbrand told Warnock that the United States, while concerned about the events in the North, would be unable to intervene in the internal affairs of the United Kingdom. The ambassador replied that the Irish government understood that there could be no official American involvement, but Dublin hoped that Washington could make it clear to the British that it was concerned about the course of events in Northern Ireland.[73]

Warnock returned to the State Department on August 20 with copies of the Lynch–Heath exchange from the previous day as well as Lynch's response from that same day. The ambassador asked about the request he had made for American help on August 13 and was informed that the State Department had considered the Irish proposal but had determined that nothing constructive could arise from any American approach to London. Warnock pressed Acting Assistant Secretary of State Russell Fessenden, arguing that "even an expression of humanitarian concern would be helpful." Fessenden rejected this idea and called American noninvolvement in Northern Ireland "a cardinal point in American policy."[74]

While Washington remained steadfastly committed to noninvolvement in Northern Ireland some elements in the State Department agreed with the Irish analysis of the problem. A State Department intelligence summary on Northern Ireland published in late August reported that internment had backfired and had little chance of reducing the violence in the province. The report concluded that London's basic policy of promoting reform in the North was being undermined by the unionist's insistence on placing security concerns ahead of any political settlement. Internment was London's reaction to this political pressure as much as it was a genuine tactic designed to defeat the IRA. According to the summary, the major effect of internment had been the damage it had caused to Anglo-Irish relations.[75]

The State Department also publicly endorsed the idea that the situation in Northern Ireland was a legitimate concern of the Irish Republic. In a routine press conference on September 2, 1971, a State Department spokesperson called the recent violence in the North tragic and distressing but insisted that the official American stance was that the problems in the province were "internal affairs of Great Britain and Northern Ireland and the Irish Republic. We have expressed the hope to those we talked to about it officially that they may reach reconciliation through diplomatic talks." When questioned by a reporter as to how the Northern Ireland crisis could be an internal affair for both the United Kingdom and the Irish Republic the spokesperson attempted to resolve the conundrum by saying that the situation was one "for the Governments—Great Britain, Northern Ireland, and the Irish Republic—to resolve."[76]

Deadly border incident

With internment still very much a raw wound, a deadly incident at the border on August 29 caused another public argument between London and Dublin. The two governments agreed on the basic facts that two British armored cars crossed into Irish territory and were prevented from returning to Northern Ireland by a large crowd and a van that was blocking the road. The angry crowd set one of the armored cars on fire and the crew had to flee to the remaining vehicle, which was then able to recross the border. During a gunfight immediately after the border incursion a British soldier was killed. Ambassador Peck called Hugh McCann later in the day to express London's outrage over the incident and to demand that the perpetrators be brought to justice. McCann reminded Peck that the incident started with a British incursion into Irish territory. The ambassador assured McCann that the two armored cars crossed by mistake and claimed that the British Army had been fired upon from the Republic's side of the border. The two men agreed that the timing of the incident was unfortunate given the already heightened state of crisis in Northern Ireland but Peck said that London had to make a public statement deploring the events and calling on Dublin to increase border security.[77]

Rather than accept the British version of events, Lynch issued his own statement on the incident in which he claimed that Garda and Irish Army patrols that responded to the incursion did see armed civilians in the area (presumably an IRA unit) but believed that the British casualty was caused from gunfire coming from within Northern Ireland. The Irish security forces believed that any gunmen on the Irish side of the border fled into the North to evade capture by the Garda or Irish Army. Lynch placed the blame for the incident on the British border incursion and pointed out that there had been over thirty such crossings in the past two years.[78]

When Ambassador Peck next spoke to Hugh McCann he pointed out that there were discrepancies in the two official views of the border incident but that the British government apologized for the mistaken incursion into Irish territory and still expected Dublin to help find the people who were responsible for the shooting of the soldier. McCann stood by Lynch's statement that the gunmen had come from Northern Ireland and that the tragedy of the fatal shooting was the direct result of the British violation of Irish territory. McCann made the general point that all the violence was a result of the basic problems in Northern Ireland and that these root problems could only be solved by an innovative political solution that Dublin and London needed to find through cooperation with each other.[79]

Abuse of internees

The controversy surrounding internment increased as reports began to surface of the mistreatment and abuse of detainees. On August 18, 1971, Ambassador Donal O'Sullivan met with Sir Stewart Crawford at the FCO to express Dublin's concerns over the increased level of British Army activity in Catholic areas of Derry and to report that over thirty credible witnesses, including John Hume, were making serious allegations of abuse of internees. The Irish government wanted the "brutality" to stop immediately and called for an impartial investigation into the claims. Sir Stewart said that he personally did not believe the charges of mistreatment and pointed out that a complaint system was already in place to deal with the allegations. O'Sullivan stressed that pursuing a military solution to the Northern crisis was counterproductive as it further alienated moderate nationalists and threatened to spread the violence to the whole of Ireland. Crawford denied that London was seeking a military solution and pointed out that Lynch's recent public statements had not been helpful. He also took Dublin to task for failing "to control IRA activities" in the Republic. While London agreed that a political solution needed to be found, Sir Stewart argued that the withdrawal of the SDLP from Stormont, which he blamed on IRA intimidation, only made a peaceful agreement harder to achieve. O'Sullivan said that Dublin had not advised the SDLP to boycott Stormont but that it believed that they would not return to government under the current circumstances.[80] Crawford reported to the Home Office that, in his opinion, the Irish complaints about internee abuse were aimed at placating a domestic Irish audience rather than a serious request for action by London.[81]

While Lynch was indeed under domestic political pressure about the issue of abuse, Dublin did, in fact, expect real action from the British. On August 25 Donal O'Sullivan met at the FCO with Sir Thomas Brimelow, deputy undersecretary of state, and Kevlin White to outline the Irish government's requests. At the top of the list was a call for London to establish an "independent inquiry into the allegations of brutality." The British officials quickly agreed to this idea and indicated that both Prime Minister Heath and General Tuzo were keen to create such a body. However, the British also indicated their firm belief that the charges of abuse of detainees "were greatly exaggerated." O'Sullivan requested that the investigative body have at least one non-British member and that it should also look into the matter of the controversial killings of nationalists by the British Army which had been the initial cause of the SDLP withdrawal from Stormont. O'Sullivan also requested the creation of an appeals body for internees as well as access to medical exams and legal advice for the prisoners. Kelvin White assured the ambassador that an appeals body would be created in due course, that the internees had already been given medical examinations, and that they were free to ask for legal counsel. In addition, White said that the International Red Cross would be allowed to inspect any internment camps that might be set up for long-term housing of detainees.

The cooperative attitude of the FCO officials changed when O'Sullivan informed them that Dublin was considering taking action at the European Court of Human Rights regarding the brutality charges. The British advised O'Sullivan that Dublin should not make a rash move in that direction until more information came to light and warned that Lynch's government might find itself embarrassed if it backed a set of baseless charges against the British Army. At the very least, the British requested that Dublin inform them before approaching the European Court and refrain from talking about this possible action with the press. Sir Thomas Brimelow urged O'Sullivan to convey to Dublin the British hope that the two governments would "get back to reasonable political dialogue as soon as possible."[82]

Under the pressure of mounting public accusations of mistreatment of internees the British government agreed to the Irish demand for a special commission to investigate the claims. On August 31 Reginald Maudling appointed Sir Edward Compton to head a special commission of inquiry into the charges of mistreatment of internees. However, the creation of the committee hardly ended the controversy as the rules of the inquiry were criticized by the Irish government and Northern nationalists and the internees refused to give testimony.[83]

Conclusions

The resignation of James Chichester-Clark and his replacement by Brian Faulkner in Mach 1971 did nothing to help Anglo-Irish relations or change the trajectory of the Troubles in Northern Ireland. London and Dublin remained divided about the efficacy of military action aimed at the IRA. While Heath's government was still interested in talking to Dublin and searching for a political solution for the North the imposition of internment was a clear indication that security considerations were being given priority over politics. To some extent this move was forced on Heath as the moderate nationalists had withdrawn from Stormont and Faulkner, whom the British wished to keep in power, faced as much right-wing pressure as Chichester-Clark had to take a firm stance against republican violence. However, it was disingenuous for Heath to have suggested to Lynch that internment was a policy that London was forced into by Stormont. If the British had hoped that internment might buy them a period of calm in which to begin a new political initiative in Northern Ireland the results must have been disappointing. The SDLP was only further alienated from Stormont and violence did not abate following internment.

From Lynch's point of view internment was yet another example of how London refused to accept the advice that was offered to it by the Irish government. Dublin saw internment as confirmation that Heath was intent on pursuing a counterproductive military strategy to return peace to the North. Even before internment Jack Lynch had adopted the idea that originated in the Department of Foreign Affairs that Britain should be pushed to support Irish unification as a part of a political solution to the Troubles. Lynch's speech on July 11, 1971, marked an important public move away from his long-standing policy of support for the reform of Stormont toward the idea that Stormont needed to be replaced. Internment only reinforced the idea in Dublin that the existing Stormont system was a failure that could not be saved.

In the immediate aftermath of interment Lynch abandoned low-key diplomacy with London for angry public exchanges with Heath when he sent his message to Chequers. According to Lynch this action was brought about because of growing despair in Dublin and among Northern nationalists that London did not have any policy beyond keeping the unionists in power in Stormont. Lynch's decision to begin such a public fight with the British may also have been driven by the fear that his brand of moderate Irish nationalism linked to cooperation with Britain was losing its appeal with Irish nationalists on both sides of the border. In addition to engaging with Heath, Dublin once again appealed in vain for Washington to put some pressure on the British to change their policies in Northern Ireland. While the Nixon administration would not agree to involve itself in the Troubles in any way, the State Department did at least publicly acknowledge that it considered that the Irish government had a legitimate interest in Northern Ireland and encouraged talks among Dublin, London, and Belfast.

The Chequers Summits and Diplomatic Stalemate: August 1971–January 1972

For the six-month period after internment Northern Ireland experienced a political stalemate that resisted efforts by Edward Heath's government to break the logjam caused by the SDLP boycott of Stormont and the Unionist Party's reluctance to embrace meaningful reform. While January 1972 saw the culmination of the joint Anglo-Irish plan to enter the European Economic Community (EEC), the two governments could not come to any agreement on the issues that divided them on Northern Ireland despite the high-profile summit meetings held at Chequers in September 1971.

The lead-up to the first Chequers meeting

Even as problems such as the deadly border crossing of August 29 and the growing controversy over the allegations of abuse of internees were adding more items to the menu of Anglo-Irish disagreements, the two governments were moving toward a final agreement on a summit meeting between the taoiseach and the prime minister. Edward Heath's government pushed for an early date for the long-discussed summit meeting. On Friday, August 27, 1971, Peter Evans of the British Embassy in Dublin phoned Hugh McCann at home to advise him that Ambassador Peck had an urgent message from the prime minister that he wanted to give to Jack Lynch no later than the following Monday. Unfortunately, Lynch was in West Cork and was not expected back by then. Evans stressed that the message had to be delivered directly to Lynch. After speaking to Lynch by phone and discovering that he did not plan to return to Dublin until Tuesday, McCann phoned Evans back to see if the message could be transmitted by McCann to Lynch. Ambassador Peck became directly involved at this point and told McCann that he was in the uncomfortable situation of being trapped between Heath's instructions and Lynch's desire not to rush back from Cork. Peck told McCann that London was most anxious to arrange for a summit within two weeks at the most. The ambassador agreed to come to McCann's home the next day with the text of the message for McCann to read to Lynch over a secure phone line. When Peck arrived the next morning with the message, he urged McCann to support the idea of an early summit. McCann expressed concern that a meeting at this point "would probably do more harm than good" unless it made a concrete step toward finding a political solution to the Troubles. Peck assured McCann that Heath understood that Lynch would need to have some kind of positive result from a summit, even if he did not get everything he wanted. After talking to McCann, Lynch agreed to a meeting in the near future and announced that he would return to Dublin on Monday night to begin planning for the summit.[1]

Despite Eamonn Gallagher's claim that Lynch had sent his provocative message to Heath and Faulkner in order to goad the British into including the Irish government in talks, he did not appear to grasp at the offer immediately and there were voices in the Irish government that continued to argue against a meeting even after Lynch had agreed to it in principle. The arguments in favor of delaying a meeting included the desire for a firm agenda to be hashed out before any summit and the belief that a continuing high level of disorder in Northern Ireland might actually force London to pay more attention to finding a permanent solution to the crisis in the province.[2]

On August 31, the Irish ambassador in London requested the British government's views on the most likely result of the summit meeting. While the British would not make a prediction about the outcome of the talks, Heath presented another set of arguments in favor of moving up the date. The prime minister contended that a summit meeting would help the two governments to communicate their major concerns to each other. Heath suggested that they both faced "acute" problems and that they could work together "to find ways and means of dealing with them," even if they could not hope to solve all the problems at once. The prime minister strongly suggested that a second summit meeting would follow if Lynch agreed to meet soon. Heath suggested meeting on September 6 or 7 to allow a little time to pass since the fatal border shooting on August 29. The prime minister did not want to give the impression that the meeting was in reaction to this incident but he did believe that a high-profile meeting would show that both governments were working to reduce tensions.[3]

After consultation with members of the Cabinet, including Patrick Hillery, who supported the idea, Lynch announced his consent to an early meeting on September 1, 1971.[4] With the dates for the summit at Chequers set for September 6 and 7, the two governments prepared their materials and plans for the meeting. The FCO produced a brief for the meeting that both surveyed the current situation and suggested goals for the prime minister. The FCO accepted that Lynch was under "considerable pressure" from the more militant wing of Fianna Fáil and could possibly be replaced. If Charles Haughey, Neil Blaney, or Kevin Boland ended up as the new taoiseach, they might give "material comfort" to the IRA. Even if the relatively moderate Patrick Hillery became the new Irish leader the FCO feared that he would be forced to take a much harder line than Lynch had done. As the FCO saw any Fine Gael-led alternative to Lynch as inherently weak, they cautioned that "Lynch... remains the best Irish Prime Minister in sight." The document argued that since internment had been imposed, support for a more hardline stance by the Irish government had spread to the Irish public at large who have come to believe that London was no longer supporting reform in the North. The brief claimed that the Irish population generally saw internment as both anti-Catholic and a failure that justified the nationalist civil disobedience campaign in the North and even gave credibility to the IRA. With the exception of sympathy for the IRA, the FCO believed that Lynch shared these perceptions and would therefore seek "some tangible success from the Chequers meeting" or to at least demonstrate that he "stood up for Ireland."

In terms of specifics, the FCO believed that Lynch would ask for Stormont to be replaced by a cross-community commission overseen by Britain or some type of power-sharing executive for the province. Problematically for London, neither Dublin nor the SDLP would trust any initiative from Brian Faulkner nor would the Unionists accept any plan that came from a summit that excluded them. In this atmosphere, the FCO suggested that Heath focus on getting Lynch to take more effective action against the IRA and to persuade the SDLP to stop the civil disobedience campaign and return to Stormont. The brief acknowledged that both of these goals would be difficult to achieve. As to the long-term Irish goal of reunification, Heath had to defend the Ireland Act of 1949 but to accept, and have Faulkner accept, that reunification was "a perfectly proper political goal."[5]

In addition to the formal brief, Heath received a personal memo from the cabinet secretary, Sir Burke Trend. Trend began by expressing his "dismay about the bareness of the landscape and the absence of any realistic progress on the basis of our present assumptions" regarding Northern Ireland. He stressed to Heath that his ideas were not to be raised with Lynch at the coming meeting, however "sooner or later—and perhaps sooner rather than later—we shall be driven to call in question some of the political and constitutional assumptions which we have hitherto accepted." Trend argued that the official brief called for Britain to maintain the status quo of "crisis management...always reacting to events and hoping that things will get better." So far, London had been able to stop the situation in the North "from...boiling over." However, the current policy offered "no permanent solution, no light at the end of the tunnel" and, given recent events, no longer seemed to be working. Trend called for "a radical new political initiative" that would at least allow London to claim credit for trying to avert disaster in Northern Ireland in case of a total breakdown in law and order. Any new solution would have to accept a change in "the basic constitutional position of Ulster." One way forward, the cabinet secretary argued, would be to impose direct rule: a move that Heath's government had so far rejected as having "appalling consequences." However, direct rule would at least eliminate the need to get Stormont to agree to any political solution and self-government could be restored as part of a solution that included "new safeguards for the rights and interests of Roman Catholics" in the North in return for the recognition of Northern Ireland by Dublin. The second option that Trend explored was for London to work for some form of Irish reunification. He suggested that rather than simple absorption of the North by the South, reunification might take the form of joint sovereignty over the province. While the unionist reaction to this move would be potentially more destabilizing than the current crisis, the danger could be mitigated if London moved slowly with the idea of "a new deal for Ireland." If the British public could be made to accept that the settlement of 1920 was a failure and needed to be replaced to end the ongoing crisis, then Dublin and Belfast might be pressured to, at least, "investigate the options." While many details would have to be worked out, Trend advised his prime minister that the British government was currently "letting events dictate to us each further step downhill" and needed to at least be seen to try to "break-out from the vicious circle."[6]

    Lynch's government was even less satisfied with the status quo than London, and the Irish preparations for the summit reflected this dissatisfaction. In a long document prepared for Lynch before the meeting, the taoiseach was presented with a suggestion for an opening statement at the summit. The draft statement provided a brief historical analysis of Northern Ireland from the point of view of the Irish government. The current violence in the North was compared to other historical episodes of coercion during British rule of Ireland which had failed to fully solve the Irish Question. While the Anglo-Irish Treaty of 1921 had been a step forward for noncoercive Anglo-Irish relations, that settlement had now unraveled in Northern Ireland. Furthermore, the Irish brief contended that the Stormont government was bound to fail from its inception because a traditional parliamentary system would not work in a situation of a divided, antagonistic society in which the permanent majority systematically discriminated against the permanent minority. While the government in Stormont could fairly claim to be democratically elected by the population of Northern Ireland, it did not function like a normal government, and never would, since there was no hope that the Unionist Party would ever lose its monopolistic control of the Stormont Cabinet. Dublin had been cheered by the Downing Street Declaration promising equal rights to the nationalist community, but this reform effort had been a failure as the Unionist Party and unionist community as a whole did not support real reform of the system and never would.

The document presented Lynch with a number of options to present to the British as an alternative to the current system in Northern Ireland. These options ran the gamut from a major restructuring of Stormont that included power sharing, to replacing Stormont with a bicommunal commission overseen by London, to an Anglo-Irish condominium for the North, to repartition, to a federation of the British Isles that would include both parts of Ireland.

The section of the brief that focused on issues which Lynch could use to end the talks included British insistence that the IRA was the real problem or Heath's refusal to accept a significant change in the government of Northern Ireland. This stance obviously ran directly counter to the FCO's plans to ask for more Irish assistance against the IRA and to push the SDLP to return to Stormont and stabilize the political situation.

The document ended with a list of suggestions of what Lynch should ask for from Heath. The first Irish goal was to end the Unionist Party monopoly on power in the North and replace it with a system that would allow moderate nationalists a share of power. In addition, Lynch was advised to seek public support from the British for the idea of peaceful reunification. In order to achieve the long-term goal of consensual reunification, an All-Ireland Council should be established to facilitate the reconciliation of the two sections of Ireland.[7] Pushing Heath hard on the issue of reunification would give Lynch cover with the more republican-leaning wing of Fianna Fáil, which was still seen as a real threat to Lynch, as well as meet the demands that John Hume and the SDLP had made of the taoiseach to focus on ending partition.[8]

First Chequers meeting

The summit meeting between Heath and Lynch commenced on the morning of September 6, 1971. The prime minister was accompanied by Sir Burke Trend while Ambassador Donal O'Sullivan accompanied the taoiseach. Heath began by saying that he wanted to move the meeting up from the original date in October because of the worsening of the situation in Northern Ireland. He claimed that British policies in the North were misunderstood and invited Lynch to raise any issues involving the province. As the United Kingdom and Ireland were soon to enter the EEC, Heath suggested that it would behoove them to settle the issue of the North now rather than drag it with them into Europe. The prime minister expressed his desire for a real breakthrough as a result of the summit.

Lynch launched into a far lengthier opening statement that summarized the Irish view of how the whole history of Northern Ireland paved the way for the current crisis. The Catholic civil rights movement was an inevitable reaction to discrimination against the nationalist community. Earlier hopes that London would force reforms on Stormont and that the British Army would be a neutral peace-keeping force had given way to despair among moderate nationalists that a peaceful solution could be achieved. Lynch warned that if the current meeting did not lead to some progress, then moderate nationalists on both sides of the border would lose influence to republican extremists. The taoiseach rejected any attempt to find a military solution to the crisis. He argued that support for the IRA would only grow without a political settlement and stated that the only way forward was to replace Stormont with a new form of government and to have London publicly support peaceful Irish reunification as the long-range, permanent solution to the underlying problems in the North. On the matter of the EEC, Lynch agreed with Heath that it was unfortunate that they were moving into the community with this problem between them but also expressed hope that joint membership in the EEC would promote Irish reunification.

Heath rejected Lynch's characterization of British policy in the North as one of seeking a military solution. He said that Dublin underestimated the extent of the IRA's campaign of violence and argued that the British Army was simply responding to an urban guerrilla war that threatened to completely undermine "the established authority" in the North. Heath claimed that neither his government nor the British Army were pro-unionist and argued that Faulkner's democratically elected government had not been given enough credit for a reform program that had accomplished the goals set out in the Downing Street Declaration.

Lynch countered Heath's claims by again stressing that the functioning of parliamentary democracy in Northern Ireland was warped by the permanent majority of the Unionist Party which made the opposition irrelevant to politics within Stormont. He criticized the reform efforts as doomed due to the Unionists' close ties to the Orange Order. Britain had only made the situation worse by allowing internment without trial as this policy had further alienated the Catholic community and weakened support for the moderate SDLP leadership. The taoiseach also complained that efforts to disarm civilians in the North had focused almost exclusively on nationalists. While reporting that Northern nationalists feared that the number of licenses issued for firearms had resulted in too many armed unionist civilians, Lynch also speculated that the threat of a Protestant backlash against reform was overblown and "more a creation of the British Government than a reality."

Heath assured Lynch that Faulkner would issue no more gun licenses but insisted that the threat of a Protestant backlash was "very real" and it was fueled by IRA violence. Heath rejected that idea of London imposing a British-appointed commission as a replacement for Stormont due to its undemocratic nature and pressed Lynch on what could be done to draw the SDLP back into Stormont.

According to Lynch, the SDLP would only return to Stormont if the internees who were not to be charged with a specific crime were released, London established a commission to administer the North, and four-way talks were opened that included the British and Irish governments along with the Unionists and the SDLP. In addition, Lynch argued, if these steps were taken, nationalists would see the start of a political solution in the North and support would be drawn away from the IRA to the SDLP. The Irish leader defended the idea of a commission as a necessary interim step on the road to a more permanent political system that nationalists, as well as moderate unionists, could fully embrace. A British policy centered on defeating the IRA would not gain any traction in the nationalist community.

Heath expressed a desire to find a policy that reduced the appeal of the IRA but he reiterated his opposition to an undemocratic commission in place of Stormont. He said direct rule from London, while arguably democratic, had its own problems, including the fact that it was a goal of the IRA. The prime minister went on to defend internment as a necessary tool to reduce violence and stated that it could not be abandoned in the short term. Heath pointed out that the Irish government had used internment during the Border Campaign and argued that the reason it had been successful during that period was because it was implemented on both sides of the border. The current situation allowed the

IRA to regroup in the South. Lynch countered that when Dublin had last used interment the IRA was deeply unpopular in the Irish Republic but that this was not currently true. The taoiseach also rejected the idea that the Irish Republic represented a safe haven for the IRA as Dublin was doing everything it could to harass the IRA in the South.

The discussion then moved onto the more specific, and equally contentious, topic of the abuse of internees. Heath claimed that allegations of mistreatment of detainees were being investigated but were likely to be proven to be exaggerated. Lynch expressed doubts that the ongoing inquiry would placate the nationalist community and indicated that he was being pressured by the SDLP and the Dáil to make a formal complaint about the abuse allegations to the European Commission of Human Rights in Strasbourg.

Following a lunch break, the talks resumed with Lynch returning to his main idea that a political solution had to be arrived at for the North if the violence were going to be curtailed. He warned that if the current meeting did not produce "something worthwhile," then moderate nationalist forces on both sides of the border would be weakened compared to the republicans. Heath replied with a repetition of his own main idea that, if Dublin would only "crack down" on IRA activity in the South, the violence in the North would be reduced and this would open the way for political progress.

Despite the seeming centrality of security concerns in London's policy for the North, Heath did raise some possibilities for political actions that could be taken even in the face of IRA violence. He mentioned the possibility of instituting proportional representation in Stormont or expanding the number of members in the Northern Irish parliament to allow for greater nationalist participation. He raised the possibility that Home Secretary Reginald Maudling, with the support of Brian Faulkner, might call for a formal dialogue with unionist and nationalist leaders to promote Catholic participation in government. Heath promised that London would guarantee the civil rights of the minority, but also stressed that they still had "to deal with the urban guerrillas."

Lynch rejected the reform ideas as insufficient and said he could not support the Maudling initiative because it did not involve Dublin. If this was the extent of the British proposals, then Lynch said the meeting had been a waste of time. Heath claimed that Lynch seemed to be rejecting the basics of democracy and was demanding too much for the Northern nationalists. He stated that the involvement of Dublin in the proposed Maudling talks would only serve to alienate the unionist community. Lynch remained unmoved and said that he had hoped that Heath would accept the idea of eventual reunification as the only permanent solution to the North's problems. Heath replied that he saw reunification as a valid goal, but that in order to achieve that goal the violence had to end and, with assurances of legal equality, Northern nationalists had to participate in government while awaiting peaceful reunification. Heath warned that if Lynch publicly denounced the British proposal of the talks to be led by Maudling, then there would be anger at Dublin in the House of Commons. He pronounced himself "perplexed" that Lynch did not see that a return to peace in Northern Ireland would actually help the prospect of reunification in the long term. The prime minister said that he supported Dublin–London talks or Dublin–Belfast talks, but that the Irish government had no standing to participate in talks on the internal arrangements of the North.

Lynch repeated that his government was already doing a great deal to combat the IRA. Lynch's handling of the Arms Crisis alone was proof of his sincerity on this issue. He suggested that Northern nationalists would only enter into talks if Dublin were included and declared that best he could say of the current meeting was that both sides had expressed their views in a frank manner. Heath characterized their discussion as "very valuable" and asked if Lynch would consider a meeting with Brian Faulkner as a means of moving forward. Lynch refused to commit to talks with the Northern prime minister and the day's meeting ended with no agreement. Both Heath and Lynch were beginning to show signs of frustration with the prime minister adamant that Dublin could get the SDLP back into Stormont if it wanted to and Lynch stating that the whole summit had been worthless if London had already settled on Maudling's initiative, with Dublin excluded, as the next step.

When the meeting resumed the next day, neither side was willing to reconsider its basic position. Lynch told Heath that for the time being he had to reject the idea of a three-way meeting with Heath and Faulkner as Faulkner was not the head of a sovereign government. Heath could only ask that Lynch not publicly call the Maudling initiative doomed to failure and that he keep the details of their discussions secret.[9]

The aftermath of the first Chequers meeting

Heath's last requests were only partially fulfilled by Lynch. When the taoiseach held a press conference upon his return to Dublin on September 7, he made little or no attempt to keep the details of the discussions from the press and freely admitted to the numerous disagreements that the two leaders had had during the summit. While he was careful not to denounce the Maudling talks as a certain failure, he did state his preference for the inclusion of the Irish government in those discussions. The most positive statement that Lynch could make about the summit was that he thought that the two sides "understand each other better" and "have established a better rapport than we had before." However, he did declare himself hopeful that his continued attempts to bring peace to Northern Ireland were not in vain.[10] As Lynch could claim no meaningful accomplishment from the summit, he was clearly aiming to portray himself in the press as having, at least, championed peaceful Irish nationalism in the face of a British government that would not compromise. He did not intend to keep his criticism of Heath's policies confined to private meetings.

The guidelines that the FCO sent out to its missions regarding London's official view of the summit agreed with Lynch's assessment that the only achievement was "a clearing of the air" between the two governments. The FCO also claimed that Lynch had formally rejected Heath's offer to include Faulkner in a tripartite summit meeting in the near future, a stance that the FCO characterized as "extraordinary" given the level of violence in the North. The cable also pointed out that Maudling would move forward on a search to find ways for Northern nationalists to participate in government in Northern Ireland.[11] London's public review of the summit attempted to portray Lynch as the intractable party who refused a reasonable offer for wider talks that would include Faulkner.

The British government was not the only party that regretted that Lynch would not meet with Heath and Faulkner. Ambassador Peck reported to the FCO that the Irish press was surprised that Lynch had announced his opposition to the offer of tripartite talks as promoting more discussions about the fate of Northern Ireland seemed to have been a major goal of Dublin. "We are of course," he added, "doing nothing to decrease or discourage their bewilderment."[12]

Lynch was quick to respond to the British reports of an offer for a tripartite meeting. In a statement issues on September 8, Lynch claimed that "while the subject was mentioned no specific offer to convene a tripartite meeting was made." The statement went on to say that as Heath had obviously meant to propose such a meeting, then Lynch was "prepared to consider his offer seriously because of the continuing grave situation in the North" despite his preference for four-way talks that would include Northern nationalists.[13] While this statement might be deemed true in a legalistic manner in that Heath did not offer a specific date for the meeting, in fact the official Irish record of the talks makes it clear that Lynch had firmly rejected the general idea of a tripartite summit during the Chequers meeting.

On September 11, Lynch formally agreed to a meeting with Heath and Faulkner "on the basis that there are no preconditions." Lynch also made clear that he still believed that the Northern nationalist leaders should be included. The taoiseach requested that the meeting take place in London rather than Chequers.[14] In the public announcement of his agreement to the meeting, Lynch stressed that he would represent the interests of the Northern minority who would not be represented by their own elected leaders. Lynch stated that an imperfect meeting was better than nothing as a means of encouraging "understanding and goodwill" and defended his decision as being in accord "with the aspiration of the majority of the Irish people who, themselves, seek the unity of the nation, by agreement, through peaceful means."[15] Heath replied the following day, expressing his happiness that Lynch would attend the meeting. He advised the taoiseach that Chequers was the best venue as any London location would become the center of "demonstrations and counter-demonstrations." He offered to ferry Lynch to Chequers by helicopter directly from the airport.[16]

Brian Faulkner was initially no more anxious for tripartite talks than Lynch had been. The Northern premier was concerned that he would face opposition from within the Unionist Party to his meeting face-to-face with Lynch while Dublin was seen as unwilling to crack down on the IRA. However, Heath forced Faulkner to agree to the talks by pointing out that the British Army was providing security in Northern Ireland and that the British public expected Faulkner to cooperate with Heath in seeking a negotiated solution to the Troubles in these circumstances.[17]

Surveying the situation after the first Chequers meeting, the US State Department issued a pessimistic intelligence report on September 21. While the report credited Heath with actively seeking a solution to the crisis in Northern Ireland, it concluded that internment "has not only failed to restore calm ... but has actually created new problems. It destroyed the confidence of the Catholic minority in the neutrality and goodwill of the UK Government in the Protestant-Catholic struggle." London's attempts to engage the Northern minority in talks were described as doomed as long as Stormont continued to exist. The State Department noted that Lynch's government had always been very moderate but that Dublin had "reacted sharply" to the imposition of internment, had "recently sided more openly with the minority," and "endorsed the passive resistance campaign," while increasingly turning "a blind eye toward IRA activity." The increased tensions in Anglo-Irish relations were driven, in part, by pressure from within Fianna Fáil. The report described the Anglo-Irish summit as "fruitless" and predicted that the upcoming tripartite talks would be equally pointless. The State Department's analysis offered little hope for the immediate future in the North noting that Heath was trapped between the need to placate nationalist demands and the desire to avoid a unionist backlash that might overthrow Faulkner's government "with the danger of chaos and civil war" following.[18]

Preparing for the second Chequers meeting

While the Irish government did not have much faith that the tripartite summit would lead to a major political breakthrough, it did prepare an ambitious list of goals to pursue at Chequers. The document assumed that reunification was not an immediate possibility and therefore focused on the reformation of the government of Northern Ireland. A number of minimum objectives were laid down that primarily focused on a power-sharing arrangement that would guarantee to the nationalist community a "substantial" input on legislation. In addition, Dublin wanted to create North–South links through a consultative Council of Ireland and increase the direct involvement of the British government in the affairs of the North. Specific details were worked out for at least two styles of power-sharing governments that would recognize "the bi-confessional nature of the Northern Ireland problem."

The brief outlined three elements of what could be considered a "satisfactory outcome" of the talks from Dublin's point of view. These elements were an "agreement in principle to minority participation in government," a "breakthrough, however tenuous," on the objective of reunification, and "the avoidance of any commitment which could be presented as acquiescence" to the status quo in Stormont. According to the analysis there was a realistic, if limited, chance that Dublin's goals could be achieved as Heath was under growing pressure, both domestically and internationally, to abandon Britain's failed military response to the Troubles and try a new political strategy. At the very least, if Heath and Faulkner would not agree to any major initiatives, then Lynch would emerge in a stronger position because he could claim to have presented some reasonable proposals.[19]

As Lynch left for the meeting from Dublin airport on September 26, he made a statement to the press assuring the public that "there are no limits to what we will talk about as far as I am concerned. Irish unity is central to the whole problem." However, once he had made this politically necessary statement on reunification, he reminded his listeners that Irish unity would be a long, slow process and that the more immediate problem was to find a way for the Northern minority to return to Stormont so that new political discussions on Northern Ireland could begin which would reduce the appeal of political violence.[20]

Officials from Britain and Northern Ireland agreed with Lynch's public assessment of the importance of getting the SDLP back into an active role in government in Northern Ireland. On September 24, the British cabinet secretary, Sir Burke Trend, held a meeting with his Northern Irish counterpart, Sir Harold Black, to discuss the upcoming meeting. Trend characterized the main goals of the summit as allowing the three leaders to better understand each other's political positions and foster cooperation on a political solution to the crisis while also working on improved security. According to Trend, it was unlikely that any detailed political solution would be worked out so the main hope was that the summit would "create a suitable atmosphere for the Home Secretary's talks and to work out incentives for the SDLP to return to Stormont."[21]

The formal brief for the summit prepared by the British government for Heath went into more details as to London's view of the situation and hopes for the meeting. The growing strength of the IRA, the SDLP-led campaign of civil disobedience, and hardline unionist opposition to any compromise with moderate nationalist demands had brought the province to brink of "catastrophe" according to the brief. The bright spot was that a majority of people in the North realized that "something radical" had to be done to arrest the downward spiral. An analysis of Irish politics portrayed Lynch as under real pressure from within Fianna Fáil to take a more aggressive stance with London and suggested that Patrick Hillery had not been fully supportive of the taoiseach's earlier meeting with Heath. However, countervailing pressure from the Irish public at large, which supported negotiations, may have forced Lynch to agree to the tripartite talks. While the exact nature of the relationship between the SDLP and Dublin was unknown, the brief expressed certainty that Lynch would have some influence on the SDLP leaders.

In terms of the Northern Irish government, the British document acknowledged that like Jack Lynch, Brian Faulkner had been under pressure from his own right wing not to negotiate with Dublin and had agreed to the three-way talks because of a desire on the part of the general public in the North to seek a solution to the Troubles. However, as Faulkner had already gained the reward of Lynch's agreeing to meet with him as a presumed equal, the Northern premier could easily walk away from the talks and still gain some political advantage.

As to the aims of Her Majesty's Government, the official brief called for Heath to "avoid sterile exchanges about historical (or even recent) wrongs" and keep the two Irish leaders focused on "practical reforms and measures designed to meet the immediate situation." One group of specific British goals dealt with improving relations between Dublin and Belfast. This would entail pressing Faulkner to accept some input from Lynch on reforms in the North, as long as the sanctity of the border did not come into question. Lynch would need to be pressed into accepting the fact that ending partition would not be a short-term goal and into urging the SDLP to abandon its boycott of Stormont, end the civil disobedience, and engage in talks with Home Secretary Maudling. Both Irish governments would be urged to increase cross-border economic cooperation and jointly reject violence and sectarian discrimination. The brief closed with a few specific points to raise, including increased border security and greater Irish cooperation on security matters in general.[22]

The official brief prepared for Brian Faulkner focused on Stormont's need to balance the desire for more enhanced security with the demands that Dublin and London would make for more political reforms in Northern Ireland. From Belfast's point of view, Heath's main goal at the meeting would be to restore "peace, with the consequent lowering of the British military, financial and diplomatic commitment to Northern Ireland." As for Dublin, the document assumed that Lynch would be under pressure from domestic public opinion that was souring on the status quo in the North. It was assumed that Lynch might in fact decide that the best course of action was to try to derail the meeting by making unacceptable demands. By killing any possible deal, Lynch would avoid any pressure to more effectively combat the IRA. With no end to the IRA campaign in sight, London might decide that reunification was the best way to extract the British Army from the North. According to the brief, the other option for Lynch would be to seek some kind of compromise that traded more political reforms for increased Irish security cooperation.

In addition to the obvious desire to safeguard the Union, the document argued that Faulkner's other main goal should be to work for some style of "package deal" on security and reform that would be acceptable to all three governments. As to the details, the brief called for any deal to include a British pledge to act with more vigor against rioters and to end the "No-Go" areas in nationalist neighborhoods that were not patrolled by security forces. From Dublin, the concessions demanded by Stormont would be more "cooperation to suppress terrorism" including "ruthless suppression of the IRA in the Republic," close coordination with the British Army and the RUC, and the introduction of interment in the South. In addition, the document called for the Irish Republic to recognize the legitimacy of Northern Ireland, amend its constitution to reflect that fact, accept the Ireland Act of 1949, promote cross-border economic ties, and end support for the SDLP's campaign of civil disobedience. In return, Stormont "might be in a position to offer" political reforms that included proportional representation, changes to the makeup of the two houses of the Northern Ireland parliament, the creation of cross-party parliamentary committees, a few minor changes to internment, and greater cross-border cooperation. The document admitted that these proposed reforms did "not seem to be enough" and went on to list some of the other concessions that Belfast might have to consider. The other reforms included, in descending order of acceptability, a bill of rights guaranteed by Westminster, veto power for the governor of Northern Ireland, reworking of the Special Powers Act, the creation of an All-Ireland Council, granting control of law and order to London, a "50-50 sharing of power" in Stormont, and dual citizenship. Only the last two were complexly ruled out as a direct threat to the Union itself. The other reforms could be considered in the context of any overall deal that arose for the tripartite meeting.[23]

Figure 5.1 Northern Ireland prime minister Brian Faulkner at Downing Street with Home Secretary Reginald Maudling. Credit: Keystone.

Second Chequers meeting

The second Chequers summit began with Heath meeting separately with Brian Faulkner and Jack Lynch. Heath, accompanied by Reginald Maudling and Minister of Defense Lord Carrington, met with Faulkner and Sir Harold Black, the secretary of the Northern Ireland Cabinet, on the evening of September 26, 1971. Heath said that they needed to set the stage for a successful meeting with Lynch which would lead to "specific agreements" on the North. He stressed that the British public would not endlessly tolerate the sight of "British troops being abused, stoned and killed" while the situation only continued to deteriorate. It was therefore vital to get Lynch to support the home secretary's political initiative to find common ground between the two communities in the North. While Heath told Faulkner that Dublin could be pressed to take specific actions to weaken the IRA, he echoed Jack Lynch's own line of argument when he stated that the best way to reduce the power of the IRA was to give nationalists "a fairer deal politically."

The Northern premier countered that the nationalist community was not as alienated from Stormont as it seemed, but was rather the victim of IRA intimidation. Faulkner also claimed that the civil disobedience campaign was driven by intimidation and, furthermore, was not as much of a problem as London believed. He stated that be believed that the SDLP could be drawn back into support of Stormont, particularly after his government issued the Green Paper it was preparing on new reforms in the province. What was needed at the present time, Faulkner argued, was increased security measures such as expanding the deployment of the UDR. "It was a minor miracle," he warned, "that, so far, the people have not taken the law into their own hands and set up some kind of 'third force.'" Heath and Carrington agreed to look more at the use of the UDR, but the prime minister told Faulkner that safeguards had to be put in place to make sure that the UDR did not become a revival of the B-Specials.

Heath then outlined his goals for the tripartite talks. He told Faulkner, "they must be prepared to discuss anything and everything; and they must do all they could to involve the other parties in Ulster in the discussion of constitutional developments." Since the SDLP would not talk to them, Lynch should be made to state the requirements, as he saw them, of Northern nationalist participation in Stormont as well as a possible All-Ireland Council for economic cooperation. Faulkner was agreeable to these ideas but insisted that no non-unionist Catholic could be expected to be a part of the Northern Irish Cabinet and that he would rather resign than change his mind on that point. Faulkner warned that even a pro-union Catholic minister might be resisted by working-class Protestants. Heath replied that this reflected the fact that the Unionist Party was a sectarian institution but Faulkner assured him the Orange Order was only a minor part of the Unionist Party as a whole.[24]

On the morning of September 27, Heath held a preliminary meeting with Lynch. Heath began by pointing to the importance of Maudling's talks being joined by the SDLP as a way to move forward on the political front while defending internment as necessary to combat IRA violence. Lynch indicated that he was willing to talk about a political solution even if reunification was not part of the current discussion. The taoiseach went on to explain the confusion over Heath's offer for tripartite talks by claiming that he thought Heath was merely asking his opinion of the idea rather than making a formal offer for them to meet with Faulkner.

Turning to the specifics of the present meeting, Lynch said that he had met with SDLP leaders and was convinced that internment was the major hurdle to the party's return to Stormont. An independent appeals process and the release of all internees who were not formally charged was the bare minimum that the SDLP would accept before talking to Maudling. Moreover, Lynch reported that SDLP leader Gerry Fitt demanded that Catholics be given "a position in Government as of right and not as a favor," which would entail a major restructuring of Stormont. While Lynch stressed that he was not a formal spokesman for the SDLP or other Northern nationalist groups, he was confident that the SDLP would stick to these demands. He suggested to Heath that if Faulkner could not agree, then London and Dublin should proceed without his cooperation.

The prime minister argued that the best way for the SDLP to make its case was to enter into the ongoing discussions with the home secretary. Heath defended the existing legal safeguards for internees and pointed out that the IRA had admitted that 160 of its members had been interned. To release these men would be a major blow to security in the North. Lynch countered that internment was simply not working as it had not helped to turn the nationalist community against support for the IRA.

Lynch moved on to the idea of a power-sharing system for Northern Ireland that could include features such as Cabinet membership proportionate to the number of seats in the parliament and a unionist prime minister coupled with a nationalist deputy prime minister. The taoiseach also supported that idea of an All-Ireland body to foster cross-border cooperation. Heath said that he was willing to discuss anything, and the two premiers agreed that they had to work together to stop the violence in the North from becoming a full-blown civil war that would also engulf the Irish Republic as well.[25]

The first tripartite session began later that day. Heath began the meeting with a call for a frank discussion and a suggestion that the three governments should agree to publicly renounce political violence and the growing disorder in Northern Ireland. Lynch agreed but also took the opportunity to present a list of Irish nationalist complaints starting with partition and ending with internment. "In short," he said, "the whole system of Stormont must be changed." As a first step, Lynch claimed that the SDLP would not engage in any political discussions until the internment question was settled.

Heath reminded Lynch that as his stance on reunification was well known and London continued to back the Ireland Act of 1949, there was no point in discussing the matter any further and the talks should focus on the reform of Stormont. Faulkner said that he joined Lynch in condemning political violence but he went on to defend internment as necessary. The Northern premier said that internment on both sides of the border had ended the IRA's Border Campaign of the 1950s and 1960s and a similar move would work in the current situation. Faulkner believed that the moderate nationalists would return to cooperation with Stormont if the violence could be halted. "It follows," he argued, "that the first priority must be to restore law and order." If Lynch could not agree to use interment in the South, Faulkner asked what Dublin could do to fight the IRA in cooperation with London and Belfast. Lynch made his standard reply that the Irish government was doing all it could to fight the IRA in the Irish Republic and said that the real strength of the republicans was in the North. Faulkner suggested that his government could provide Dublin with specific intelligence about IRA training bases and the location of fugitives in the South. As no agreement could be reached on the security issue, Faulkner moved on to the topic of further reforms in the North and announced that he would move ahead with or without the SDLP in Stormont.[26]

After a break for lunch the talks resumed. Faulkner presented more details of his own plans to increase nationalist participation in Stormont. The main point of the reform would be the creation of four parliamentary committees that would be responsible for commenting on proposed legislation related to the committees' area of responsibility. Membership on the committees would be drawn proportionally from the parliament and the opposition would be allowed to nominate two chairmen subject to the approval of the Cabinet. Faulkner said that the US Congress was the model for the concept and the general idea had been popular with SDLP leaders when it was first proposed before the boycott of Stormont. Faulkner indicated that he could not foresee SDLP members of the Cabinet itself as they differed so radically on the issue of reunification from the Unionist Party.

Lynch predicted that the SDLP would reject any reforms that did not guarantee them membership in the Cabinet. Faulkner argued that Gerry Fitt in particular was anxious to end the boycott of Stormont and might urge the SDLP to accept the idea of parliamentary committees as an effective reform. Lynch, while again stressing that he was not an official spokesman for the SDLP, said that unless internment was ended on a "release or charge" basis, then the SDLP boycott would remain in place regardless. Heath countered that this was not practical as there were good reasons to hold some of the detainees even without trail, while Faulkner added that even special nonjury trials would put witnesses in danger of IRA retaliation.

Faulkner asked Lynch why the SDLP had really begun the boycott in the first place as he doubted that the shootings of the two civilians in Derry were the true cause. Lynch replied that the SDLP "were completely disillusioned by the reform programme" which they believed was having no real-life impact. Lynch told Faulkner and Heath that "the existing system was no longer acceptable" and the "IRA campaign was ... only a by-product of the situation."

Heath redirected the conversation to the issue of the Maudling talks, pointing out that the other non-unionist parties, like Northern Ireland Labor and the Alliance Party, were taking part and arguing that the SDLP should do so as well if only to discuss internment. Faulkner and Lynch agreed that discussing internment might draw in the SDLP but Lynch pointed out that the SDLP still rejected the inclusion of nonelected officials in Maudling's list of participants in his talks. Lynch contended that it was up to London and Belfast to decide whether or not to meet the basic demands of the SDLP while Heath argued for more flexibility from the Northern nationalists.

The three men briefly discussed the EEC. They all agreed that having the United Kingdom and Ireland join the EEC was a reason to increase North–South economic cooperation but Lynch warned that his government had been so distracted by the Troubles that they had had little time to promote the idea of entering the Common Market with the Irish public. Heath ended the day's discussions by suggesting that they all spend the night reflecting on their meeting so they could come up with a joint statement. Lynch again warned that Heath and Faulkner had to try to meet the minimum demands of the SDLP or risk even greater problems in Northern Ireland.[27]

Heath and Lynch met separately on the morning of Tuesday, September 28, to discuss a draft communiqué that had been prepared by the British. Lynch objected to the fact that the draft called for support of the Maudling talks and seemed to support Faulkner's general arguments. During the course of the discussion neither side would agree to make any changes that would bridge the many disagreements of the previous day's tripartite meeting. The taoiseach warned that by failing to make concessions designed to lure the SDLP into negotiations, Heath was risking a scenario in which his next talks would have to be with the IRA. Lynch stated that any joint statement would have to limit itself to a promise that the three governments would continue to look for a peaceful solution without supporting any specific plan.[28]

The addition of Faulkner to the meeting later that afternoon did nothing to produce any more consensus and the three premiers argued about the semantics of a draft statement that Lynch had offered as an alternative to the earlier British draft. Lynch continued to insist that any joint communiqué should avoid supporting any specific political initiatives and therefore a very vague document was all that could be agreed to. The final draft began by recognizing the differing, and unchanged, opinions on reunification and continued to a joint condemnation of political violence and discrimination. The three governments promised to try to stop violence and seek an early end to internment while promoting improved relations between the two communities of Northern Ireland. The communiqué characterized the summit as having "helped to create an atmosphere of greater understanding between us" and promised more meetings in the future. It ended with Heath and Lynch promising to remain in close contact on all aspects of Anglo-Irish relations.[29]

Lynch decided not to let the communiqué speak for itself and held a press conference following the meetings. He made no attempt to paper over the disagreements and spent a good deal of time discussing internment. He expressed his view that internment remained a major stumbling block to political progress and explained that he and Faulkner fundamentally disagreed about whether or not internment was a solution to, or a cause of, violence in the North. The taoiseach also expressed his desire that the SDLP would engage in talks with Maudling and return to Stormont. However, he made it clear that this was not Dublin's decision and predicted that this would not happen without an end to internment. Lynch denied that he supported "civil disobedience" by Northern nationalists but indicated that he would support "passive resistance," although he did not clearly define the differences between the two terms. Putting the talks in the best light possible, Lynch said that despite fundamental disagreements among the parties at Chequers, including the issue of reunification, it was valuable to continue to talk because "as long as we can talk there is some hope…for a political reconciliation." Lynch told the assembled press that the most significant result of the meetings was that the joint communiqué reinforced the Downing Street Declaration's call for equality in the North and that Dublin was now acknowledged as having a role in achieving that aim.[30] The FCO's public reaction to the tripartite talks mirrored Lynch's view that any discussion among the three governments was of some benefit as it kept open the lines of communication while a permanent solution was sought.[31]

Analyses of the Chequers meetings

The two Chequers summit meetings represent the most high-level public diplomatic talks of the early years of the Troubles and as such are an important historical event even though they produced no breakthrough agreement. Some historians who have studied the meetings in depth agree that having held the talks at all was an achievement. Commenting on the first summit, Thomas Hennessey has argued that both sides had the limited objective of being publicly "seen to do something" to address the deepening crisis in Northern Ireland. While nothing of importance was achieved, Hennessey believes that "for the first time, both Premiers had a real idea of each other's position." The next step for London would be to try to include Faulkner in another meeting to try to find common ground from which to formulate a plan of action.[32] Hillery's biographer Patrick Walsh agrees that despite the lack of any tangible results from the first meeting, "the summit was important as the first step in Anglo-Irish dialogue at the highest level about the major unresolved issue between the two countries."[33] According to Stephen Kelly, the importance of the summits rest in the fact that Heath was effectively acknowledging that Dublin had a right to be included in the discussion about Northern Ireland.[34]

On the other hand, Anthony Craig has a more jaundiced analysis of the first Chequers meeting in that he believes that the British were unhappy to have rewarded Lynch for his belligerent public attitude of August by moving up the date of the summit, but that Heath had taken to heart Sir Burke Trend's warning that it was politically dangerous for London to be seen to be simply supporting the status quo in Northern Ireland. In Craig's analysis, the most important outcome of the first meeting was that Heath was able to raise the issue of tripartite talks and, despite the fact that Lynch clearly rejected that idea at Chequers, push the taoiseach into accepting the meeting by revealing the offer to the press. Lynch could not resist the public pressure for continued negotiations and maintain his status as the voice of moderation in Irish nationalism.[35]

However, while Heath may have achieved his goal of convening a three-way meeting, Craig's view of the tripartite talks themselves is that they were bound to fail and that "success…was never really a possibility…as nothing had been put forward initially to discuss." He argues that while the talks did make Heath seem like the reasonable party in the eyes of the public, and were thus a partial political success for London, they actually made North–South relations worse. However, Craig still accepts the idea that Anglo-Irish diplomatic dialogue, even if fruitless at this point, was better than not talking at all.[36]

It is obvious that in the short term the two Chequers meetings produced nothing but a public restatement that all three governments wanted an end to the violence in the North and hoped to create a normal political atmosphere that would lead to a long-term solution. While the meetings did demonstrate to the public in both the United Kingdom and Ireland that their governments were working on a solution to the Troubles, the outcome also demonstrated the limits of the ability of Dublin, London, and Belfast to control events in Northern Ireland or even agree on which direction a peaceful solution lay. The first meeting showed that politics in Northern Ireland had been deadlocked since the beginning of the SDLP boycott of Stormont and that internment had only made the political situation worse without reducing the IRA's ability to wage a campaign of violence. While Heath hoped that the Maudling talks in Northern Ireland would be the vital first step toward a political settlement, he could not agree that Dublin should play a role in the talks or abandon the need to keep up the security pressure on the IRA. This left little area of agreement for Dublin and London.

The tripartite talks, which Heath essentially forced on the reluctant Jack Lynch and Brian Faulkner, were equally sterile. In fact, Faulkner's presence only exacerbated the divide between Dublin and London as the Unionist leader showed little appetite for compromise beyond his own anemic reform proposals. Lynch continued to insist that the SDLP would not participate in the Maudling talks unless internment was effectively ended, and Heath was forced to back Faulkner's defense of internment or risk the collapse of Faulkner's government. In his memoir, Edward Heath claimed that he was an early proponent of the idea of power-sharing and cross-border institutions and that he hoped these concepts would be accepted by all three parties at the second Chequers summit.[37] While Heath's later enthusiasm for these ideas is shown by the details of the Sunningdale Agreement, the records from September 1971 do not show him as having advocated for power sharing at Chequers despite Lynch's having raised the concept. In his study of British policy toward Northern Ireland, Peter Neumann agrees that Heath's government only began to move in the direction of power sharing after Lynch pushed the idea at Chequers.[38]

Instead of an agreement on power sharing, the discussions at Chequers highlighted the impasse that London and Dublin have arrived at over Northern Ireland. While there were voices in the British government, such as Sir Burke Trend and Ambassador John Peck, who argued for radical rethinking about London's policies toward Northern Ireland, Heath was still determined to keep the Troubles at arm's length as much as possible by supporting the survival of Faulkner at Stormont. Despite his promises to Dublin that the first summit would achieve a positive result, Heath chose to disregard Trend's advice to look for a radical solution for the Troubles and instead adhered to the more limited goals set forth by the FCO. Since the FCO itself predicted that getting Dublin to crack down on the IRA or push the SDLP back into Stormont were objectives that would be hard to achieve, Heath could not have had much hope that his meeting with Lynch would have a major impact on events in Northern Ireland. Adding Faulkner to the mix for the second round of discussions changed nothing and British hopes that Maudling would be able to start a political process in the North could not come to fruition without the participation of the moderate Northern nationalist leadership.

While it makes sense to view the Chequers summits as having accomplished nothing in their own right, an alternate interpretation of the talks is that they set the stage for later important developments in Anglo-Irish attempts to find a peaceful solution to the Troubles, such as the power sharing arrangement envisioned by the Sunningdale Agreement in 1973. One key component of the Chequers summits that had an impact on future developments was that in calling for public meetings with Lynch, Heath's government had effectively acknowledged that Dublin had to play a role in any political solution in Northern Ireland. This recognition of the importance of the Irish government by London went far beyond the limited nature of the Anglo-Irish discussions up to this point which had mainly consisted of the exchange of ideas and information. The meetings also made it clear to the British that Dublin no longer had any faith in the idea of reforming the existing Stormont system and gave Lynch an opportunity to argue in favor of the alternative idea of a power-sharing arrangement as a method to remake politics in Northern Ireland. Heath could not accept any power-sharing plan at this point because of the rejection of any such idea by Brian Faulkner. However, the intransigence of Faulkner, which was one of the major reasons that the summits achieved nothing in the short term, may have helped to move Heath in the direction of accepting that direct rule as a transitional step to a radical restructuring of the government of Northern Ireland, in line with the advice of Sir Burke Trend and others, was the only way to break the political stalemate in the province.

After the Chequers meetings

Whatever their long-term importance may have been, the Chequers summits did little to lift the sense in Dublin that the situation in Northern Ireland was getting worse. From Ambassador Peck's point of view, the summits had changed nothing. On September 30, 1971, he reported to the FCO that Lynch had met the day before with the leadership of the Northern opposition but could make no headway in getting them to change their demands over returning to Stormont or talking with Maudling. Peck found that Hugh McCann was "sunk in gloom" over the North and reported that Faulkner's public statement that he would only accept Catholic unionists in his government was seen as an attempt "to sabotage the Home Secretary's talks."[39]

In October, Peck wrote a lengthy analysis of the Irish situation which called on London to radically rethink its strategy. In the cover letter to the memorandum, the ambassador asked Sir Denis Greenhill to initially show the document to only a couple of people, including Sir Burke Trend. Peck wrote to Greenhill that joint entry of Ireland and the United Kingdom into the EEC was the best moment for London to reassess the seemingly intractable problem of Northern Ireland and to state that the British government had decided that Irish reunification was the best long-term solution.[40] In the body of the memorandum, Peck noted that Anglo-Irish relations in general were very good and that the two governments had many shared interests in the fields of economics and trade but that Northern Ireland was a "festering wound" that could sour the relationship as a whole. Peck argued that the main problem was partition and that it did London no good to simply stand by the Ireland Act of 1949 as the final word on the border. The Irish government did not accept partition and neither did Irish nationalists on the whole. The IRA was simply the violent expression of a demand for unification that peaceful Irish nationalists on both sides of the border shared. Partition also warped democracy in the North as the whole structure of Stormont was created and maintained on the basis of a unionist majority. The Unionist Party, Peck contended, would never compromise on reunification, or truly seek to make nationalists equal citizens, as long as it had the effective backing of London. In the current situation the IRA, which showed no sign of being militarily defeated, would only grow in appeal and the British Army would have to deal with the violence. Peck's memo urged Heath's government to accept that it had to change course on Northern Ireland. He urged four basic steps for a future policy: continuation of the campaign against the IRA, talks with Dublin regarding "harmonization" of the two parts of Ireland with the aim being eventual reunification, use of these talks to lure Northern nationalists back into public life, and ending the unionist monopoly in Stormont by any means, including direct rule.[41] Unlike Sir Burke Trend, whose earlier memo to Heath urging a rethinking of the border included consideration of the political value of even an empty gesture by London, Peck presented his ideas as simply the best policy available. Peck's advice also coincided almost exactly with the view of Jack Lynch's government. According to Anthony Craig, London believed that John Peck had been acting as an "apologist" for Lynch since early 1971 and that the ambassador was no longer trusted at home.[42] Peck's October memorandum would certainly not dispel the idea that the ambassador was going native in his views on Northern Ireland even though Sir Burke Trend's earlier memo showed that there were other British officials who were also advocating a reconsideration of partition.

Edward Heath was well aware that the tripartite talks had not accomplished anything. On October 7, Heath and Faulkner met in London. Heath warned the Northern premier that their two governments had to stop simply reacting to events and create a path forward to a political solution. Faulkner refused to change his stance on the exclusion of any nationalist from his Cabinet, even those who rejected the use of violence to achieve Irish unification. Heath, fearful that Stormont, without the SDLP, was too weak to survive, expressed his opposition to Faulkner's intransigence to no effect. However, Thomas Hennessey has characterized this meeting as significant in that Heath had moved away from defending the structure of Stormont as he had done at Chequers and had accepted some of Lynch's argument.[43]

This view of Heath as anxious to force Faulkner to compromise is undercut by the actual results of the Heath–Faulkner meeting. In a message to Lynch describing the meeting, the prime minister mentioned that he still supported the idea of including the SDLP in Maudling's talks and in making sure that the internees were given a chance to appeal their detentions; however, the main point of the communication to Lynch was that Heath and Faulkner agreed that "more drastic measures must be taken to make more difficult the passage of men, arms and explosives across the border." In order to achieve this aim, the British planned to block some eighty-four unofficial crossings on the border by cratering the roads and increasing security at the authorized checkpoints. Knowing that this move would be unpopular in the Irish Republic, Heath apologized for the inconvenience but blamed the "campaign of terrorism" for forcing the new measures. Heath claimed that without increased security there could be no political movement in the North.[44] The day before he sent the message to Lynch outlining the border measures, Heath had told the Cabinet Committee on Northern Ireland that the government's priority had to be to the "defeat of the gunmen using military means, and in achieving this we should have to accept whatever political penalties were inevitable."[45]

Lynch's reply to Heath reiterated his view that the Stormont regime was incapable of any real reform and that the SDLP would not enter any talks at this point. He criticized Britain for continuing to focus on a military solution when the violence was, in fact, "a direct product of the determination of Unionism to govern as it pleases." Increasing border security was an example of focusing on "the wrong problem, in the wrong place." Not only would the new measures not help, Lynch argued, "they will aggravate a deteriorating situation" and strengthen the appeal of the IRA at the expense of moderate nationalists. Lynch told Heath that he had hoped that the summits had helped to restore "harmony in Anglo-Irish relations" but that the new barriers would "serve as a milestone in the already long history of the failures by British Governments to realize the nature of this island." He closed by asking Heath to reconsider his "approach to the whole subject."[46]

Heath replied to Lynch a few days later, stating that he could not change his mind on the new border measures. He expressed his distaste for cratering the roads and admitted that it was not a complete solution to border infiltration by the IRA, but claimed that it was a necessary step toward better security. Heath maintained that Faulkner was committed to reform and that London was set on obtaining "an active, permanent and guaranteed role for the minority in Northern Ireland's political life" but that the refusal of the SDLP to talk was delaying progress.[47] What the prime minster did not reveal to Lynch was that the British government had very little faith in the efficacy of the border measures but felt compelled to stick with the policy because they had promised Faulkner that they would do so.[48]

As the Chequers summits had not seen any breakthrough, Dublin put some international pressure on Britain to accept Lynch's ideas by raising the issue of Northern Ireland at the UN. On October 7, 1971, Patrick Hillery addressed the General Assembly of the United Nations and outlined Dublin's views on Northern Ireland. He began by pointing out that Ireland had been proud to provide soldiers for UN peacekeeping missions throughout the world but that Ireland itself now faced a rising tide of violence. The Irish foreign minister then presented his government's analysis of the problem in the North. Hillery denounced Stormont as "a tragic failure" that had presided over the collapse of law and order in Northern Ireland. The Irish government supported peaceful reunification as the only permanent solution in the North that would provide justice for all the people of Ireland. Hillery placed responsibility for bringing peace to the province squarely at the feet of the British government and charged that London was the proximate cause of the current violence because it had not lived up to the promises of the Downing Street Declaration of August 1969. He criticized the British Army for having become an instrument of unionist hegemony instead of a neutral force and called for "dialogue" to create a new political system in the North that would guarantee the minority a share in government and acknowledge their desire for reunification.[49]

While the United States had so far maintained a strict policy of noninvolvement in Northern Ireland, both Dublin and London kept an eye on Washington's attitude. During September, Trevor West, a Protestant member of the Irish Seanad, was on holiday in America. He took the opportunity to meet in an unofficial capacity with the head of UK and Irish relations at the State Department as well as a number of important US senators and congressmen, including Edward Kennedy and Thomas P. "Tip" O'Neil. In a letter to Lynch, West explained that he had stressed to the Americans the peaceful nature of Protestant–Catholic relations in the South as compared to the North and the need for Britain to completely restructure Stormont. While West came away from his meetings convinced that the Irish-American community was very concerned about Northern Ireland, he also understood that Washington was not anxious to become involved. However, he maintained his belief that "America will prove to be a good and influential friend to us as she has so often in the past."[50]

On October 20, Senators Kennedy and Abraham Ribicoff introduced a resolution in the US Senate calling on President Nixon to seek a solution to the violence in Northern Ireland and for the British Army to be withdrawn.[51] The FCO immediately approached the US Embassy in London and, while acknowledging that neither the State Department nor the White House could control Kennedy, lodged a complaint that Kennedy was making matters worse.[52] While the British Embassy in Washington was not overly concerned about the American public's view of Northern Ireland as a whole, it did warn that Irish-Americans were more concerned about the Troubles and that there was an Irish caucus in Congress that could cause some trouble by putting pressure on Nixon. However, the embassy concluded in general that the American people were preoccupied with the war in Vietnam and were not looking to become involved in Ireland.[53]

The Dáil debated Northern Ireland in late October 1971 and Jack Lynch made it clear that his government no longer supported the idea of internal reform by Stormont. After outlining his well-known views about the illegitimate nature of partition and the discriminatory practices of Stormont, Lynch told the Dáil that London had the ultimate responsibility over Northern Ireland. He claimed that "British public opinion, if it fully recognized the nature of the North, would not tolerate it for a moment" and would not support the use of the British Army to keep Stormont in operation. Pointing out that Faulkner had rejected the idea that nationalists should have a "guaranteed part in the life and public affairs of Northern Ireland," Lynch wondered how long London would continue to support "the impertinent demand of a very small minority of these islands to dictate policy to the British Government in their own sectarian interest?" Fine Gael's Liam Cosgrave agreed with Lynch that Britain was to blame for the situation in the North. Cosgrave said that British policy on Northern Ireland was characterized "at times by malice, at times by ignorance, but almost always by stupidity and that stupidity has been shown clearly in recent actions." However, Lynch was criticized by Brendan Corish, leader of the Labour Party, who, while acknowledging British folly, also charged that Fianna Fáil had failed to promote unity between the two Northern communities as a means of promoting Irish unification.[54]

Other TDs raised complaints about Lynch's record. Neil Blaney, rejecting the idea of working with London, called for "Britain to take her paws out of the nest" so that the Northern crisis could be solved by the Irish people. Fine Gael TD Garett FitzGerald, hardly an ally of Blaney, pointed out that Jack Lynch had so far failed to get London to adopt any Irish ideas and that the British continued to foolishly pursue a military solution to the crisis. Speaking in defense of the taoiseach, Patrick Hillery claimed that the violence in the North had grown with the despair of the minority but that Dublin could alleviate this despair "by approaching its fundamental cause, injustice, and approaching it through the British Government.... What is wrong in Northern Ireland is the Stormont

Administration." The foreign minister told the Dáil that the recent summits had been successful in getting Heath to recognize that Dublin had a role to play in the North and in admitting that reunification was "a natural aspiration."[55]

Treatment of internees

The issue of the abuse of internees moved to the forefront of Anglo-Irish relations beginning in October 1971. The Irish government formally notified London that it was "seriously considering taking a decision to have recourse to the European Commission on Human Rights" on October 19, 1971. This fulfilled a promise made in August by Dublin that they would provide Heath's government with advanced warning of any such move.[56] London urged the Irish to at least wait until the Compton Report was issued, cautioning Dublin that "allegations of abuse are part of the stock-in-trade of the I.R.A."[57] However, by the time the Compton Report was issued, Dublin had already received an independent investigation of the allegations conducted by Amnesty International. Amnesty International had found "a prima facie case of brutality and torture in contravention of Article 5 of the Universal Declaration of Human Rights and Article 3 of the European convention on Human Rights." The report, which had been given to the Irish government on October 30, was released to the press on November 8, 1971.[58]

On the release of the Amnesty International document, American Ambassador John Moore reported to the State Department that Lynch, with the support of Fine Gael, was planning to take the matter to the European Commission on Human Rights once the Compton report, which the Irish considered a certain "whitewash," was released. Moore concluded that the allegations of "brutality/torture in Northern Ireland sound disturbing and credible" and that Dublin's reaction was not based on political calculations but on "humanitarian concerns."[59] Moore's faith in the Amnesty International report was buttressed by the fact that the US Embassy in Dublin had recently received a detailed complaint of abuse from a Belfast woman who wanted the American government made aware of the situation. Moore found the report of the abuse of her brother, Colum Meehan, which was backed up by written testimony from a priest and a doctor, to be credible and indicative of "a distressing violation of human rights.[60]

The inquiry headed by Sir Edward Compton issued the formal British governmental report on the allegations of abuse on November 16, 1971.

The report found that various forms of abuse, including the techniques of placing hoods over prisoners' heads, keeping prisoners in stress positions, subjecting prisoners to loud noises, sleep deprivation, and a bread and water diet, rose to the level of "ill-treatment," or "hardship" but not brutality, which the inquiry defined as "an inhuman or savage form of cruelty."[61] In his introduction to the report, Reginald Maudling wrote that "it is clear ... that the security forces have discharged their onerous duties with the utmost restraint .... [while] conducting their fight against a vicious and ruthless enemy."[62]

Once the Compton report was issued, the Irish Department of Foreign Affairs prepared a secret memo for Patrick Hillery on the advisability of taking Britain to the European Commission on Human Rights at Strasbourg. There were a number of factors that argued against making a formal case. The document warned that the EEC might not look favorably at two nations in the process of joining the Common Market engaging in such a public dispute. The Department of Foreign Affairs section in charge of the EEC treaty advised waiting until Ireland formally joined the body. In addition, a case brought to Strasbourg would harm Anglo-Irish bilateral relations as Heath "would probably be furious" and Ambassador O'Sullivan advised against "taking action at the present time." The arguments in favor of pursuing the case included the hopes that it would cause the remaining internees to be treated with much greater care by the British and sap London's will to seek a military solution to the Troubles thus increasing pressure for a political solution. The memo also pointed out that public opinion in the Irish Republic as well as among the Northern minority was strongly in favor of taking action against Britain. On balance, the document advised Hillery that it would be unwise to ignore the weight of public sentiment on the matter, despite the obvious drawbacks, and argued in favor of bringing a case to Strasbourg.[63]

Anticipating this analysis by the Irish, London was concerned that Lynch, despite his personal reluctance to do so, would be forced to bow to public pressure and begin legal action against Britain.[64] On November 29, the British Embassy in Dublin delivered a message to the taoiseach from Heath offering an argument against going to Strasbourg. Heath urged Lynch to reject calls for him to bring a case, not because Britain had anything to hide, as the Compton Report showed, but because it would cause the two governments to be seen as opponents "in a public forum." Heath warned that a broad case brought forward by Dublin would open the door to a wide-ranging investigation by the Commission on Human Rights that would be bound to raise acrimonious issues such as IRA support in the Irish Republic. The prime minister held out hope that Dublin and London might need to closely coordinate on a political settlement for the North in the near future if the security situation improved and argued that this would be made difficult if they were engaged at Strasbourg. Finally, Heath urged that all the parties that rejected political violence needed to maintain a common front against extremism coming from either community in the North.[65]

Heath's appeal was in vain, and on November 30, 1971, Lynch announced on television that the Irish government planned to refer Britain to the European Commission on Human Rights based on Irish concerns about the brutal treatment of internees. The taoiseach condemned the Compton Report as inadequate and stated that Dublin would not have had to take this step if British had done a more serious job of investigating the charges of abuse.[66] On December 16, the Irish government filed a complaint with the European Commission on Human Rights that made reference not only to the abuse of the internees but also to specific shooting deaths in Northern Ireland as well as challenging internment itself and the entire Special Powers Act as violations of the Convention on Human Rights.[67]

Ambassador Moore advised the State Department that in his opinion, the Irish actions were the "first step in a new policy of confrontation" with Britain as Dublin's "policy of friendly negotiations with Britain had appeared [to have] failed completely." Moore said that this new public stance matched what Irish officials had been saying in private for some time about the state of Anglo-Irish relations. A possible bright spot, according to Moore, was that the Irish believed that "Heath is badly informed and advised rather than ill-intentioned."[68]

British Labour Party's Northern proposals

While relations between the governments of Jack Lynch and Edward Heath were mired in ever increasing disagreement, the British Labour Party offered an alternative scenario. On November 25, Labour leader Harold Wilson outlined his proposals for a change in policy toward Northern Ireland. He reported to the House of Commons that he had recently returned from a trip to both Northern Ireland and the Irish Republic and that he had come away convinced that the Northern nationalists would never join the Maudling talks "in present circumstances." Wilson was careful to praise the efforts of the British Army despite mistakes made "in the heat of the moment." He supported the idea that a permanent political solution could not be arrived at until "the security problem is solved" but added that discussions toward a political solution should begin before the security task is finished as this would help "in winning the hearts and minds which have been desperately alienated." Wilson contended that the reform efforts in the North had been continually undermined by events on the ground that made the reforms inadequate once they were adopted and that internment had once again changed the parameters of what was needed for a peaceful solution. Most of what the opposition leader said matched the policies of Heath's government in terms of defending the Ireland Act of 1949, maintaining a strong security stance, rejecting direct rule, and promoting improved cross-community relations in the North. The major innovation revealed in the speech was that Wilson believed that "it is impossible to conceive of an effective long-term solution" that did not accept Irish unification as a goal. Once the violence had stopped, Wilson proposed all-party talks within Northern Ireland that would be a precursor to a tripartite conference involving London, Dublin, and Belfast, to create a "constitutional commission" that would find an agreeable reunification plan. Unification itself would be delayed for 15 years after the constitutional arrangement was arrived at and Wilson added that any constitution would have to guarantee minority rights, remove clerical influence from public policy, and include a provision by which a united Irish Republic would join the Commonwealth. "No one," Wilson said, "underrates the immensity of the task of reconciliation but still less will anyone underrate the alternative to reconciliation in terms of bitterness and violence."[69]

On November 29, the Tories pushed back at Wilson's initiative and a Labour motion of censure condemning "the failure of Her Majesty's Government's present policies in Northern Ireland." Reginald Maudling acknowledged that Wilson's proposals deserved serious discussion but he doubted that "in present circumstances" the majority of people in Northern Ireland would support any plan for reunification or that the Irish Republic would ever enter the British Commonwealth. If, at some point, the Irish people on both sides of the border wanted reunification, the home secretary said that "not only would we not obstruct that solution but, I am sure, the whole of the British people would warmly welcome it." However, until that time, Maudling argued that the task of the British government was to get the two communities in the North to live peacefully "together within Northern Ireland as it is constituted at present." Maudling said that the way forward was to fully implement the equal rights guaranteed by the Downing Street Declaration and to find a way for nationalists to enjoy "an active, guaranteed and permanent role in the life of the Province." The home secretary defended Faulkner's record on reform and called on nationalists to enter into discussions with him but warned that nationalists could not expect "a right of the minority to outvote the majority."

Prime Minister Heath ended the debate with a catalogue of his government's efforts to promote peaceful dialogue on the North. This included, Heath noted, an open invitation to talk with Jack Lynch whenever the taoiseach wished to meet with him. "But what some would like," Heath said, "would be for us to say to Northern Ireland that Her Majesty's Government want, and that Northern Ireland ought to want, a united Ireland. That we cannot do, because it would be usurping the right of choice of the people of Northern Ireland." Heath called on Jack Lynch to help create the conditions for reunification by trying to harmonize the economic and social parts of life on the island and to "restore more confidence in the North" by cracking down on IRA activity in the Republic. The debate concluded with the Commons rejecting the condemnation of British policy in the North by 293 to 259 votes.[70]

Lynch had an opportunity to publicly comment on Harold Wilson's proposals and to change Heath's mind when the taoiseach traveled to London on December 6 to give a speech at Westminster during a luncheon hosted by the Parliamentary Press Gallery Group. The taoiseach began his remarks by predicting that Wilson's speech in the House of Commons "will be seen to be a turning point not only in British domestic politics but also in Anglo-Irish relations." While Lynch rejected the idea of Irish entry into the Commonwealth as pointless given the uniquely close ties between the two counties, he praised Wilson for making Irish reunification "no longer unmentionable in British politics." Lynch tried to bridge the gap between Labour and the Tories by pointing out that there was very little difference between Wilson's proposal that London support reunification and Maudling's statement in the Commons that the British public would welcome Irish unity. The taoiseach criticized Heath's comments that if London embraced Irish unity, it would be "usurping the right of choice of the people of Northern Ireland" and claimed that the real problem was that the British government had "usurped the right of choice of the Irish people as a whole" when it imposed partition fifty years earlier. However, Lynch stated, he was willing to move past the history of partition and work toward a negotiated reunification that would be acceptable to unionists. "It is wrong," he said, "terribly wrong- to coerce the Northern minority, at the expense of the Army, of finances and prestige of the British people in order to avoid asking the Northern majority to think again." Lynch went on to claim that Unionist Party rule of the North was finished and that not even a military victory over the IRA would change that the fact that Northern nationalists rejected the legitimacy of Stormont. He argued that while London could continue to prop up Stormont for a short time, this policy only caused the British government to avoid the fact that "negotiations aimed at an independent, unified Ireland must begin." As "Unionism as a political philosophy has reached the end of the road," it was time, Lynch argued, for the British and Irish governments, in coordination with both communities in the North, to establish "a new order of things in Ireland as well as between Ireland and Britain." Even if reunification was in the works, Lynch declared that the government of Northern Ireland could not continue as it was, a unionist monopoly, although the exact form of the provincial administration was open to discussion. Lynch closed by saying that entry into the EEC only made it more vital that Ireland would be able to achieve economic development as a unified island.[71]

Lynch and Heath met briefly in private after the taoiseach's speech. Lynch said that while he hoped that the two would be able to continue to meet, since there had been no progress from their Chequers talks, further meetings were unlikely. The two men then covered some well-worn paths of discussion, with Lynch criticizing the cratering of the border roads and Heath calling for more rigorous measures against the IRA. Lynch warned that the influence of his moderate government was declining compared to the IRA and claimed that a political initiative was therefore vital. He asked about the likelihood that Wilson's proposals would move forward. Heath replied that he hope to convene an interparty meeting at Westminster to discuss Labour's ideas but insisted that the violence in the North had to end before any political solution could take hold. Lynch said that he believed that if London came out in favor of Irish unity, then the unionist community would at least begin to contemplate the idea. Heath stood by his stance that while London would not stand in the way of reunification, his government would not be in the business of telling the people of the North what they should think about the idea and expressed doubt that the unionists in the North would accept unification any time soon.[72]

Assessments at the new year

As 1971 drew to a close, there was no Anglo-Irish agreement on how to proceed toward a peaceful resolution of the Troubles. Ambassador John Peck expressed pessimism in his annual review to Douglas-Home. He told the foreign secretary that it was "politically impossible" for Dublin to publicly cooperate with "any aspect of our Northern Ireland policy." Peck suggested that from the Irish point of view Anglo-Irish relations on the North had been reduced to an endless series of disagreements and a total failure by London to accept any advice from the Irish government. Lynch's only hope of maintaining a policy of moderation was for London to help push unionists toward acceptance of gradual, but inevitable reunification. The dire alternative to cooperation on this issue, Peck warned, was that the government of the Irish Republic would collapse and be replaced by one of the wings of the IRA.[73]

The Irish Department of Foreign Affairs' Eamonn Gallagher produced his own evaluation of 1971 for Iveagh House in January 1972. Gallagher, like Peck, saw Anglo-Irish relations as frozen in conflict, but he had a more optimistic view of the future than Peck had shared with London. In examining the recent past, Gallagher argued that there had been some hope for progress until Faulkner came to power at Stormont. Faulkner had not pursued any real reforms and Heath's government has allowed the Northern premier to set the general policy of the British as London hoped of keeping a working devolved government in place. According to Gallagher, by the summer of 1971 the Irish government had given up on the reformation of Stormont and began to focus more on reunification as the ultimate solution to the Northern problem while Faulkner doubled down on keeping the Union intact by imposing internment. So far, Heath had supported keeping the North in the United Kingdom. Gallagher went on to state that, in his opinion, the British Army could win a "victory" over the IRA, if victory was defined as establishing a manageable level of violence, even though current British military tactics were counterproductive. He warned that the possibility of a military solution could not be ignored and therefore Dublin had to find a way to convince the British public to support reunification even without the threat of expanding violence in the North. Gallagher's suggested plans for achieving this aim included continuing Dublin's "tough attitude against current British military repression of the minority," support for passive resistance by the minority, encouraging the Labour Party to break with Heath on Northern Ireland, attempting to internationalize the conflict as much as possible, and building support among Northern Protestants to consider reunification as a "valid alternative to what is in fact a police state." If these policies were followed in a firm but judicious manner, Gallagher believed that they could succeed in achieving peaceful reunification because the Unionist Party's monopoly on power was unsustainable and, in private, even unionists were accepting that change would have to come.[74]

Entry into the European Economic Community

In an odd contrast to the acrimony between Dublin and London over Northern Ireland, the two governments had continued to cooperate on their joint entry into the EEC. The two states were set to sign the treaty of accession on January 22, 1972.[75] While there had obviously been concerns in London that the Troubles would have an impact on Ireland's entry into the EEC, an FCO report in late December 1971 correctly predicted that Ireland had too much to lose to derail entering the European Community. James Cable, head of the FCO's Planning Staff, wrote to the UK delegation to the EEC at Brussels that "the Irish tend, in their relations with Her Majesty's Government to make a distinction between the Northern Ireland situation...and all other questions involving bilateral contacts and consultations on matters economic, social, etc. The maintenance of this dichotomy is part of the Irish charm."[76]

In spite of this compartmentalization of different facets of Anglo-Irish relations, Lynch and Heath agreed that they would meet to discuss Northern Ireland, without prior announcement, when the two men were at Brussels for the EEC treaty signings.[77] Lynch began their meeting by detailing his growing concern with developments such as the opening of a new internment camp at Magilligan in County Derry that was provocatively close to Donegal, the possibility that women might be interned, and high unemployment on both sides of the border which helped the IRA with recruiting. He urged Heath to join him in a reappraisal of "the whole situation, to see if it were possible to find solutions without taking old stands." However, Lynch then proceeded to take an "old stand" himself and renounced the idea of Britain seeking a military victory over the IRA. Even if this were possible, Lynch argued, it would allow unionists "to freeze their position" and reject any further compromise. The taoiseach suggested that a "new angle" to pursue would be for him to "take up a position of leadership for all people of moderation and good will in the whole of Ireland." He hoped that moderate unionists might welcome this now that it was clear, at least to Lynch, that an unreformed Stormont was no longer viable.

Heath said that the British government was willing to discuss any peaceful solution but that with the SDLP boycotting all talks it would be hard to find people to represent the Northern nationalists. Heath also defended the campaign against the IRA, claiming that the Provisionals were on the ropes and asked for Lynch's help to extradite IRA suspects from the Republic. Lynch suggested that this was the best time to make a dramatic political initiative, coupled with a move to end internment, since this might induce the IRA to "come off the streets" and allow moderate nationalists leadership to reclaim strength in the Catholic community. The taoiseach said that he was willing to say to all the Irish people that reunification was not possible until the Northern Protestants could be satisfied with the structure of an all-Ireland state. He asked Heath to pressure Faulkner to accept that the status quo was not sustainable. The prime minister replied that while Faulkner was in no position to talk about reunification but he would talk about a new political arrangement within the province. Lynch concluded with a warning that the violence in the North was growing worse and might spread to the South as well as mainland Britain unless something were done to stop the "drifting" that characterized the current situation.[78]

At a post-meeting press conference Lynch admitted that the two governments had major disagreements on Northern Ireland but that "neither of us wanted to bring the … problem into Europe. I noted that six nations in Europe were able to get together even though there were serious differences between them." The taoiseach ended his press conference with the upbeat assessment that Heath was coming "to understand my point of view."[79] However, instead of continued dialogue, within a week, the drift that Lynch warned about would land Anglo-Irish relations on the rocks of Bloody Sunday.

Conclusions

The months following the imposition of internment saw a great deal of Anglo-Irish diplomatic activity regarding Northern Ireland but the two states did not come to any agreement on how best to end the Troubles. The meetings at Chequers show that London was not only willing but eager to engage in high-profile talks with the Irish government regarding the North but these talks produced nothing positive in the short term. In fact, Lynch's government, under pressure from public opinion, returned to a level of confrontation with the British not seen since 1969. Lynch publicly stated that the reform movement in the North had failed and increased calls for reunification. In addition, Dublin prepared a case against the United Kingdom in the European Court of Human Rights despite British lobbying against the move. While Heath was willing to talk to Lynch and clearly saw that the Irish government had some role to play in Northern Ireland, he would not acknowledge any specific right of Dublin to be involved in formal discussion of the future of political life in the province. With the Maudling talks going nowhere without the participation of the SDLP, the only steps that London could take were increased security measures, such as closing roads on the border, that were very unpopular in Dublin. While the Irish and British governments cooperated on their joint entry into the Common Market, they only moved farther apart on Northern Ireland. Tragically, the political and diplomatic deadlock in Northern Ireland left plenty of room for violence to flourish as the death toll of 127 fatalities between the imposition of internment and the end of year grimly testified.[80]

Bloody Sunday and Direct Rule:
January–April 1972

The dramatic events that took place from the end of January through March 1972 brought the first phase of the Troubles to a close. In the wake of Bloody Sunday, as violence in Northern Ireland reached an unprecedented level, London finally abandoned its attempt to encourage reform at Stormont and instituted direct rule. Anglo-Irish relations were placed under a great strain during this period and Irish diplomats focused more attention on securing some kind of assistance from the US government than they had since 1969.

Bloody Sunday

The shooting deaths of thirteen nationalist protestors in Derry on January 30, 1972, by British paratroopers, an event immortalized as Bloody Sunday, was the most shocking act of violence during the early years of the Troubles and had an important impact on Anglo-Irish relations and the future of Northern Ireland. The general outline of what happened that day is not disputed. The NICRA scheduled a protest march in Derry on Sunday January 30 to protest internment. The protest, while designed to be peaceful, was illegal as all marches had been banned since August 1971. The British Army plan for the day was to contain the marchers in the Catholic Bogside neighborhood with a series of barricades and, if possible, make arrests of any violent rioters who accompanied the peaceful protesters. The locally deployed 8 Infantry Brigade was reinforced by 1 Battalion, Parachute Regiment which was to act as the arresting force. The majority of the marchers turned back from the army barricades but some people remained to throw stones at the soldiers who initially responded with tear gas and a water cannon. At about four in the afternoon the paratroopers were sent in to make arrests. During the course of this operation the paratroopers shot

27 Catholics; 13 died on the scene and a fourteenth died from his wounds months later. These basic facts are not disputed.[1]

While the basic facts are agreed upon the exact details of what transpired on Bloody Sunday, as well as the motivation of the British Army, have been in dispute since. Even the publication of the British government's *Saville Inquiry* in 2010, which found that none of the people killed on Bloody Sunday were armed or posing a threat to the soldiers, did not fully end the controversy.[2] In one of the most detailed studies of the events leading up to the shootings Niall Ó Dochartaigh concluded that Bloody Sunday was neither a planned massacre as republicans believed, nor an unforeseeable consequence of soldiers placed in a stressful and dangerous position as London contended immediately after the events.[3] According to Ó Dochartaigh, General Robert Ford, Commander of Land Forces, Northern Ireland, along with other aggressive minded officers, disagreed with the established, government sanctioned policy in Derry of avoiding confrontations between the British Army and nationalists.[4] Ford ordered the use of the Paras to make mass arrests specifically to create a confrontation and Ó Dochartaigh believes that the shooting of civilians in this atmosphere was a predictable outcome. While the British government did not sanction the shootings it did support the military after the fact, thus linking London to the massacre.[5] While there are certainly some disagreements about specific details among historians who have investigated Bloody Sunday, there is a general consensus that while the shootings were not premeditated, the army was totally unjustified in its actions and that the fatal shootings were the result of the employment of overly aggressive tactics during the protest march. In addition, Bloody Sunday is regarded as having been a great recruiting tool for the Provisional Irish Republican Army.[6]

Initial Irish response to Bloody Sunday

Dublin reacted very quickly to the news of the shootings. On January 31 Jack Lynch gave a special broadcast to the nation in which he said that the government was "satisfied that British soldiers recklessly fired on unarmed civilians in Derry yesterday and that any denial of this continues and increases the provocation offered by present British policies." He acknowledged that all of the Irish people felt "the shock of horror and indignation" at the killings but declared that "our policies and our reactions must be calculated and our decisions must be taken calmly and with determination." Lynch told the public that he had already met with the leaders of Fine Gael and the Labour Party and that all three were united in this "critical situation." As a first response Lynch announced that Dublin had recalled its ambassador to London. Lynch then outlined three immediate demands for the British government which included the withdrawal of British troops from nationalist areas in the North, the end of internment, and a declaration of Britain's intention "to achieve a final settlement of the Irish question and the convocation of a conference for this purpose." Lynch speculated that the British public was unhappy with its own government's handling of Northern Ireland and did not support the maintenance of Stormont.

"We are a small nation," Lynch said, "placed by destiny close to a larger and more powerful neighbor. For too long throughout our history might has been always the ultimate arbiter in our relationship. In recent years there have been indications of welcome and fruitful changes in this pattern.... The present British Government, however, appears to have reverted to the old unprincipled doctrine that might is right. We must and will turn to other nations for support." In order to achieve this international support Lynch announced that Patrick Hillery would be dispatched to seek the assistance of the UN and a number of foreign governments. The taoiseach also pledged that Dublin would provide financial support "for political and peaceful action by the minority in Northern Ireland to obtain their freedom from Unionist mis-government." He maintained that moderate unionists in the North would now support the idea "that a peaceful solution to Ireland's problem can be worked out between Irishmen." After declaring a national day of mourning for the following Wednesday, Lynch called on the Irish people to "show to the world their patriotism by their dignity and discipline."[7]

Lynch addressed the Dáil the next day. "This is the saddest occasion on which I have ever addressed this House," Lynch began. "We share with the people of Derry the tragedy which has befallen them." The taoiseach proclaimed that the task for the Irish government was "to ensure that these days and months, indeed years, of refusal to govern justly in Northern Ireland shall end and never again return." Lynch told the Dáil that this was the minimum requirement to achieve peace in the North. The taoiseach called on all the people of Ireland "to stand behind and support this united endeavor to secure the unity that really matters and which alone will be enduring—the unity of minds and hearts of all Irish people."[8]

Speaking after the taoiseach, Fine Gael leader Liam Cosgrave agreed with Lynch's assessment that British governmental policy was to blame for the tragedy. Cosgrave warned that "we should realize that it is predictable that something like this could happen again unless the British Government and people move towards making a political solution possible." Like Lynch, Cosgrave called for calm and unity in Ireland and supported the plans to approach the UN and other governments that were friendly to Ireland. The Fine Gael leader also suggested that he, Lynch, and Labour Party leader Brendan Corish should seek a meeting with Heath. Corish also spoke in support of the actions that Lynch had taken and his plan to move forward "to shake the British Government out of its indolence, indifference, lethargy and apathy."[9]

Lynch's public comments on Bloody Sunday both reflected the shock, anger, and sorrow of the Irish people and firmly maintained his government's commitment to a nonviolent solution to the Troubles. The demands that the taoiseach made of the British government, with the exception of the withdrawal of troops from Catholic areas in the North, were consistent with the stance that Dublin had held since the Chequers meetings. Lynch put the responsibility for the shootings, as well as the general state of crisis in Northern Ireland, at the feet of Heath's Northern policies which Dublin saw as overly military in nature. The Dáil statements of Cosgrave and Corish demonstrate that the other main parties in Ireland generally agreed with Lynch's assessment of the situation.

Initial British response to Bloody Sunday

The initial response to the Derry shootings by the British government was defensive. On the day following Bloody Sunday the House of Commons experienced a contentious debate regarding the shootings that contrasted sharply with the calm unity displayed by Dáil Éireann. Home Secretary Reginald Maudling defended the actions of the army, claiming that the troops were responding to an armed attack and had only fired on "those who were attacking them with firearms and bombs." Acknowledging the disputed nature of the shootings, he also announced that the government would "set up an independent inquiry." Bernadette Devlin, who had been in Derry on Bloody Sunday, accused Maudling of lying and referred to him as a "murdering hypocrite" before famously launching a physical attack on the home secretary. Gerry Fitt demanded that any inquiry be international but Maudling refused to support that idea as, he said, the government did "not intend to hand over our responsibility for any part of the United Kingdom to an international body." Harold Wilson, as he had initially done back on November 25, 1971, called for all security matters to be handled directly from Westminster and pressed for negotiations among all parties in Northern Ireland to be followed by talks that included Dublin.[10]

When debate on the topic resumed on February 1 Prime Minister Heath announced that Lord Widgery, the Lord Chief Justice of England, had agreed to form a one-man Tribunal of Inquiry to investigate the shootings. While the idea of an official inquiry was supported in the Commons, Harold Wilson questioned the wisdom of a single-person tribunal while ex-Northern premier Chichester-Clark argued that the inquiry should not take place in Derry as the city was "in the grip of the most appalling IRA intimidation."[11] Labour MP Merlyn Rees spoke about his concerns that many in the nationalist population of Derry were convinced that the killings were a premeditated act and that the British military in Northern Ireland had been given "a task almost impossible to perform." Lord Balniel, the minister of state for defense, gave a detailed account of the army's actions on Bloody Sunday that absolved the military of blame and warned against "bitter, intemperate and, to the best of my belief, inaccurate or untrue statements" that were likely supported by IRA propaganda. Devlin and Fitt rejected Lord Balniel's report of events and Fitt called on the army to withdraw from Northern Ireland as it was not acting as a peacekeeping force any longer. Harold Wilson cautioned that everyone should wait until the inquiry before deciding the facts, but renewed his call for reforms in the North

Figure 6.1 Funeral of Bloody Sunday victims, Saint Mary's Church, Derry, February 1972. Credit: M. Stroud.

along the lines he had announced in November. Reginald Maudling countered Wilson by pointing out that Heath's government was attempting to hold all-party talks in the North but that the nationalist parties refused to participate.[12]

Anglo-Irish relations and Bloody Sunday

The official exchange between the Irish and British governments was no less contentious than the debates in Westminster. On January 31, the Irish chargé d'affaires in London, Charles Whelan, met with Kelvin White, the FCO's head of the Irish division, to present a copy of Lynch's public statement and an Aide Memoire to the British government. White complained that Lynch's statement had already assigned blame to the soldiers before any investigation could be launched. The first reports of the army in Northern Ireland, according to White, were that the troops had returned fire on militants armed with guns or nail-bombs. White added that he could not believe that soldiers as highly trained as the paratroopers would open fire on unarmed civilians. Whelan countered that the Irish government was convinced that the impartial witnesses, including members of the press, were correct in reporting a massacre of unarmed protestors. When White asked if Whelan was claiming that the British Army was lying about the shootings he replied that the army had a "credibility" problem with civilian deaths and that "Irish people and neutral observers alike" did not accept the army's account. Whelan argued that, as London had announced an official inquiry into the shootings, it was clear that the British government itself, the British public, and world opinion were not prepared to accept the army's initial report as the last word on the subject. White continued to defend the army's record and asked Whelan if he would withdraw his remarks if the inquiry showed that all the casualties were indeed armed.

Moving on to the three demands made by Lynch, White complained that the Irish government seemed to be "lecturing the British Government on how they should carry out policy in the United Kingdom and this was hardy acceptable." He argued that withdrawing troops would only lead to more problems as the military's tactics had been effective in curbing violence. White produced charts that showed a reduction in bombing incidents since the imposition of internment and road cratering and that only an end to violence would justify an end to internment. On the issue of a conference to discuss the future of the North, White pointed out that London was already engaged in an effort to conduct talks within Northern Ireland and planned to include Dublin at a later date. He suggested that Dublin only wanted talks if they led to a united Ireland and complained that the public nature of Lynch's demands were counterproductive and reduced Brian Faulkner's ability to make a compromise.

Whelan disagreed on each point. He said that the army's tactics, even if they had had some success, which he believed was doubtful, "had completely alienated the Catholic minority." The charge d'affaires pointed out that internment should be phased out as it was the main hurdle to beginning intercommunity talks in the North. As far as the call for a conference, Whelan admitted that reunification was Dublin's long-term aim as a final solution but that any talks would be aimed at an interim settlement that would allow for peaceful coexistence within Northern Ireland. Whelan said that the whole tone of White's response showed that London was too focused on achieving a military solution while it ignored the alienation of the nationalist minority. As the two officials parted company they expressed mutual regret at how bad the state of Anglo-Irish relations had become. White's parting comment was that "we had both lost and the only people to have gained were the IRA."[13]

Anglo-Irish relations were further complicated by the burning of the British Embassy in Dublin on February 2, 1972. During the national day of mourning in Ireland a large crowd of trade unionists, students, and republicans marched in Dublin to protest Bloody Sunday and call for the withdrawal of British troops from the North. Some of the participants in the march gathered outside the already evacuated embassy on Merrion Square and began to attack the building with stones and eventually firebombs. The small Garda contingent could not halt the attack and the efforts of the fire brigade to put out the flames were frustrated by the mob.[14]

Irish charge d'affaires Whelan was summoned to a meeting with Joseph Godber, the minister of state for foreign and commonwealth affairs, to receive a protest about the destruction of the embassy. Godber complained that Dublin had ignored British warnings regarding the safety of the embassy and had failed to adequately protect the building. Whelan told him that the Irish government had decided that only the Irish Army could adequately provide security but that the government had determined that deploying troops would not be wise and that the Garda detail had been easily overwhelmed by a crowd estimated at 25,000. Whelan expressed the regret of Dublin for the events, agreed to pay restitution, and assured the British that Ambassador Peck and his staff would be fully protected. Godber replied that the burning of the embassy "was bound to be very seriously regarded in this country."[15]

During a Cabinet meeting the following day Foreign Secretary Douglas-Home assured his colleagues that he planned to make a statement in the Commons warning Dublin that any repeat of this type of violence "would lead to a serious deterioration in the relations between the two countries." However, Douglas-Home argued against any retaliatory measures as he did not want to further inflame the already volatile state of Anglo-Irish relations.[16] When Ambassador Peck met with Jack Lynch that same day he did not dwell on the arson attack, although he did extract a promise from the taoiseach that every effort would be made to protect Glencairn, the ambassador's residence.[17] In his memoir Peck explained that while he did not "mince words" about the attack on the embassy he did accept that the arson was an expression of "a national rage deeply and widely felt" in Ireland. Peck wanted to reduce Anglo-Irish tensions and move past what he hoped was "the lowest point in Anglo-Irish relations."[18] Heath shared Peck's hope that relations between the two states could be quickly repaired and indicated to the British Cabinet that he was still willing to meet with Lynch, if the taoiseach requested such a meeting, as Heath preferred to keep Lynch in power rather than face an alternative Irish government that would be less moderate.[19]

For its part, the Irish government was very clear in condemning the embassy attack. Lynch made a public statement in the Dáil on February 3 in which he denounced the burning of the embassy as the act of a "small minority—men who, under the cloak of patriotism, seek to overthrow … this State…. We must show the world that, with dignity and restraint, we can express our grief and support for the minority in the North without, at the same time, playing into the hands of those who would destroy our fundamental institutions."[20]

As Anthony Craig has pointed out it is possible that the burning of the embassy, and the calm official reaction of the British government, coupled with Dublin's apology, helped to restore a measure of stability to diplomatic relations between the two states.[21] It certainly did not serve the purposes of either government to allow the destruction of the embassy to further harm Anglo-Irish relations. Nor could the destruction of property by a civilian mob be equated with the shooting deaths of thirteen people by the British Army. London was in no position to express extreme outraged over the embassy burning. In fact, both governments saw the need to keep the lines of communication open to try to avoid another clash between protesters and the British Army at a civil rights march scheduled to be held at Newry on February 6 to protest Bloody Sunday.

Even as Whelan had been called into the FCO to protest the embassy attack he warned Godber that Dublin was "extremely concerned that there should be no mis-judgement in regards to the week-end march at Newry" since a repeat of Bloody Sunday would be a disaster. Godber reminded Whelan that all parades were banned by a decree that Lynch supported and the law had to be maintained but the charge d'affaires replied that a confrontation had to be avoided.[22] When Whelan met with Sir Denis Greenhill and Kelvin White the next day to discuss the safety of Ambassador Peck the conversation turned to Newry. The British warned that the situation might be exploited by the IRA but pledged that "every possible precaution would be taken." Greenhill suggested that a rally in a single spot would be better than a protest march and asked if Jack Lynch could request that the organizers of the event move it to a sports field.[23]

When Ambassador Peck spoke to Lynch on February 3 he also raised the issue of the Newry march, expressed fear that the IRA would be able to provoke a repeat of Bloody Sunday, and asked Lynch to try to get the event canceled in order to avoid trouble. Lynch replied that the underlying problem was that London was being intransigent and that the British Army should not be used to "suppress the only form of peaceful demonstration open to the minority." The taoiseach said he was not inclined to take the political risk of asking for the march to be canceled.[24] On February 3 Lynch told the Dáil that the Newry protest would take place and that he hoped it would be peaceful and "not provide any cloak or alleged excuse for the British Army to behave again as they did in Derry last Sunday."[25] Lynch's hopes came to pass, for when the Newry march was held on February 6 it went off without a major incident. The army provided a large security presence and the protest organizers maintained effective control of the demonstration.[26]

International diplomacy and Bloody Sunday

As Lynch had announced the day after Bloody Sunday, the Irish government immediately began an international diplomatic campaign to gain support for its views with Hillery visiting the United States to meet with officials of the American government and the United Nations. Following meetings at the UN on February 2 Hillery spoke to the press about his mission. He began by admitting that there was nothing that the UN could do on an official basis regarding Northern Ireland without the approval of the British government and he did not intend to make any formal appeal to "the Security Council or any other UN body." He described his mission as one designed to convince governments friendly to Britain to urge London to change its "lunatic policy." Hillery told the press "the British government have gone mad. We hope their friends can put them back on line." The Irish foreign minister went on to say that British policy had changed since Heath replaced Wilson at 10 Downing Street. He characterized British policy under Heath as "brutal repression" which had led to a major increase in support in the North for the IRA. "'The strength of the IRA in the North' he said, 'and many of our problems in the South are the result of British policies.'" In spite of this, Hillery restated Dublin's total rejection of political violence.[27]

In an interview on an American television program Hillery repeated his harsh condemnation of British policy telling his interviewer that they were "lunatic, they're aggressive, they're war-like policies on a peaceful nation. They're going to cause war in our country." Hillery said that London's main goal was to maintain Stormont by any means necessary including "internment, torture, and now open warfare on the innocent people." He claimed that as long as British troops remained in the North they would face increasing attacks by the IRA which was growing in popularity on both sides of the border. Hillery said that Dublin, while committed to peace, could not stop all IRA activity without creating a "concentration camp type of society" in Ireland.[28]

Hillery's next stop was Washington to meet with Secretary of State William Rogers and a number of congressional leaders. The American Embassy in Dublin had already warned the State Department that "Irish sensitivity over Northern Ireland" was at a high point and that Dublin harbored some resentment over Washington's failure to involve itself at all in the situation. The embassy advised that Washington agree to "approach Britain and ask them to take steps to relieve tensions in [the] North" such as had been suggested by the Irish government. According to the embassy staff there was more danger to Irish-US relations in doing nothing than there was to Anglo-American relations by taking this step.[29] The embassy also argued that Dublin's more confrontational stance since Bloody Sunday was a political necessity given the anger of the Irish people but that Lynch remained flexible on most of the details of any Northern settlement. On the other hand, the embassy stressed that the Irish were very much "unified in basic convictions, one of which is that they are right and that Britain will have to come around eventually."[30] The embassy also advised that it was in the best interests of the United States to pressure Britain to change its policy on Northern Ireland as the present situation, if unchanged, might lead to a full-scale civil war that would draw even more British troops from NATO service and might cause a radical change in government in Dublin that would have "significant consequences for ourselves, the EEC and Western Europe."[31]

The State Department received the opposite advice from Ambassador Walter Annenberg in London. He cautioned against "abandoning our basically neutral position on Northern Ireland" warning that it might become a slippery slope of increasing involvement. Annenberg also believed that an American approach to London would be deeply resented by the British government.[32]

The British were not relying on the support of Ambassador Annenberg to sway Washington. Douglas-Home sent instructions to Lord Cromer, British ambassador in Washington, to meet with Secretary of State Rogers and explain London's views on Northern Ireland before Hillery's meeting with Rogers. Douglas-Home wanted Rodgers to know that the British did not accept the narrative that the victims of the Derry shootings were unarmed civilians and that an inquiry was underway to determine the truth. Despite the fact that the Widgery Inquiry had been established to investigate the events, Cromer was instructed to remind Rodgers that, in any case, the march was illegal and that the British Army was doing the "thankless task of keeping the peace." In terms of a political solution to the Troubles, London wanted to stress that Home Secretary Maudling was seeking talks with all parties but that Northern nationalists refused to participate. Cromer was to argue that Lynch's recent public proposals would do more harm than good and that Washington should urge the Irish to do more to fight the IRA within its own territory and to push the SDLP to enter negotiations.[33]

Ambassador Cromer duly delivered the foreign secretary's message to Rodgers. The secretary of state replied that political pressure was building in the United States among the general public, as well as Congress, for the Nixon administration to do something about Northern Ireland. On February 2 Senators Kennedy and Buckley had called on the White House to urge Britain to withdraw its troops while British government offices in the United States faced thousands of Irish-American demonstrators. Rodgers explained that under the circumstances he had to "do or say something constructive" that would "appease some of the domestic lobbying … while at the same time being acceptable" to the British government. He promised to consult with the British Embassy regarding any statement he made after meeting with Hillery.[34]

Hillery had his meeting with Rogers on February 3. He outlined Dublin's well-known views on Northern Ireland and urging Washington to make a friendly approach to the British, arguing that they should end internment and withdraw troops from nationalist areas. Hillery contended that these steps would lead to a major reduction in violence and thus pave the way to a political settlement. The foreign minister complained that all the Anglo-Irish talks that had taken place so far had only been used by Heath to further his own agenda and had resulted in ever increasing "repressive measures" so that any future talks would be pointless if London continued to pursue a military solution in the North. Hillery even suggested that Ireland would build up its own armed forces to counter British militarism if that was necessary. Rodgers assured Hillery that the US government was concerned about the "tragic situation" but that Washington could not "judge, condemn, [or] advocate any particular solution," even in a private meeting with the British, or "intervene" in any way. The best that the American government could do, barring a request for aid from both London and Dublin, was to urge the Irish and British to work together to find a peaceful solution. Rodgers closed by urging Hillery not to harshly attack the British in the press during his visit.[35]

In his own press briefing following the meeting Rodgers laid out Washington's neutrality on Northern Ireland. Not only would the United States not get involved, he told the press, it would not judge any past actions by any party or make any suggestions for future actions. The secretary of state said that Hillery had clearly understood that the United States could not intervene, and in fact, claimed that Hillery had not asked for American intervention in the North. Rodgers said that the Troubles were fueled by "animosities and hatreds that existed in that area … for centuries" and they could only "be solved fundamentally and basically by the people in the area."[36] The British Embassy in Washington, which had been consulted by the State Department before the Secretary of State's remarks, deemed Rodgers's response to Hillery "about as good as we could hope for."[37]

On the surface Hillery's visit to America was a failure as he was unable to convince either the UN or Washington to put any pressure on Britain to change its Northern Ireland policy. However, the aim of the Irish diplomatic offensive was not focused entirely on international relations. In his biography of Hillery, John Walsh argues that in addition to putting international pressure on Britain, Hillery's trip, and the harsh rhetoric that he employed in public, was designed to appeal to the anger of the Irish domestic audience and reduce the ability of the IRA to exploit Bloody Sunday. Lynch's government had not changed its moderate stance on the North and in Walsh's words, "Hillery's uncompromising rhetoric concealed the essential moderation of his position."[38] In addition, Hillery had taken the opportunity of his trip to Washington to meet with friendly congressional leaders, like Senator Edward Kennedy, in order to begin to form a better partnership with the Irish-American community in support of Dublin's policies regardless of the formal stance of the White House and State Department.[39]

In fact, the domestic impact of Ireland's diplomatic actions may well have been paramount from Dublin's point of view. Judging by Hillery's own public statements, he had no hope that the UN would actually take action on Northern Ireland and there was no repeat of the attempt in 1969 to have the issue formally discussed by the Security Council or the General Assembly. While there was more hope that Washington might have a friendly word on Dublin's behalf with London regarding the efficacy of Britain's Northern Ireland policy, Hillery certainly undercut that possibility by announcing to the press ahead of time that this was his purpose. Quiet diplomacy and rhetorically violent press conferences are not normally compatible. Hillery's high-profile trip to America seems to have been primarily aimed at showing that Dublin was deeply concerned about Northern Ireland, was outraged over Bloody Sunday, and could at least do something to try to have an impact on Northern Ireland. Lynch's government had to show the Irish people that there was an alternative to throwing their support behind the IRA.

Following Hillery's inability to solicit help from friendly states, Lynch's government kept the anti-British rhetoric at a high level and publicly speculated that they might turn to other sources for aid. In the Dáil, Finance Minister George Colley said that Ireland expected more than expressions of concern from nations like the United States. He stated that Ireland had always maintained a policy of not allowing its territory to be used as a base from which to threaten Britain but that it was hard for Ireland to cling to that policy in the face of British "ruthlessness and bloodletting." During a press conference Lynch was asked about the possibility of seeking help from the communist world. The taoiseach replied that if the "neutral and friendly countries do not support us, we would have to consider the situation....But we cannot continue as we are, a small country, with relatively little or any military strength compared to a large power. If Britain continues to use that power in the situation that now exists in Ireland.... Then we will have to consider what peaceful measure we should have to undertake." The America Embassy in Dublin believed that while an Irish turn to the Eastern Bloc was unlikely, it could not be ruled out if there was no political progress in Northern Ireland.[40] Although there is no evidence that Dublin was seriously considering an appeal to the Soviet Union, these types of confrontational public statements helped to protect Lynch from more republican-minded critics. At the same time, Lynch made it clear that he did not intend to stray from his commitment to a peaceful solution even if Dublin did seek help from communist nations.

US Congress and Northern Ireland

After Bloody Sunday there was growing concern among Irish-Americans about the situation in Northern Ireland and, as Hillery's meeting with figures like Senator Kennedy demonstrate, members of Congress were taking more of an interest as well. Senator Kennedy and fellow Democratic legislators Senator Abraham Ribicoff of Connecticut and Congressman Hugh Carey of New York had sponsored a Congressional resolution regarding Northern Ireland months before Bloody Sunday. The resolution called for the suspension of Stormont, the temporary establishment of direct rule, a gradual withdrawal of British troops, and an all-party conference to settle the conflict in Northern Ireland. Kennedy himself indicated that he believed Irish unification was the best solution.[41] The British Embassy saw this Congressional involvement as one sign of a growing British public relations problem after Bloody Sunday. Donald Tebbitt, an embassy official, warned the FCO that "there is a danger of our losing the propaganda battle" as Irish-American activists have made headway in spreading doubt about British neutrality in the press, the government, and in public perception since the killings in Derry. The embassy was particularly concerned about a House Foreign Affairs Committee hearing concerning Northern Ireland that was scheduled to begin on February 28. Tebbitt's message outlined a number of steps that the embassy saw as important in winning the propaganda battle. These ideas included making sure that any British political initiative was given "maximum coverage," sharing information with the State Department to shore up its continued support for American nonintervention, and fostering a corps of friendly journalists in the United States who could argue in favor of British policies in the American press.[42]

The State Department was certainly a willing partner for the British when it came to presenting London's view to Congress. The US Embassy in London helped to arrange a meeting between Assistant Secretary of State for European Affairs Martin Hillenbrand and FCO and Home Office officials in advance of Hillenbrand's testimony to the House Committee on Foreign Affairs.[43] The meeting, which took place well before Bloody Sunday, consisted largely of Hillenbrand asking for London's take on issues he believed would be raised in

Congress. On the issue of internment, Philip Woodfield of the Home Office told the American that the tactic had been used before in both the United Kingdom and Ireland and that it was a necessary response to IRA violence. Woodfield added that a judge, who was Catholic, reviewed all the internments and had suggested release for 10 percent of the detainees. With regard to the need for the deployment of British troops, Woodfield said that they were needed to stop "something like a civil war between [the] Protestant and Catholic communities." Woodfield said that London was determined to avoid direct rule if possible, in part because it was "the immediate objective of the IRA," and that Heath's government was seeking a way "to give the minority a role in government" that they had historically lacked in Northern Ireland. Kelvin White told Hillenbrand that in the long-term London would be "perfectly willing to see Northern Ireland united with [the] Republic if that is what the population wish" but that reunification had to be agreeable to both communities. After thanking the British officials for their input Hillenbrand expressed the hope that he "would be able to leave the problems of Northern Ireland to them."[44]

In spite of opposition from the White House and the State Department, the Congressional hearings were held from February 28 to March 1, 1972. Senator Kennedy and thirteen other members of Congress addressed the House Foreign Affairs Subcommittee on Europe. Another twenty-two legislators had statements read into the record of the hearings. These comments were universally critical of Britain's handing of Northern Ireland. The Irish witnesses who were on hand to testify included individuals, like Father Edward Daly, who gave firsthand accounts of Bloody Sunday. All the witnesses were chosen by Senator Kennedy and his Democratic Party allies with the exception of the State Department's Martin Hillenbrand.[45]

When Martin Hillenbrand testified at the hearings on February 29 he gave a firm defense of American noninvolvement to the members of Congress. He began by reminding the committee that Secretary of State Rodgers had already given the official administration view on Northern Ireland following the visit of Patrick Hillery earlier in the month, that Hillery had understood the American stance, and that nothing had changed since then. Congressional resolutions calling on the Nixon administration to use its good offices to help the situation or push the UN to intervene could not be acted upon, as to do so would be unacceptable involvement by the American government according to Hillenbrand. He reminded those calling for Irish unification that this was only possible if it were agreed to by all the people of Ireland and that Jack Lynch had been unambiguous in supporting the idea of unification by agreement and condemning the use of violence to achieve Irish unity. In fact, Hillenbrand pointed out that Lynch had recently called violence a hindrance to his hopes for reunification. Nor had Dublin supported the call to withdraw all British troops from the North. Lynch had called for the much more limited goal of the removal of troops from nationalist areas. Hillenbrand warned that "people who are closer to the situation than we are" believed that a withdrawal of British troops would actually lead to a surge in violence. Hillenbrand admitted that the American public was very critical of interment without trial, and declined to defend it as a "principle or a policy" but he did state that it had been used in the past by both the British and Irish governments and that Washington should refrain from judging the decision. Once again pointing to the public statements of Jack Lynch, Hillenbrand praised the taoiseach's moderate and unemotional response to the crisis and called on all the friends of Ireland in the United States to follow his lead.[46] The British were very pleased with Hillenbrand's performance. The FCO praised him for using Lynch's comments to bolster his case, and deemed his testimony "both effective and helpful."[47]

In fact, while Hillenbrand's testimony pleased London it also painted an accurate picture of Lynch's stance on certain issues related to Northern Ireland which was not always in line with that of the Irish-American caucus in Congress. In an interview Lynch gave to the *Washington Post* in early March he repeated some of the points Hillenbrand had raised. Lynch criticized Senator Kennedy's calls for Britain to withdraw all of its troops from the North while promoting his own demand that the British Army stop patrolling in nationalist neighborhoods. The taoiseach also urged Irish-Americans not to give money to the IRA as republican violence only helped to drive a wedge between the two Northern communities.[48]

The only problem that appeared in US-Irish relations as a result of the hearings of the House Committee on Foreign Affairs arose from an issue of semantics that pointed to the domestic political agenda of Hillery's February visit. Hillery called Ambassador Moore on March 4 to inform him that Irish politicians who had been in Washington for the House hearings had reported that Hillenbrand had stated that Hillery had not asked for US intervention in Northern Ireland. Hillery said that this had left the impression that "I had crossed the Atlantic and did not ask for anything, which is not true." According to Hillery, Lynch's government would face embarrassment in the Dáil because of this and if Washington did not confirm that Hillery had asked for help, Lynch would have to make a formal request to the US government for clarification.[49]

As Hillery predicted, he was questioned in the Dáil about the allegation that he did not request "US intervention." The foreign minister replied that it was "quite clear that we asked the US Government and other Governments to speak to Britain and to encourage Britain to seek a political rather than a military solution" but that the term "intervention" was not an accurate representation of the Irish government's request "for action" by Washington to advise Britain to change its policy.[50] Ambassador Moore reported to Washington that "Hillery handled the challenge effectively and tried to avoid damaging relations with the U.S. in part because he could not admit dissatisfaction without confirming" that his critics were correct.[51] The State Department instructed Moore that Washington had no desire to get involved in "some semantic difficulty over the word 'intervention'" and that if asked, the embassy should say that Hillery had asked for "'help' without being specific and that the U.S. had explained why it couldn't 'intervene in any way.'" In addition, Moore was instructed to point out that President Nixon had recently met Heath in Bermuda and discussed the "tragic situation and our support for any efforts to put Northern Ireland on [the] road to peace and justice. So far as we know, no other country has done more, or has discussed [the] subject with Britain at [the] highest level."[52]

Attempts at informal diplomacy

While Jack Lynch and Patrick Hillery had publicly condemned British policies in the North, and Lynch's government in general was making undiplomatic public statements, there was at least one actual attempt being made at a semiprivate diplomatic initiative from the Irish. The move came from Ken Whitaker, Lynch's influential adviser on Northern Ireland and the governor of the Central Bank of Ireland, whom the taoiseach encouraged to make informal contacts with the British and Northern unionists.[53] Whitaker, in personal correspondence with David James, a Tory MP, outlined his own thinking on a political solution to the crisis in the North on February 15. Whitaker explained that he was "not a Stormont-abolitionist" and that he hoped that a reformed Stormont would be an effective government in Northern Ireland. Mirroring Lynch's policy, Whitaker called for peaceful and consensual Irish reunification as the final solution to the Northern problem and as a method of promoting development in Ireland as a whole. Again following the outlines of Lynch's ideas, Whitaker suggested that London should help to promote gradual reunification among the unionist community in the North. He also wrote about the need to reject violence and replace "majority rule" with "representative rule" in Northern Ireland to increase political participation by nationalists. He declared that the current form of government in Stormont had no future. Lastly, Whitaker called for an All-Ireland Council that would slowly take over control of cross-border issues while an "Anglo-Irish consultative council" would allow coordination among London, Belfast, and Dublin. Whitaker envisioned a thirty-year process of reunification to allay unionist fears of a rapid takeover by Dublin and allow for moderates in both communities to create support for the idea.[54]

In a meeting on March 12 with Sir Leslie O'Brien, governor of the Central Bank of England, Whitaker continued to express his ideas. He wrote to O'Brien a few days later, sharing with him the letter he had sent to James, and adding that he believed that the initiative for the ideas he proposed had to come from Britain in a "bold" policy announcement.[55] While this initiative by Kenneth Whitaker did not lead to any diplomatic breakthrough it was, unlike the confrontational public face of Dublin's reaction to Bloody Sunday, a real expression of Lynch's hope for Ireland and Anglo-Irish relations.

Harold Wilson also engaged in a bit of private diplomacy in mid-March 1972. During a visit to Dublin, ostensibly to talk to Lynch, the Labour leader held a secret meeting with a group of Provisional IRA leaders. The PIRA had called a 72-hour cease-fire on March 10, demanding the withdrawal of British troops, release of prisoners, and an end to Stormont as the price for a lasting peace. While the Provisional leaders saw their talks with the former prime minister as a sign of their growing power nothing came of the discussions.[56] Although Dublin had supported Wilson's public stance on the North as an improvement over Heath, the Labour leader's meeting with the Provisionals only succeeded in angering Lynch and embarrassing his government.[57]

London contemplates direct rule

The overall picture of Anglo-Irish relations on Northern Ireland was bleak in March 1972. There had been no headway on a political solution and, since even before internment, the main Northern nationalist political parties had withdrawn from Stormont and were refusing to have any discussions with London. Despite the seventy-two-hour PIRA truce that began on March 10 there had been no reduction in violence in Northern Ireland since Bloody Sunday. From February 1 until March 20, 1972, there were fifty-nine deaths due to the Troubles, including twenty-three civilians, sixteen republican militants, ten RUC or UDR members, and ten British soldiers.[58] Heath's government was forced to contemplate direct rule as the only plausible way forward for Northern Ireland.

London had been looking at direct rule for some time. A secret government document from December 1971 entitled "The Probable Effects of Direct Rule in Northern Ireland" provided some speculation on the outcome of abolishing Stormont. The memo assumed that London would continue to stand by the Ireland Act of 1949 and maintain British military forces in the province. While there would be general nationalist "relief" at direct rule, it was still likely that the SDLP would continue to refuse to participate in government in Northern Ireland as long as internment continued. As far as Dublin was concerned, the document argued that Lynch's government would welcome the step, particularly if it was seen as "the prelude to radical change in the North." However, Dublin would still not "endorse any settlement" that did not involve the Irish government. It was also deemed unlikely that direct rule would satisfy republican demands and thus end IRA violence. Another problem that the document identified was that both communities in the North would see direct rule as a step on the road to reunification and therefore it would "raise Catholic hopes and Protestant fears." There would have to be close cooperation with the Irish government to moderate both exaggerated hopes and fears over reunification. One of the memo's main conclusions was that the price for Irish cooperation would be that direct rule would have to be sold as a "new start" with any new provincial government having a guarantee of nationalist participation, an acknowledgment that Dublin had some role to play in the North, and an acceptance that peaceful reunification would be the stated goal of Dublin and Northern nationalists. However, even these moves were not seen as insuring that the IRA's campaign would be easily defeated.[59] Clearly, direct rule was not seen as a magic bullet by London and the debate continued.

On March 3 Reginald Maudling outlined his thinking about the situation in the North to his Cabinet colleagues. He acknowledged the danger of taking any step forward but warned against the equal danger of continuing to do nothing. Maudling did not believe that the British Army would be able to wipe out the IRA and that, in the present situation, the Troubles were driving the two Northern communities farther apart and hurting the UK's international standing. He argued that if the border could be guaranteed unionists would be satisfied while nationalists would settle for equality within the United Kingdom for the time being. Rather than call explicitly for direct rule, Maudling argued that all security matters should be transferred from Stormont to Westminster as the British Army was the main security force. Internment would then be phased out while a new power-sharing system of government was worked out.[60]

The Cabinet discussed the home secretary's memo when it met on March 7. Maudling admitted that as it was unlikely that Faulkner would accept the transfer of security powers, there would have to be a period of direct rule until a new administration could be established. He argued that as there was no military solution, there had to be a way forward politically that would include the nationalists. Plenty of objections were raised including the fear of a unionist backlash, the possibility that direct rule might be seen as an IRA victory, and the danger that Dublin would not support direct rule if it was seen as helping to make partition more stable.[61]

Lynch's government had been arguing for some months that London should actively support Irish reunification and Sir Alec Douglas-Home supported that as a better alternative to direct rule. He wrote to Heath on March 13 to argue against direct rule as he did not believe that the people of Northern Ireland "are like the Scots or the Welsh and I doubt if they ever will be." He argued that Britain's real "interest would … be served best by pushing them towards a United Ireland rather than tying them closer to the United Kingdom."[62] After further Cabinet discussions Heath decided that Maudling's plan to transfer security to London had to be tried even if it led to Faulkner's refusal and the imposition of direct rule.[63]

Direct rule

Faulkner and Heath met in London on March 22. While Heath stressed that London was still committed to the Ireland Act of 1949, he told Faulkner that London did not believe that a purely military solution was possible. Heath told Faulkner that while the British Army already had seventeen battalions deployed in Northern Ireland the security forces had only reduced, not eliminated, IRA violence. Progress had been made in Belfast, but to secure the border and restore calm to Derry would take major military operations that would be too costly in terms of resources, add additional strain to the army's ability to meet its international commitments, and further alienate the nationalist community in the North. With no military solution in sight, Heath argued that they had to move forward on a political solution for the North. In order to break the current political deadlock the prime minister said that internment would have to be wound down. To achieve this aim London would have to have responsibility for all aspects of law and order including policing, courts, and the penal system. Heath said that London might consider periodic referenda on maintaining the border but the main problem that had to be solved was how to give the nationalists a "permanent, active and guaranteed role" in government in Northern Ireland. Faulkner rejected these proposals arguing that the transfer of power would make Stormont a mere puppet of London. On March 23 the Northern Ireland Cabinet agreed to resign rather than accept the loss of control over law and order in the province.[64]

On March 24, 1972, Heath informed Parliament about his discussions with Faulkner and the need for London to now take "full and direct responsibility for the administration of Northern Ireland until a political solution to the problems of the Province can be worked out in consultation with all those concerned." The prime minister called for the House of Commons to pass legislation to implement direct rule for a year and to create a secretary of state for Northern Ireland who would appoint a commission to "advise and assist him." Harold Wilson spoke in favor of passing the needed legislation thus giving direct rule the backing of the Labour Party.[65]

Ambassador Peck delivered a message from Heath to Lynch an hour before the prime minister spoke at Westminster informing the taoiseach about the imposition of direct rule. Heath gave Lynch an outline of his talks with Faulkner and the new plans for government in the North. He pointed out that London had "also decided that it would be right in principle to bring internment to an end, when respect for the law and a normal situation of order has been restored." Certain detainees could be released very soon and if violence abated there might be further releases but Heath warned that if violence persisted "we must retain the power to arrest and intern" those responsible. Heath explained that the purpose of the border plebiscites would be to "ensure a period of stability and enable Northern Irish politicians to be concentrated on matters other than the border." The prime minister closed his message by stating that he did "not pretend that what we are now doing constitutes the whole answer" to the crisis as the vital step of integrating the nationalist community into political life in Northern Ireland still had to be accomplished. "This is a difficult period," Heath wrote, "difficult not only for us and for Northern Ireland, but also, I recognize for the Republic, and I ... hope that I can now look to you ... to prevent troublemakers from exacerbating the situation." In particular, Heath wanted Lynch to help calm unionist fears about a quick move for reunification and to counter any suggestion that direct rule was a victory for the IRA. He asked for Lynch to urge all Irish nationalists to cooperate "with the forces of law and order" and to seek "peace and justice" in the North before turning their attention to Irish unity and to help the whole process by being "seen to be taking effective action against the IRA."[66]

Peck reported to London that Lynch "was clearly impressed by the magnitude of the step taken" when he delivered Heath's message. Peck said that he urged Lynch to take into consideration the political risk that Heath was taking with direct rule and that it was vital for Dublin to support the move with "a strong reaction ... against all gunmen and men of violence." When Lynch expressed some trepidation about the idea of border plebiscites Peck argued that they demonstrated that London was open to the idea of consensual reunification and did not intent to integrate Northern Ireland into the rest of the United Kingdom on a permanent basis.[67]

Lynch's official statement, issued later that day, praised the announcement of direct rule "as a step forward in seeking a lasting solution to the remaining problem in Anglo-Irish relations." Avoiding a call for reunification, he urged "all Irishmen to find a new way forward towards a society in which peace, justice, understanding and friendship will prevail." Lynch also announced that the Irish ambassador, who had been recalled after Bloody Sunday, would return to London.[68]

In addition to the taoiseach's formal statement Peck was also able to provide the FCO with an account of some "off the record" remarks that Lynch had made to the Irish media. Lynch told the journalists that direct rule was more than he had expected from Heath's government and that the move was a vindication of his own policies for the North. The taoiseach warned his ministers "not to gloat" but to focus on improving North–South relations. Lynch also said that "he was determined that much stronger measures would be taken against the IRA in the Republic." Peck told the FCO that he believed that Lynch was sincere in his desire to fight the IRA but that London could not expect "that this will happen in a matter of days or that he will publically seek a confrontation with the IRA."[69]

In a separate message that same day Peck urged a note of caution regarding Dublin's attitude toward the IRA. The Irish, he warned, did not believe that cooperation with the British Army or the RUC were necessary for the IRA to disappear. Rather, they "foresee the IRA in the North evaporating in the same way that it always has: public support withers away, they just bury their arms ... and the struggle is either dormant or non-violent." In that situation Dublin would expect a reduction in police and military action against the IRA "and any evidence that direct rule has produced no change after a fairly short period will lead to widespread disillusionment." Peck concluded that, overall, direct rule was a positive development for Anglo-Irish relations but that Dublin would expect real progress in the North.[70]

Jack Lynch sent a formal reply to Heath on March 29 promising that the Irish government would do all that it could to help direct rule achieve the aim of bringing "an end to violence on the one side whilst also avoiding violence on the other." Lynch reported that he had met with leaders of the SDLP and Nationalist Parties and that they supported direct rule and, "with the speedy end of internment," the two parties would "engage in the discussions you envisage in an effort to reach agreement on a new way forward." The taoiseach predicted that Northern nationalists would move away from support for the IRA and that "the broad mass" of unionists would join them in rejecting all political violence. Lynch's only complaint was with the plan for plebiscites on the issue of the border. He claimed that Northern Ireland did not have the right to decide by itself an issue that affected all of Ireland. Furthermore, Lynch argued that the plebiscites would give rise to periods of tension in the North that ran counter to Dublin's hope for a gradual "softening of opinion" among unionists in favor of peaceful reunification.[71]

The US State Department's analysis of the impact of direct rule expressed fear that the move only had a 50 percent chance of creating a stable political solution. An internal memorandum stressed that direct rule was not welcomed by unionists and that "if Heath's efforts fail, the British forces will face armed hostility not only of Catholics but also of Protestants."[72] The State Department's official response to the imposition of direct rule did not mention these concerns but called for "all those involved in the Northern Ireland problem to now proceed in the spirit of compromise to secure peace with justice." It also repeated the Nixon administration's firm policy that "the United States ... is not itself involved in the problem but ... has many close links to both Ireland and Great Britain."[73]

President Nixon wrote to Heath on March 29 to thank him for having provided advance notice to Washington about direct rule and to express Nixon's hope that the policy would "break the cycle of violence and bring about the restoration of order and peace in Northern Ireland." Nixon assured Heath that he was "fully sympathetic to the problems you face ... and I ... will do nothing to add to those problems." However, the president cautioned that he could not answer "for certain elements of the Congress which are beyond my control." Nixon informed the prime minister that he had had a conversation with Irish ambassador Warnock on St. Patrick's Day and had praised both Heath and

Lynch "as just and honorable men devoting their utmost energies to the solution of an inherited problem with a long and melancholy history" while also making it clear to Warnock that his administration could not support "intervention in any form."[74]

In late April, Heath sent a letter to Lynch expressing his happiness that Ambassador O'Sullivan had returned to London and voicing a cautious optimism that the "prospects for peace have improved but we still have a long way to go." The prime minister claimed that the IRA was now the major hurdle in establishing a peaceful settlement in the North and asked for Dublin's help in defeating "terrorism." He also laid out for Lynch his plans for the future, "assuming peace returns," which included all-party talks in the North to establish a new form of administration for the province. Heath defended the border plebiscites as acknowledging the legitimacy of unification as a political goal while also serving to reassure unionists that they would remain in the United Kingdom for the foreseeable future. He advised Lynch that they should refrain from meeting for a time as not to further alarm unionists. Heath returned to the threat of the IRA at the end of his message claiming that if direct rule was to be "a turning point for Ireland, the IRA must be hit hard and hit now" and urging Lynch to move toward greater cooperation with the British security forces.[75]

While direct rule was clearly welcome by Dublin, and improved Anglo-Irish relations in the wake of Bloody Sunday, it did not bridge the major divide between the two governments as to how to best achieve peace in Northern Ireland. A meeting between Patrick Hillery and Sir Alec Douglas-Home on April 27, 1972, demonstrated how the two governments still had the same fundamental difference of opinion on how to deal with the violence in Northern Ireland. Sir Alec pressed the Irish to crack down on the IRA as London believed that reducing violence was the next step on the road to a settlement in the North. Hillery countered that Dublin was doing the best that it could against the IRA and contended that nationalist support for the IRA would fade away "if there is no further need for the gunmen and the important political developments leading to a United Ireland are on the way."[76]

Although the imposition of direct rule did not immediately transform Anglo-Irish relations it was a still a major development in the opinion of most scholars of the period. In his biography of Jack Lynch, Dermot Keogh called direct rule a victory for Lynch's government that moved Anglo-Irish relations "to another level" in which Heath would move "away from a purely military solution" toward a more constructive focus on finding a peaceful solution with Irish participation.[77] According to historian Anthony Craig the British government made the move because it was primarily focused on the security situation and the failure of Faulkner "to keep the province under control." Direct rule was popular with both moderate Northern nationalists and Dublin and helped "to put Bloody Sunday in the past." Craig has described direct rule as a "radical change in how Northern Ireland was governed" and in the way "intergovernmental relations" between Dublin and London worked as Belfast had been taken out of the equation.[78]

By suspending, and later abolishing, Stormont London had acknowledged that the status quo in the North was unsustainable. This moved the British position much closer to that of Lynch's government which had been arguing for some time that Stormont could not be reformed and had to be replaced with a different type of government. However, in the short term, Heath expected more Irish cooperation on security issues while Lynch believed that direct rule was only the first step that London needed to take on the road to a political settlement that would cause political violence to be abandoned by the people of Northern Ireland.

Conclusions

Bloody Sunday was the greatest challenge to Anglo-Irish relations since the outbreak of the Troubles in August 1969. While Lynch's government had been moving in a more confrontational manner since the start of internment, the shootings in Derry pushed this policy to a new level. Although Lynch's government clearly saw Bloody Sunday as the inevitable result of the overly aggressive British military actions it had been warning against, it is also clear that Dublin's anti-British rhetoric and diplomatic moves in New York and Washington were intended to reflect the anger of the Irish public and defend the political stability of Lynch's government as much as to accomplish any diplomatic goal. The sadness and outrage expressed by Lynch's government was real but it did not overwhelm the government's dedication to a peaceful solution to the Troubles. While London's public defense of the British Army's version of Bloody Sunday only increased the outrage of the Irish public, Heath's government made some effort to calm the situation and support Lynch by keeping its reaction to the burning of the British Embassy to a bare minimum. Heath understood that Lynch was still the best option as taoiseach from Britain's point of view.

The Derry shootings also caused the British government to accept that the status quo in Northern Ireland was too unstable to sustain and that it had to abandon its long-standing commitment to keeping a government in Stormont. The imposition of direct rule was a major development in Northern Ireland and in Anglo-Irish relations but it was obviously not a solution in and of itself. The Irish government reacted in a positive manner to London taking direct control of the province, and relations between the two states rebounded from the low point of Bloody Sunday, but Dublin and London remained divided on the vital issue of how much emphasis should be placed on security issues versus the search for a political settlement. Dublin argued that a de-escalation of military action coupled with a new political structure in the North would cause the IRA to wither away while London called for increased pressure on the IRA to help facilitate political talks.

Conclusion

The period from the deployment of British troops on the streets of Northern Ireland in August 1969 until the suspension of Stormont in March 1972 saw many dramatic developments and events that gave the Troubles the basic shape that the conflict would retain for the next quarter of a century. During these early years of the Troubles the Provisional Irish Republican Army emerged as the chief paramilitary organization pursuing a violent reunification of Ireland, the moderate nationalist community of the North largely united behind the SDLP, the Unionist Party was divided into moderates who would accept reform and compromise and hardliners who rejected change, the security forces struggled to reduce violence in the province, the government in London looked for a permanent solution to the conflict, and the Irish government sought a role for itself in Northern Ireland. The main focus of this book has been to examine the details of Anglo-Irish relations in regard to Northern Ireland and the impact that those relations had on the evolution of the Troubles during the first phase of the conflict.

Anglo-Irish relations evolved over the period in question. In the wake of the breakdown of law and order that necessitated the use of British troops to keep the peace in August 1969 the government in Dublin was divided as to what course of action to take. The initial Irish response toward Britain was antagonistic, confrontational, and focused on partition as the cause of the violence. Harold Wilson's government reacted to Dublin's apparent animosity by claiming that the government of the Irish Republic had no legal right to be involved in Northern Ireland in any way and pointed to the promise of reforms in the province, as outlined in the Downing Street Declaration of August 19, 1969, as the way forward. Rather than accept the idea that Northern Ireland was not a concern for Dublin, Jack Lynch's government quickly turned to the United Nations to draw world attention to the Northern crisis and demonstrate to the Irish people in general, and the more republican leaning elements of Fianna Fáil in particular, that Dublin could have an impact on events in the North. This sharp Anglo-Irish public conflict did not last long. London quickly came to the realization that Jack Lynch was the best, most moderate leader that it could hope to see in Dublin. The Irish initiatives at the UN ended in a compromise that satisfied Lynch's political need to be seen to act while having no real impact on British policy on Northern Ireland.

Jack Lynch's speech at Tralee in September 1969 outlined his essentially moderate stance on Northern Ireland and helped to set the stage for less contentious Anglo-Irish relations. In line with the traditions of Fianna Fáil, he rejected partition but also renounced the use of force to reunify Ireland. Lynch called for reunification to be gradual, peaceful, and with the consent of the unionists. He also claimed that Dublin had a right to be consulted on the future of Northern Ireland. Anxious to reduce confrontation and improve Anglo-Irish cooperation over Northern Ireland, Wilson's government agreed to the Irish call for low-profile bilateral discussions about the North. A series of talks between the two governments began in December 1969. These talks on the margins were the major conduit for Anglo-Irish relations regarding the effort to reform Northern Ireland for the rest of Wilson's time in office. While Harold Wilson would become much more open to dramatic changes in Northern Ireland during his stint as leader of the opposition, in 1969 and 1970 his government believed that implementing the Downing Street Declaration would solve the crisis in the North and keep the responsibility for running the province in Stormont. As a result, his government was seemingly more interested in keeping Lynch placated by talks than in actually following any advice that Dublin offered regarding the pace or scope of the ongoing reforms. Although the Irish government expressed concern that the reform efforts were either coming too slowly or were incomplete, both governments, during this period, supported the basic concept that reforming Stormont, rather than radically restructuring Northern Ireland's government, was the first step on the road to restoring peace to Northern Ireland.

The period of calm in Anglo-Irish relations that had emerged in September 1969 ended during the summer of 1970 as the level of violence in Northern Ireland increased, Edward Heath replaced Wilson as prime minister, and Lynch's hold on power in Dublin was challenged by the Arms Crisis. Events on the ground in Northern Ireland had a central role in shaping Anglo-Irish relations during this next phase of the Troubles. The increased activity of the IRA coupled with British military efforts to stop the violence led to the souring of relations between the Northern nationalist community and the British Army. Lynch's government, under pressure from the more militant wing of Fianna Fáil to defend Northern nationalists, reacted with a return to diplomatic confrontation as symbolized by the unannounced visit of Patrick Hillery to Belfast. The Irish government began to express serious doubts to London that Stormont could be reformed in the face of hardline unionist opposition. Heath's government responded to the provocation of Hillery's visit by downplaying any disputes in order to maintain good relations with Dublin. Seeking to keep open the lines of communication, Heath and Lynch agreed to meet in New York to exchange ideas, but the prime minister was also keen to avoid any drastic political change in the North as he hoped to keep Chichester-Clark in power and avoid direct rule. Partly due to the need to take a strong security stance to help Chichester-Clark to survive politically, and partly because of genuine military concerns over the growing effectiveness of the IRA, Heath began to stress the need for greater security cooperation from Lynch's government. London's argument that reform in the North could not be accomplished until the violence was reduced was countered by the Irish view that only meaningful reforms would undercut the appeal of the IRA and thus reduce its power. This disagreement on whether to emphasize security or political initiatives became a central divide in Anglo-Irish relations on Northern Ireland.

After the resignation of Chichester-Clark in March 1971 Lynch signaled that he would continue to support the reform movement under the new Northern premier Brian Faulkner, but by July the taoiseach issued a call for the British government to give their active support to the idea that peaceful Irish unification was the best method of ending the Troubles and cementing close Anglo-Irish relations. However, London was not interested in changing its self-described neutral stance on partition or in reducing its focus on security in Northern Ireland. The withdrawal of the SDLP from the Northern Ireland parliament in July 1971 seriously damaged the effort to reform Stormont and added to the growing push for internment as a means of restoring law and order to the province. The introduction of internment without trail in August 1971 caused another public dispute between Dublin and London as Lynch's government categorically condemned the use of internment. Over the next few weeks Dublin first expressed to the British the idea that Stormont should be replaced by a bi-communal power-sharing body and Heath and Lynch engaged in an acrimonious public war of words that was almost on par with the crisis of August 1969. Internment also further alienated moderate Northern nationalists making it even less likely that the SDLP would end its boycott of Stormont.

London quickly sought to limit the damage to Anglo-Irish relations caused by internment and to coax the SDLP back into political life by pressing Lynch to meet with Heath at Chequers and shortly afterward to come to a tripartite meeting that included Faulkner. These two meetings proved fruitless, at least in the short term, as the Irish pushed for an immediate end to internment and a power-sharing arrangement to replace Stormont while Faulkner offered only token concessions and, barring the return of the SDLP to political life, Heath was left to focus on the need for more security cooperation from Dublin. With Heath still hoping to keep a functioning Unionist government in Stormont to avoid direct rule by London, Anglo-Irish relations seemed frozen in a state of disagreement over how to achieve any political breakthrough in the North.

At the start of 1972 there was no meaningful political engagement by Northern nationalists and internment had not stopped the violence. The British and Irish governments could not agree on a strategy to try to end the Troubles. The impasse was broken by the Bloody Sunday shootings on January 30 that initially placed a severe strain on Anglo-Irish relations. The understandable uproar in Dublin was made worse by London's defense of the British Army's actions in Derry. In a move reminiscent of August 1969 the Irish government dispatched Patrick Hillery to the United States to lobby the UN and the American government for help in moving London away from what the Irish saw as a disastrous militarization of British policy. Hillery received no help in the United States but his harsh public rhetoric against Britain reflected the anger of the Irish people and helped to provide political cover for the fact that Lynch's government maintained its essential moderation on the North even after Bloody Sunday. With Northern Ireland seemingly trapped in a state of violence, Heath's government finally abandoned Stormont and imposed direct rule in March 1972. Lynch quickly welcomed the announcement as a positive step forward and Anglo-Irish relations were able to refocus on the search for a political solution to the Troubles.

While Anglo-Irish relations evolved during the first years of the Troubles the stance of the American government to the conflict remained consistent. The Nixon administration and the State Department had no intention of becoming involved in Northern Ireland. Although the Americans were unfailingly polite to the Irish and were willing to hear Dublin's complaints about British policy, Washington clearly had no intention of attempting to influence British actions at the behest of the Irish government. American noninvolvement served British interests more than Irish interests and, in fact, while the public stance of the American government was that it was strictly neutral with regard to Anglo-Irish disputes on Northern Ireland, the State Department coordinated many of its responses to the conflict directly with the British government to avoid any embarrassment to America's NATO ally.

The Irish had a more sympathetic audience in the American Congress but Lynch's government made no attempt to rally or direct its Congressional supporters. While the pro-Irish caucus on Capitol Hill helped to draw attention to the Troubles, without coordination from Dublin members of Congress were apt to make statements that were actually at odds with Irish policy, such as when Senator Kennedy called for a total withdrawal of British troops from Northern Ireland. Dublin would only begin to effectively cooperate with Congressional allies in 1973 after Liam Cosgrave replaced Jack Lynch as taoiseach.[1]

A number of general observations about Anglo-Irish relations and the early years of the Troubles can be drawn from this study. While Anglo-Irish relations were very complex in the decades that followed, the general outline of the relationship between the Irish and British governments was set during the period under consideration in this book. Once Heath dissolved Stormont he accepted the general ideas put forward by Lynch that Northern Ireland needed some type of power-sharing government and that Dublin had to play a role in the North.[2] In 1973 the British government published a white paper entitled "Northern Ireland Constitutional Proposals" outlining its plan to reestablish an assembly in the province that would have a power-sharing executive and links to Dublin in a Council of Ireland. The details were worked out by the Northern Irish parties along with Irish and British officials at Sunningdale in December 1973. While the executive collapsed in 1974 due to the opposition of a majority of unionists the general idea was not abandoned.[3] The Anglo-Irish Agreement of 1985 revived and codified the idea of an "Irish dimension" in Northern Ireland with the creation of the Anglo-Irish Intergovernmental Conference that gave Dublin a voice in most aspects of government in the province.[4] The Good Friday Agreement of 1998, while a very complex compromise, had power-sharing and cross-border institutions at its heart.[5] Of course many things had changed politically and militarily in Northern Ireland since the early 1970s, and the US government took an active role in promoting the peace process that led up to Good Friday, but the two core concepts of power sharing and a role for Dublin in the North were ideas that were first raised in Anglo-Irish relations during the early years of the Troubles.

Another general conclusion is that Anglo-Irish relations were very much shaped by political actors and events in Northern Ireland that were outside of the control of either London or Dublin. The civil rights movement and the Stormont's response to this movement set the Troubles in motion in the first place. The revival of armed republicanism in general, and the creation of the PIRA in particular, shaped the nature of the Troubles and frequently caused the

British and Irish governments to be more reactive than proactive in dealing with Northern Ireland and with each other. Dublin and London could not even control the moderate nationalist and unionist political leaders in the North. The SDLP's decision to boycott Stormont and wage a campaign of civil disobedience as well as the Unionist Party's unwillingness to compromise with Northern nationalists limited the actions that the British and Irish governments could take as they sought a political solution to the Troubles. The lack of political progress tended to push security considerations, on which the two governments fundamentally disagreed, to the front of Anglo-Irish discussions.

The historical evidence also shows that domestic political considerations played a major role in Anglo-Irish relations during this period. Jack Lynch was continually under threat from the more republican leaning wing of Fianna Fáil and needed to be concerned with the sometimes emotional reaction of the Irish public in general to the dramatic events in Northern Ireland. Lynch's government was able to use public confrontation with London and diplomatic appeals to the United Nations and foreign governments to show that it was willing to stand up to the British and attempt to influence events in the North. These periodic diplomatic confrontations helped to keep Lynch in power while not forcing his government to abandon its basic policy of support for a peaceful compromise on Northern Ireland. For its part, the British government under both Wilson and Heath recognized that Lynch was London's best option as taoiseach and accepted some public criticism as the price that needed to be paid to keep Lynch in power. London's own domestic political considerations were largely confined to concerns about the unionist community in the North. As long as London was wedded to the idea of avoiding direct rule it had to try to protect the moderately pro-reform governments of James Chichester-Clark and Brian Faulkner from the more hardline unionists. British options were also constrained by the fact that even relatively moderate unionists like Chichester-Clark and Faulkner were resistant to dramatic political change and adamant that there should be no reconsideration of Northern Ireland's place in the United Kingdom.

On the whole, Anglo-Irish diplomacy in the early years of the Troubles failed to offer an immediate solution to the conflict. In fact, the violence of the Troubles steadily increased from 1969 to 1972 and the two communities in Northern Ireland became more polarized. However, relations between Dublin and London did help to avoid an even worse political crisis. The danger that a Fianna Fáil government might have become an apologist and enabler of armed republicanism in the North was a very real possibility as the events of the Arms Crisis demonstrate. Jack Lynch's firm policy of a peaceful response to the Troubles was appreciated by London and the fact that the two governments were in frequent communication with each other provided Lynch with political cover as his government alternately cooperated, or publicly argued, with the British government. Diplomacy was the primary peaceful method that Dublin could employ in an attempt to have an impact on Northern Ireland. In London, the British government eventually came to accept the fact that it would need the help of the Irish government in order to promote political moderation and achieve a peaceful settlement in the North.

The attempts at cooperation between the British and Irish governments in this period were an important break with the established historical pattern. Both Dublin and London had a history of unrealistic policies on Northern Ireland before the Troubles began. Although there was some attempt at cross-border détente starting with the government of Sean Lemass, Dublin had basically adhered to a sterile policy of condemning partition as an historical injustice perpetrated and perpetuated by Great Britain. In London, successive British governments had studiously ignored the internal affairs of Northern Ireland since partition. The outbreak of the Troubles in 1969 forced both the Irish and British governments to develop more realistic policies toward the complex situation in Northern Ireland. While Dublin still hoped for eventual Irish unification, Lynch's government accepted that this could not be accomplished without some type of settlement between the two communities in the North that acknowledged the reality of partition, while giving the nationalists a role in government. Rather than simply condemning Britain's role in partition, Ireland now embraced the idea of cooperation with Britain to facilitate a more just society in the North and to work toward the goal of Irish unity. The British government, which had long avoided becoming involved in Northern Ireland's internal affairs, could no longer ignore the province once the Troubles began. London was forced to assume the responsibility for security in the province and eventually accept the necessity of a period of direct rule. Anxious to find a peaceful solution to the conflict, London began to diplomatically engage with Dublin regarding the future of the North. While the two governments disagreed on many particular issues relating to Northern Ireland during the first years of the Troubles, and in the many violent years that followed, Dublin and London were able to set the pattern of attempting to cooperate with each other in order to help the people of Northern Ireland achieve a durable peace. This diplomatic cooperation between Dublin and London, combined with a new willingness on the part of the US government to involve itself in the conflict, was vital to the peace process of the 1990s that effectively ended the Troubles.

Notes

Introduction

1 Henry Patterson, *Ireland since 1939: The Persistence of Conflict* (New York, 2006), 193–94.

2 J. Bowyer Bell, *The Irish Troubles: A Generation of Violence, 1967–1992* (New York, 1993), 8, 64–66; Richard English, *Armed Struggle: The History of the IRA* (New York, 2003), 98; Simon Prince, *Northern Ireland's '68: Civil Rights, Global Revolt and the Origins of the Troubles* (Dublin, 2007), 5.

3 Niall Ó Dochartaigh, *From Civil Rights of Armalites: Derry and the Birth of the Irish Troubles* (Cork, 1997), 20–21.

4 Bell, *The Irish Troubles*, 76–80; Patterson, *Ireland since 1939*, 207.

5 Bell, *The Irish Troubles*, 4, 75–76, 91–92; Peter Rose, *How the Troubles Came to Northern Ireland* (New York, 2001), 171; Anthony Craig, *Crisis of Confidence: Anglo-Irish Relations in the Early Troubles, 1966–1974* (Dublin, 2010), 40–42.

6 Catherine O'Donnell, *Fianna Fáil, Irish Republicanism and the Northern Ireland Troubles, 1968–2005* (Dublin, 2007), 4–9, 12–13.

7 Dermot Keogh, *Jack Lynch: A Biography* (Dublin, 2008), 135–37.

8 Keogh, *Jack Lynch*, 123, 147–48; John Walsh, *Patrick Hillery: The Official Biography* (Dublin, 2009), 167–68; Bell, *The Irish Troubles*, 158.

9 Keogh, *Jack Lynch*, 141–46, 149–59.

10 Walsh, *Patrick Hillery*, 3–4; Craig, *Crisis of Confidence*, 47–48.

11 Craig, *Crisis of Confidence*, 20–22, 28–29.

12 Craig, *Crisis of Confidence*, 39–40; Keogh, *Jack Lynch*, 139.

13 Stephen Kelly, *Fianna Fáil, Partition and Northern Ireland, 1926–1971* (Dublin, 2013), 297.

14 Walsh, *Patrick Hillery*, 172.

Chapter 1

1 Bell, *The Irish Troubles*, 100–06; O Dochartaigh, *From Civil Rights to Armalites*, 119–23; Patterson, *Ireland since 1939*, 211–13.

2 Keogh, *Jack Lynch*, 166–70, 174; Walsh, *Patrick Hillery*, 173; Pádraig Faulkner, *As I Saw It: Reviewing Over 30 Years of Fianna Fáil and Irish Politics* (Dublin, 2003), 89;

Michael Kennedy, *Division and Consensus: The Politics of Cross Border Relations, 1925–69* (Dublin, 2000), 336–42.

3   NAI, DT 2000/6/657, August 13, 1969, "Statement by the Taoiseach."

4   NACP, RG 59, 1967–69, POL 23–8 UK, 1/1/67, Box 2569, August 14, 1969, John Moore to Secretary of State.

5   Kennedy, *Division and Consensus*, 338–39; Kelly, *Fianna Fáil, Partition and Northern Ireland*, 302–03; Keogh, *Jack Lynch*, 170; Walsh, *Patrick Hillery*, 174; Craig, *Crisis of Confidence*, 50.

6   NAI, DT 2000/5/38, August 14, 1969, Kevin Rush to Hugh McCann, "Demarche to Lord Chalfont, Minister of State, Foreign and Commonwealth Office regarding Northern Ireland."

7   NAI, DFA 2000/5/33, August 14, 1969, "Announcement issued by Government Information Bureau on the Taoiseach's instructions."

8   TNA, PRO, FCO 33/757, 122626, August 14, 1969, Sir Andrew Gilchrist to the FCO.

9   NAI, DT 2000/5/38, August 15, 1969, "Report of Discussion at the Foreign and Commonwealth Office, London … concerning Northern Ireland."

10 TNA, PRO, CJ 4/122658, August 19, 1969, "Northern Ireland, Note of a Meeting held at 10 Downing Street."

11 NAI, DFA 2000/14/465, August 16, 1969, Irish Embassy, Washington to the DEA, "Northern Ireland: Interview with Acting Secretary of State Johnson"; NACP, RG 59, 1967–69, POL 23–8 UK, 1/1/70, Box 2569, August 15, 1969, Charge d'affaires, Irish Embassy, Washington to Secretary of State.

12 NAI, DFA 2000/14/465, August 26, 1969, Secretary of State to Irish Charge d'affaires, Washington.

13 NAI, DFA 2000/14/465, August 28, 1969, Sean OhEideain to Sean Ronan.

14 NACP, RG 59, 1967–69, POL 23–8 UK, 1/1/67, Box 2569, August 21, 1969, US Embassy, London to Secretary of State.

15 TNA, PRO, FCO 33/757, 122626, August 16, 1969, Sir Andrew Gilchrist to FCO.

16 TNA, PRO, FCO 33/757, 122626, August 17, 1969, Sir Andrew Gilchrist to FCO.

17 Bell, *The Irish Troubles*, 113; NAI, DT 2000/6/658, August 20, 1969, Secret Memorandum by Hugh McCann.

18 TNA, PRO, FCO 33/757, 122626, August 22, 1969, Sir Andrew Gilchrist to FCO.

19 TNA, PRO, FCO 33/766, 122689, August 22, 1969, "Issued on behalf of the Government of Ireland by the Department of External Affairs: The Situation in the North of Ireland."

20 NAI, DT 2000/6/657, August 16, 1969, Memorandum for the Information of the Government.

21 NAI, DT 2000/6/659, August 17, 1969, Text of a Letter from Con Cremin to Jaime de Pinies.

22 NAI, DFA 2000/5/28, August 18, 1969, "Implementation of Government decisions: External Affairs."

23 TNA, PRO, FCO 33/772, 122689, August 18, 1969 "Northern Ireland: Security Council" Memorandum by Anne W. Warburton, UN (Political) Department, FCO.

24 TNA, PRO, FCO 33/772, 122689, August 18, 1969, Lord Caradon to FCO.

25 TNA, PRO, FCO 33/722, 122689, August 19, 1969, Michael Stewart to UK Mission, to the UN.

26 NACP, RG 59, 1967–69, POL 23–8 UK, 1/1/67, Box 2569, August 18, 1969, US Mission at UN to Secretary of State.

27 NAI, DT 2000/6/658, August 20, 1969, "Secret" Memorandum by Hugh McCann.

28 NACP, RG 59, 1967–69, POL 23–8 UK, 1/1/67, Box 2569, August 17, 1969, State Department to US Mission at UN.

29 TNA, PRO, FCO 33/772, 122689, August 18, 1969, Michael Stewart to William Rogers.

30 NACP, RG 59, 1967–69, POL 23–8 UK, 1/1/67, Box 2569, August 18, 1969, Rogers to US Mission at UN.

31 NAI, DT 2000/6/659, August 25, 1969, Con Cremin to Sean Ronan, DEA.

32 NACP, RG 59, 1967–69, POL 23–8 UK, Box 2569, August 19, 1969, US Mission at UN to Secretary of State and Rogers' reply to US Mission.

33 TNA, PRO, FCO 33/773, 122689, August 20, 1969, "United Nations Security Council: Provisional Verbatim Record of the Fifteenth Hundred and Third Meeting."

34 NAI, DT 2000/6/658, August 21, 1969, Record of Telephone call from Con Cremin to unnamed official in Dublin.

35 NACP, RG 59, 1967–69, POL 7 IRE, Box 2222, August 23, 1969, US Embassy, Dublin, to Secretary of State.

36 NAI, DT 2000/6/658, August 21, 1969, Statement issued by the Government Information Bureau on behalf of the Irish Government.

37 NACP, RG 59, 1967–69, POL 23–8 UK, 1/1/67, Box 2654, August 21, 1969, US Embassy, London (Mr. Cleveland) to Secretary of State.

38 NAI, DT 2000/6/659, August 26, 1969, Patrick Hillery to Jack Lynch.

39 NAI, DT 2000/6/659, September 5, 1969, Irish Permanent Representative to the UN (Con Cremin) to Secretary General U Thant.

40 TNA, PRO, FCO 33/773, 122689, September 9, 1969, Lord Caradon, UK Mission, to the UN, to FCO.

41 TNA, PRO, FCO 33/758, 122626, September 10, 1969, Michael Stewart to UK Embassy, Dublin.

42 TNA, PRO, FCO 33/773, 122689, September 11, 1969, Andrew Gilchrist, UK Embassy, Dublin, to FCO.

43 TNA, PRO, FCO 33/773, 122689, September 12, 1969, Andrew Gilchrist, UK Embassy, Dublin, to FCO.

44 TNA, PRO, FCO 33/774, 122689, September 16, 1969, Michael Stewart to UK Mission, to the UN.

45 TNA, PRO, FCO 33/774, 122689, September 16, 1969, Lord Caradon, UK Mission to UN, to FCO.

46 NAI, DT 2000/6/661, September 16, 1969, Memorandum of a Meeting at the Irish Mission to the UN.

47 NAI, DT 2000/6/661, September 1969, "Extract from Provisional Summary Record of General Committee Meeting of 17 September 1969"; NAI, DT 2000/6/661, September 1969, "Request for inclusion of the item 'The Situation in the North of Ireland' in the agenda of the twenty-fourth session of the General Assembly."

48 NAI, DT 2000/6/661, September 23, 1969, Patrick Hillery to Jack Lynch.

49 TNA, PRO, CAB 128/44, CC (69) 45th Conclusions, September 25, 1969.

50 TNA, PRO, FCO 33/758, 122626, September 25, 1969, Michael Stewart to UK Mission, to the UN.

51 Walsh, *Patrick Hillery*, 199, quoting Hillery's Private Papers.

52 NACP, RG 59, 1967–69, POL IRE-US, 1/1/67, Box 2223, September 22, 1969, "Memorandum of a Conversation" between William Rogers and Patrick Hillery.

53 Kennedy, *Division and Consensus*, 355–58; Walsh, *Patrick Hillery*, 199–200; Craig, *Crisis of Confidence*, 63.

54 Kennedy, *Division and Consensus*, 358.

55 Kennedy, "'This Tragic and Most Intractable Problem': The Reaction of the Department of External Affairs to the Outbreak if the Troubles in Northern Ireland," *Irish Studies in International Affairs* (Volume 12, pp. 87–95, 2001), 89–90.

56 Craig, *Crisis of Confidence*, 51–52.

57 Craig, *Crisis of Confidence*, 63.

58 Bell, *The Irish Troubles*, 118.

59 Ronan Fanning, "Playing it Cool: The Response of the British and Irish Governments to the Crisis in Northern Ireland, 1968–9," *Irish Studies in International Affairs* (Volume 12, pp. 57–85, 2001), 77–78.

60 Walsh, *Patrick Hillery*, 178, 185–89.

61 Walsh, *Patrick Hillery*, 200–01.

62 Keogh, *Jack Lynch*, 191–92.

63 Kennedy, *Division and Consensus*, 336.

64 Craig, *Crisis of Confidence*, 49.

65 Fanning "Playing it cool ..." 57.

66 O'Donnell, *Fianna Fáil, Irish Republicanism and the Northern Ireland Troubles*, 28.

67 Keogh, *Jack Lynch*, 475–76.

68 Keogh, *Jack Lynch*, 170

69 Walsh, *Patrick Hillery*, 174–76.

Chapter 2

1   TNA, PRO, FCO 33/758, 122626, September 17, 1969, Andrew Gilchrist, UK
    Embassy Dublin, to FCO.
2   Craig, *Crisis of Confidence*, 44–45.
3   TNA, PRO, FCO 33/771, 122689, September 18, 1969, MISC 244 (69) 4th Meeting:
    Cabinet: Northern Ireland.
4   NAI, DT 2001/6/514, September 20, 1969, "Speech by Jack Lynch at Tralee."
5   Keogh, *Jack Lynch*, 201–05; Craig, *Crisis of Confidence*, 62.
6   TNA, PRO, FCO 33/767, 122689, September 22, 1969, Sir Andrew Gilchrist,
    "Options Available: Ireland."
7   TNA, PRO, FCO 33/759, 122626, September 24, 1969, "Northern Ireland: Relations
    with the Irish Republic."
8   TNA, PRO, FCO 33/759, 122626, September 23, 1969, James Callaghan to Harold
    Wilson "Northern Ireland."
9   TNA, PRO, FCO 33/758, 122626, September 25, 1969, Michael Stewart, FCO to Sir
    Andrew Gilchrist, UK Embassy, Dublin.
10 TNA, PRO, FCO 33/759, 122626, November 10, 1969, Michael Stewart, FCO to Sir
    Andrew Gilchrist, UK Embassy, Dublin.
11 TNA, PRO, FCO 33/759, 122626, November 19, 1969, Sir Andrew Gilchrist, UK
    Embassy, Dublin, to FCO.
12 Craig, *Crisis of Confidence*, 64.
13 Kelly, *Fianna Fáil, Partition, and the Northern Ireland Troubles*, 311.
14 NAI, DFA 2000/5/12, October 3, 1969, Eamonn Gallagher to Sean Ronan, "Policy
    questions raised by the embassy in London."
15 http://www.oireachtas.ie/parliament, Parliamentary Debates, Dáil Éireann,
    October 22, 1969, Volume 241, No. 9 "Private Business: Situation in the Six
    Counties"; Dáil Éireann Debate, 22 October 1969, Volume 241, No. 10 "Situation in
    the Six Counties: Motion (Resumed.)
16 TNA, PRO, FCO 33/759, 122626, October 24, 1969, Andrew Gilchrist, UK
    Embassy, Dublin, to Edward Peck, FCO.
17 TNA, PRO, CJ 3/100, 122700, November 5, 1969, Andrew Gilchrist, UK Embassy
    Dublin, to FCO.
18 TNA, PRO, FCO 33/760, 122626, November 7, 1969, "Anglo-Irish Talks,"
    Memorandum by M. MacGlaghan.
19 TNA, PRO, FCO 33/759, 122626, November 19, 1969, Andrew Gilchrist, UK
    Embassy, Dublin, to FCO.
20 NAI, DFA 2000/5/12, November 28, 1969, "Memorandum for the information of
    the Government: Policy in Relation to Northern Ireland" prepared by the DEA.

21 TNA, PRO, FCO 33/760, 122626, December 8, 1969, HT. Morgan, Western European Department, FCO to Edward Peck, "Irish Republic: 'Talks in the margin' with Dr. Hillery."

22 Walsh, *Patrick Hillery*, 204.

23 TNA, PRO, FCO 33/760, 122626, December 10, 1969, "Record of a Conversation between the Chancellor of the Duchy of Lancaster and the Minister for External Affairs of the Irish Republic ..."; NAI, DT 2000/6/662, December 12, 1969, Report by J.G. Molloy of meeting between Patrick Hillery and George Thomson on December 10, 1969.

24 NAI, DT 2001/6/513, February 20, 1970, "Report of discussion concerning the North of Ireland situation between the Minister for External Affairs and the Chancellor of the Duchy of Lancaster."

25 NAI, DFA 2001/43/1296, March 3, 1970, "Secret" Record of talks between Kelvin White, Sean Ronan, Eamonn Gallagher on March 2 and 3, 1970.

26 NAI, DFA 2001/43/1407, March 6, 1970, Donal O'Sullivan, Irish Embassy, London to Hugh McCann, DEA.

27 TNA, PRO, PREM 13/3276, 122658, March 18, 1970, "Prime Minister: Relations with the Irish Republic."

28 NAI, DFA 2001/43/1407, March 25, 1970, "Report of Discussion about the North of Ireland at the Foreign and Commonwealth Office" by Kevin Rush.

29 Cain.ulst.ac.uk, CAIN Web Service, A Chronology of the Conflict, 1970, Sunday March 29, 1970, and Tuesday March 31, 1970, and Wednesday April 1, 1970.

30 Cain.ulst.ac.uk, CAIN Web Service, A Chronology of the Conflict, 1970, Thursday April 16, 1970.

31 NAI, DFA 2001/43/1407, April 29, 1970, "Report of Discussion about the North of Ireland at the Foreign and Commonwealth Office on 27 April 1970" by Kevin Rush

32 NAI, DFA 2000/5/38, May 4, 1970, "Secret" DEA Memo.

33 TNA, PRO, CAB 170/98, 122689, May 4, 1970, John Peck, UK Embassy, Dublin, to FCO.

34 TNA, PRO, CJ 4/23, 122658, May 6, 1970, "Luncheon at the Irish Embassy, London."

35 NACP, RG 59, 1970–73, POL 23–9 UK, 1/1/70, Box 2654, May 15, 1970, "Department of State Memorandum of Conversation"; NACP RG 59, 1970–73, POL 23–9 UK, 1/1/70, May 22, 1970, "Department of State Memorandum of Conversation."

36 TNA, PRO, FCO 33/1081, 122719, June 11, 1970, John Peck, UK Embassy, Dublin, to W.K.K. White, FCO.

37 Craig, *Crisis of Confidence*, 50–51, 67; Bell, *The Irish Troubles*, 159; English, *Armed Struggle*, 119.

38 Eunan O'Halpin, *Defending Ireland: The Irish State and Its Enemies since 1922* (New York, 1999), 306–08; Bell, *The Irish Troubles*, 159.

39 Keogh, *Jack Lynch*, 257–65; Walsh, *Patrick Hillery*, 218–20, 223–25; Patterson, *Ireland since 1939*, 175.

40 Justin O'Brien, *The Arms Trial* (Dublin, 2000) XVI, 216; Diarmaid Ferriter, *The Transformation of Ireland* (New York, 2004), 688–89.

41 O'Donnell, *Fianna Fáil, Irish Republicanism and the Northern Ireland Troubles*, 24–5.

42 Keogh, *Jack Lynch*, 257, 476–77.

43 Walsh, *Patrick Hillery*, 214–16.

44 Craig, *Crisis of Confidence*, 67–68, 71.

45 Kelly, *Fianna Fáil, Partition and Northern Ireland*, 315.

46 Faulkner, *As I Saw It*, 92–94, 98–100.

47 TNA, PRO, FCO 33/759, 122626, November 10, 1969, Andrew Gilchrist, UK Embassy, Dublin, to FCO.

48 TNA, PRO, CJ 4/23, 122658, May 6, 1970, C.C.C. Tickell, Office of the Chancellor of the Duchy of Lancaster to P.J.S. Moon, 10 Downing Street.

49 TNA, PRO, CAB 128/45, CC (70) 21st Conclusions, May 7, 1970.

50 TNA, PRO, CJ 4/23, 122658, May 8, 1970, David Blatherwick, UK Embassy Dublin, to Maureen McGlashen, Western European Department, FCO.

51 TNA, PRO, FCO 33/1206, 122689, May 28, 1970, John Peck, UK Embassy, Dublin, to Michael Stewart, FCO.

52 www.oireachtas.ie/parliament, Parliamentary Debates, Dáil Éireann, Volume 246, May 14, 1970, Confidence in Government: Motion (Resumed) Jack Lynch.

53 TNA, PRO, CJ 4/23, 122658, May 19, 1970, W.K.K. White to Edward Peck.

54 NAI, DFA 2001/43/1407, May 25, 1970, "Notes for the Minister in regard to six Parliamentary Questions on Dr. O'Sullivan's visit to the Foreign and Commonwealth Office on 20th May."

55 NAI, DFA 2001/14/1407, May 25, 1970, "Note on press reaction to Ambassador O'Sullivan's call to the Foreign and Commonwealth Office on 20th May"

56 TNA, PRO, CJ 4/23, 122658, May 26, 1970, Ronnie Burroughs, UK Representative in Belfast to FCO.

57 TNA, PRO, CJ 4/23, 122658, May 27, 1970, Memorandum to Mr. Cairncross, Home Office.

58 TNA, PRO, FCO 33/1206, 122689, May 27, 1970, John Peck, UK Embassy, Dublin, to FCO.

59 TNA PRO CJ 4/23, 122658, May 29, 1970 Home Office Memorandum to the Secretary of State: "The Affair of the Dublin Intelligence officers in Northern Ireland."

Chapter 3

1 Bell, *The Irish Troubles*, 175.
2 Cain.ulst.ac.uk, CAIN Web Service, Sutton Index of Deaths, Chronological List of Deaths 1969 and Chronological List of Deaths 1970.
3 NAI, DFA 2000/5/33, June 23, 1970, "Note" reporting telephone call from Ambassador John Peck.
4 NAI, DFA 2002/19/369, June 18, 1970, "Inter-Departmental Unit on the North of Ireland: Minutes of the First Meeting"
5 TNA, PRO, CJ 3/24, June 30, 1970, John Peck to Alec Douglas-Home.
6 Thomas Hennessy, *Evolution of the Troubles, 1970–72* (Dublin, 2007), 31–37, and cain.ulst.ac.uk, CAIN We Service, A Chronology of the Conflict, 1970: June 26, 1970, June 27, 1970, and June 28, 1970.
7 Hennessy, *Evolution of the Troubles*, 343.
8 English, Armed Struggle, 105–08.
9 Walsh, *Patrick Hillery*, 256.
10 NAI, DFA 2001/43/1296, June 26, 1970, "Report of discussion about the North of Ireland at the FCO."
11 TNA, CJ 4/23, 122658, June 29, 1970, "Northern Ireland: Conversation with the Ambassador of the Irish Republic, June 27, 1970."
12 NAI, DT 2000/5/38, June 28, 1970, "Bernadette Devlin: Taoiseach's Statement."
13 TNA, PRO, FCO 33/1610, June 29, 1970, "Record of a Conversation between the Foreign and Commonwealth Secretary and the Minister for External Affairs of the Republic of Ireland."
14 Geoffrey Warner, "Falls Road Curfew Revisited," *Irish Studies Review* (Volume 14, pp. 325–42, 2006), 329–30 .
15 Tim Pat Coogan, *The IRA: A History* (Niwot, Colorado, 1994), 262; Bell, *The Irish Troubles*, 178–79; Thomas Hennessey, *A History of Northern Ireland: 1920–1996* (Dublin, 1997), 174–75; Warner "Falls Road Curfew Revisited," 326–27
16 Hennessey, *A History of Northern Ireland*, 175; Bell, *The Irish Troubles*, 179; Coogan, *The IRA*, 262; Patterson, *Ireland since 1939*, 218; David McKittrick and David McVea, *Making Sense of the Troubles: The Story of the Conflict in Northern Ireland* (Chicago, 2002), 61–62; Ed Maloney, *A Secret History of the IRA* (New York, 2002), 90–91 .
17 Warner, "Falls Road Curfew Revisited," 337.
18 Walsh, *Patrick Hillery*, 259–60; English, *Armed Struggle*, 136
19 www.oireachtas.ie/parliament, Parliamentary Debates, Dáil Éireann—Volume 248, 7 July 1970—Private Notice Questions—Northern Situation.
20 NAI, DT 2001/6/516, July 6, 1970, "Text of Press Conference given by Dr. Patrick Hillery."

21 Cain.ulst.ac.uk, CAIN Web Service, PRONI Records on CAIN: PRONI, Public Records, CAB/9/U/6/1, July 7, 1970, Statement issued by the Prime Minister of Northern Ireland.

22 NAI, DFA 2000/5/38, July 7, 1970, Donal O'Sullivan to Department of Foreign Affairs.

23 TNA, PRO, CAB 128/47 (part 1) July 7, 1970, CM (70) 4th Conclusions.

24 NAI, DFA 2001/43/1351, July 7, 1970, Photocopy of House of Commons Debate.

25 TNA, PRO, CJ 3/24 122700, July 7, 1970, John Peck, UK Embassy, Dublin, to FCO.

26 TNA, PRO, CJ 3/24 122700, July 7, 1970, Ronnie Burroughs, UK Representative, Belfast, to FCO.

27 NAI, DFA 2003/17/296, July 8, 1970, "Meeting between Dr. P.J. Hillery ... and Sir Alec Douglas-Home."

28 NAI, DT 2001/6/516, July 8, 1970, "Text of Press Conference by Dr. Patrick Hillery ..."

29 NAI, DFA 2001/43/1351, July 8, 1970, "Note" by Hugh McCann.

30 NACP, RG 59, 1970–73, POL 23–9 UK, 1/1/70, Box 2654, July 16, 1970, John Moore, US Embassy, Dublin, to Secretary of State.

31 TNA, PRO, FCO 33/1214/122751, July 9, 1970, John Peck, UK Embassy, Dublin, to FCO.

32 Cain.ulst.ac.uk, CAIN Web Service, A Chronology of the Conflict, 1970, July 13, 1970.

33 TNA, PRO, FCO 33/1209, 122689, July 6, 1970, Note: "Confidential: Ireland" by Edward Peck, FCO.

34 NAI, DFA 2000/5/5, July 5, 1970, "Secret" DEA Memorandum.

35 NAI, DT 2001/6/516, July 6, 1970, "Text of interview with the Minister of External Affairs Dr. Patrick Hillery ... on July 6, 1970."

36 NAI, DFA 2000/5/38, July 7, 1970, "Note" Donal O'Sullivan, Irish Embassy, London, to DEA.

37 NAI, DFA 2003/17/304, July 7, 1970, Jack Lynch to Edward Heath.

38 NAI, DFA 2003/17/296, July 8, 1970, "Meeting Dr. P.J. Hillery ... and Sir Alec Douglas-Home."

39 TNA, PRO, CJ 3/24, 22700, July 8, 1970, "Record of a meeting between the Chancellor of the Duchy of Lancaster and the Foreign Minister of the Irish Republic."

40 NAI, DT 2001/6/516, July 8, 1970, "Text of Press Conference given by Dr. Patrick Hillery."

41 TNA, PRO, FCO 33/1214, 122751, July 9, 1970, John Peck, UK Embassy, Dublin, to FCO.

42 NACP, RG 59 1970–73, POL 23–9 UK, 1/1/70, Box 2654, July 6, 1970, US Embassy, Dublin, to the Secretary of State.

43 NA, PRO, CJ 3/24, 122700, July 7, 1970, Denis Greenhill to Edward Peck.

44 NAI, DFA 2003/17/304, July 11, 1970, Edward Heath to Jack Lynch.

45 NAI, DFA 2003/17/304, July 15, 1970, Edward Heath to Jack Lynch.

46 TNA, PRO, FCO 33/1214, 122751, July 16, 1970, John Peck, UK Embassy, Dublin, to J.K. Drinkall, FCO.

47 NAI, DT 2001/6/550, July 10, 1970, "Department of Justice: Note of interview between the Minister for Justice and the British Ambassador."

48 www.oireachtas.ie/parliament, Parliamentary Debates, Dáil Éireann, Volume 248, Number 7, July 14, 1970, 'Ceisteanna—Questions. Oral Answers–Border Violations.

49 TNA, PRO, FCO 33/1212, 122689, July 29, 1970, J.K. Drinkall, FCO, to Thomas Brimelow, FCO.

50 NAI, DFA 2001/43/1296, July 30, 1970, Record of Meeting in London.

51 NAI, DT 2001/6/517, July 31, 1970, Edward Heath to Jack Lynch.

52 TNA, PRO, CJ 3/24, 122700, August 11, 1970, "Text of a message from the Taoiseach, Mr. John Lynch, T.D. to the Prime Minister, The Right Honorable Edward Heath."

53 TNA, PRO, CJ 3/24, 122700, August 26, 1970, I. McCluney, FCO, to P.J.S. Moon, Esq., 10 Downing Street.

54 NAI, DT 2001/6/517, August 31, 1970, Edward Heath to Jack Lynch via the UK Embassy in Dublin.

55 Jeremy Smith "'Walking a Real Tight-Rope of Difficulties' Sir Edward Heath and the Search for Stability in Northern Ireland, June 1970–March 1971," *Twentieth Century British History* (Volume 18, pp. 219–53, 2007), 233–34.

56 Sean Farren, *The SDLP: The Struggle for Agreement in Northern Ireland, 1970–2000* (Dublin, 2010), 29–30, 38.

57 Farren, *SDLP*, 34–35.

58 Hennessey, *Evolution of the Troubles*, 21.

59 Kelly, *Fianna Fáil, Partition and Northern Ireland*, 325–30.

60 NAI, DT 2001/6/517, September 7, 1970, "Memorandum for the Information of the Government … Policy in Relation to Northern Ireland."

61 TNA, CJ 3/24, 122700, September 1970 (exact date unknown) "Secretary of State's Visit to the XXVth Session of the United Nations General Assembly … Meeting with … Dr. Patrick Hillery … Steering Brief."

62 NAI, DT 2001/6/517, September 22, 1970, Edward Heath to Jack Lynch.

63 NAI, DFA 2003/17/304, September 23, 1970, "Summary of remarks made by Taoiseach to Mr. R.W. Piper, British Charge d'affaires."

64 NAI, DFA 2003/17/345, September 23, 1970, Sean Ronan, DEA, to Peter Berry, Department of Justice.

65 TNA, PRO, FCO 33/1209, 122689, September 24, 1970, Ronnie Burroughs, UK Representative, Belfast, to Ministry of Defence and John Peck, UK Embassy, Dublin.

66 NAI, DFA 2001/43/1296, October 5, 1970, "Meeting in London on 5th October 1970," and TNA, PRO FCO 33/1212, 122689, October 7, 1970, Stewart Crawford, FCO, to John Peck, UK Embassy, Dublin, "Meeting with the Irish Ambassador, October 5, 1970."

67 NAI, DT 2001/6/550, October 14, 1970, Sean Ronan to An Roinn Dii agus Cirt.

68 TNA, PRO, FCO 33/1209, 122689, October 22, 1970, Ronnie Burroughs, UK Representative, Belfast, to the Home Office and TNA, PRO, FCO 33/1209, 122689, October 27, 1970, John Peck, UK Embassy, Dublin, to the FCO.

69 NACP, RG 59, 1970–73, POL IRE-US, 10/8/70, Box 2384, September 17, 1970, John Moore, US Embassy, Dublin, to State Department, "US Policy Assessment: Ireland."

70 NACP, RG 59, 1970–73, POL UK-US, Box 2657, October 8, 1970, John Moore, US Embassy, Dublin, to State Department, "Report on Exchange of views between the President and Taoiseach at Dublin Castle, Monday October 5."

71 NACP, RG 59, 1970–73, POL IRE-US, 10/8/70, Box 2384, October 8, 1970, US Embassy, Dublin, to State Department, "Summary of Discussion ... between Secretary Rogers and Minister for External Affairs Dr. Hillery at Dublin Castle on October 5, 1970."

72 NAI, DFA 2003/17/296, date uncertain, "Meeting between the Taoiseach Mr. John Lynch T.D. and the British Prime Minister Mr. Edward Heath, M.P., New York, October 21, 1970."

73 TNA, PRO, FCO 33/1210, 122751, October 30, 1970, Alec Douglas-Home, FCO, to UK Embassy, Dublin.

74 NAI, DT 2001/6/517, October 23, 1970, "Prime Minister's Press Conference in New York."

75 NAI, DT 2001/6/517, October 22, 1970, "Text of Taoiseach's Address to the General Assembly of the United Nations."

76 Keogh, *Jack Lynch*, 265, 267–70.

77 TNA, PRO, FCO 33/1207, October 23, 1970, Alec Douglas-Home, FCO, to UK Embassy, Dublin, and NAI, DT 2001/6/517, October 26, 1970, "Note: Situation in the Six Counties" by Eamonn Gallagher.

78 TNA, PRO, FCO 33/1207, 122689, October 27, 1970, John Peck, UK Embassy, Dublin, to FCO.

79 www.oireachtas.ie/parliament, Parliamentary Debates, Dáil Éireann, Volume 249, Number 1, October 28, 1970, "Ceisteanna—Questions. Oral Answers. Discussion with British Prime Minister."

80 TNA, PRO, FCO 33/1212, 122689, October 30, 1970, "Record of a Meeting with Dr. Hillery in the Department of External Affairs" by John Peck.

81 TNA, CJ 3/101, 122700, November 3, 1970, "Meeting with the Taoiseach" by John Peck.

82 Keogh, *Jack Lynch*, 270.

83 TNA, PRO, CJ 4/46, 122658, October 29, 1970, P.J. Woodfield, Northern Ireland Department, to Mr. Angle, Home Office; TNA, PRO, CJ 4/46, 122658, October 30, 1970, "Discussion with the Prime Minister of Northern Ireland at Claridges, Friday 30th October."

84 TNA, PRO, FCO 33/1209, 122689, November 25, 1970, Stewart Crawford, FCO, to Philip Woodfield, Home Office.

85 NACP, RG 59, 1970–73, POL 32, IRE, BOX 2384, November 12, 1970, US Embassy, Dublin, to Secretary of State.

86 www.oireachtas.ie/parliament, Parliamentary Debates, Dáil Éireann, Volume 248, Number 8, November 12, 1970, "Adjournment Debate: Boarding of Irish Vessels."

87 NAI, DFA 2002/19/384, November 13, 1970, Donal O'Sullivan, Irish Embassy, London, to Hugh McCann, DEA.

88 www.oireachtas.ie/parliament, Parliamentary Debates, Dáil Éireann, Volume 249, Number 9, 17 November 1970, "Ceisteanna—Questions. Oral Answers—Boarding of Irish Ships."

89 TNA, PRO, CJ 3/101, 122700, November 19, 1970, John Peck, UK Embassy, Dublin, to Kelvin White, FCO.

90 TNA, PRO, CJ 3/101, 122700, 20 November 1970, Nicholas Barrington, FCO to A.R.M. Jaffray, Ministry of Defence; TNA PRO, CJ 3/101, 122700, 23 November 1970, P.L. Gregson, 10 Downing Street, to Nicholas Barrington, FCO.

91 TNA, PRO, CJ 3/101, 122700, November 26, 1970, British Embassy, Dublin, "Naval Incidents."

92 NAI, DFA 2001/43/1296, date uncertain, "Brief for Meeting of December 4, 1970."

93 NAI, DFA 2001/43/1296, December 4, 1970, "Meeting in London on December 4, 1970."

94 TNA, PRO, CJ 3/101, 122700, December 4, 1970, "Text of a Statement made by the Taoiseach and The Minister for Justice on December 4, 1970."

95 O'Halpin, *Defending Ireland*, 315, 325.

96 TNA, PRO, CJ 3/101, December 7, 1970, Kelvin White, FCO, to J.K. Drinkall and Stewart Crawford, FCO.

97 TNA, PRO, CJ 3/101, December 10, 1970, "Reference" by John Peck.

98 TNA, PRO, CJ 3/101, 122700, December 30, 1970, "Summary: The Threat of Internment." by the UK Embassy, Dublin.

99 English, *Armed Struggle*, 137.

100 Bell, *The Irish Troubles*, 187–88.

101   Hennessey, *Evolution of the Troubles*, 85–86.

102   Walsh, *Patrick Hillery*, 237, 241–42; Keogh, *Jack Lynch*, 279–87; Kelly, *Fianna Fáil, Partition and Northern Ireland*, 330–34.

103   NAI, DT 2002/8/76, February 5, 1971, "Call on Dr. Hillery, Minister of External Affairs, by Mr. James Callaghan, M.P."

104   www.oireachtas.ie/parliament, Parliamentary Debates, Dáil Éireann, Volume 251, Number 7, February 10, 1971, "Northern Ireland Situation: Statement by Party Leaders."

105   www.oireachtas.ie/parliament, Parliamentary Debates, Dáil Éireann, Volume 251, Number 7, February 10, 1971, "Northern Ireland Situation: Statement by Party Leaders."

106   TNA, PRO, FCO 33/1610, 122676, February 23, 1971, Stewart Crawford, FCO, to John Peck, UK Embassy, Dublin, "Meeting with the Irish: February 16, 1971."

107   TNA, PRO, FCO 33/1609, 122676, February 24, 1971, W.K.K. White, FCO, to Private Secretary of Alec Douglas Home, "Republic of Ireland: Dr. Hillery's Visit."

108   NAI, DT 2002/18/76, date uncertain, "Minster's meeting with British Foreign Secretary 25/2/71."

109   Henry Patterson, *Ireland's Violent Frontier: The Border and Anglo-Irish Relations during the Troubles* (London, 2013), 25, 31–33.

110   TNA, PRO, FCO 33/1610, 122676, February 25, 1971, "Record of the Meeting between the Secretary of State for Foreign and Commonwealth Affairs and the Minister of External Affairs of the Irish Republic."

111   TNA, PRO, CJ 3/101, 122700, February 26, 1971, FCO to P.L. Gregson, 10 Downing Street.

112   Walsh, *Patrick Hillery*, 170–71.

113   NAI, DT 2002/8/440, March 10, 1971, Eamonn Gallagher, Department of Foreign Affairs, to Dan O'Sullivan, Department of the Taoiseach.

114   NACP, RG 59, 1970–73, POL 23–8 UK, 1/19/70, Box 2653, February 25, 1971, Department of State Intelligence Note, "UK: Continued Trouble in Northern Ireland."

115   NACP, RG 59, 1970–73, POL 7 IRE, 1/31/70, Box 2383, March 12, 1971, "Memorandum for the President—The Lynch Visit: Perspectives."

116   NAI, DT 2002/8/440, March 16, 1971, "Draft Notes on Conversation of the Taoiseach with President Nixon."

117   NAI, DT 2002/8/440, March 17, 1971, "Radio, TV Reports … An Interview with Prime Minister Lynch."

118   NAI, DT 2002/8/440, March 16, 1971, Irish Embassy, Washington, Decoded Message for Lynch from Hillery.

119   NAI, DFA 2003/17/304, March 17, 1971, Edward Heath to Jack Lynch.

Chapter 4

1 Bell, *The Irish Troubles*, 198–99.

2 Cain.ulst.ac.uk, CAIN Web Service, PRONI Records on Cain, "'Note of a Meeting in London on 16 March', Meeting between British Home Secretary and the Prime Minister of Northern Ireland" (March 16, 1971) (internment; law and order), [PRONI Public Records HA/32/3/6: 7pages].

3 Bell, *The Irish Troubles*, 199–200; Craig, *Crisis of Confidence*, 95.

4 Hennessy, *Evolution of the Troubles*, 89–91.

5 Hennessy, *Evolution of the Troubles*, 85.

6 Barry Flynn, *Soldiers of Folly: The IRA Border Campaign 1956–1962* (Dublin, 2009), 186–87

7 NAI, DT 2002/8/77, March 22, 1971, "Secret" Memorandum by Hugh McCann.

8 NAI, DFA 2002/19/528, March 22, 1971, Memorandum by Eamonn Gallagher.

9 NACP, RG 59, 1970–73, POL 15–1 UK, 1/1/71, Box 2652, April 5, 1971, Department of State: Intelligence Note: Bureau of Intelligence and Research.

10 TNA, PRO, CJ 4/38, 122658, April 3, 1971, "Record of a Conversation with the Taoiseach at Dromoland Castle" by John Peck.

11 www.oireachtas.ie/parliament, Parliamentary Debates, Dáil Éireann, Volume 252, Number 9, March 25, 1971, "Ceisteanna—Questions. Oral Answers—Northern Ireland Developments."

12 TNA, PRO, CJ 3/101, 122700, March 26, 1971, John Peck, UK Embassy, Dublin, to FCO: Lynch message for Heath.

13 TNA, PRO, CJ 4/66, 122658, April 20, 1971, "Prime Minister's Meeting with Mr. Faulkner."

14 Hennessy, *Evolution of the Troubles*, 94–95.

15 TNA, PRO, CJ 4/37, 122658, May 3, 1971, FCO Memorandum, "Meeting of Mr. Lynch and Mr. Faulkner and Visit of Mr. Lynch to London."

16 TNA, PRO, FCO 33/1481, 122719, May 10, 1971, John Peck, UK Embassy, Dublin, to FCO.

17 TNA, PRO, FCO 33/1468, 122689, May 27, 1971, John Peck, UK Embassy, Dublin, to Howard Smith, UK Representative to Northern Ireland, Belfast.

18 TNA, PRO, FCO 33/1481, 122719, June 8, 1971, Alec Douglas-Home, FCO, to UK Embassy, Dublin.

19 TNA, PRO, CJ 4/37, 122658, June 11, 1971, John Peck, UK Embassy, Dublin, to FCO.

20 TNA, PRO, FCO 33/1481, 122719, July 17, 1971, Alec Douglas-Home, FCO, to UK Embassy, Dublin; NAI, DFA 2003/17/345, July 17, 1971, UK Embassy, Dublin, to the DFA.

21 NAI, DT 2002/8/77, May 25, 1971, "Note on Events in Belfast May 20–22, 1971."

22 NAI, DT 2002/8/78, May 24, 1971, Record of Hugh McCann visit to John Peck on May 21, 1971.

23 Hennessy, *Evolution of the Troubles*, 99.

24 NAI, DT 2002/8/77, May 26, 1971, "Note" by Hugh McCann.

25 NAI, DFA 2001/43/1296, May 24, 1971, Record of a Meeting at the Foreign and Commonwealth Office.

26 NAI, DT 2002/8/78, June 2, 1971, Donal O'Sullivan, Irish Embassy, London, to Hugh McCann, DFA.

27 NAI, DFA 2002/19/384, June 15, 1971, C.V. Whelan, Irish Embassy, Dublin, to Sean Ronan, DFA.

28 NAI, DT 2002/8/78, June 16, 1971, CV. Whelan, Irish Embassy, Dublin, to Secretary DFA, "attention … Mr. Eamonn Gallagher."

29 NAI, DT 2002/8/78, June 21, 1971, "Memorandum Prepared for the Minister of Foreign Affairs—Secret."

30 NAI, DFA 2001/43/1356, July 11, 1971 "Address by the Taoiseach … at the Garden of Remembrance Ceremony, Sunday, the July 11, 1971."

31 TNA, PRO, FCO 33/1606, 122676, July 12, 1971, Mr. Williams, UK Embassy, Dublin, to FCO.

32 TNA, PRO, FCO 33/1606, 122676, July 14, 1917, Mr. Williams, UK Embassy, Dublin, to FCO.

33 TNA, PRO, FCO 33/1606, 122676, July 21, 1971, John Peck, UK Embassy, Dublin, to FCO.

34 Cain.ulst.ac.uk, CAIN Web Service, A Chronology of the Conflict—1971—Thursday July 8, 1971.

35 Ó Dochartaigh, *From Civil Rights to Armalites*, 269–71.

36 Hennessy, *Evolution of the Troubles*, 104–07.

37 NAI, DT 2002/8/416, July 15, 1971, Minutes of the 14th Meeting of the Inter-Departmental Unit on the North of Ireland.

38 NAI, DFA 2002/19/384, July 20, 1971, Donal O'Sullivan, London, to Sean Ronan, DFA and TNA, PRO, FCO 33/1610, 122676, July 20, 1971, Steward Crawford, FCO, to Philip Woodfield, Home Office.

39 TNA, PRO, FCO 33/1601, 122676, July 21, 1917, John Peck, UK Embassy, Dublin, to FCO.

40 NAI, DFA 2003/17/304, July 23, 1971, Jack Lynch to Edward Heath.

41 TNA, PRO, CJ 4/56, 122658, July 27, 1971, Alec Douglas-Home to John Peck, "Personal for Ambassador: M.I.P.T. Security Situation in Northern Ireland."

42 TNA, PRO, CJ 4/56, 122658, July 28, 1971, John Peck, UK Embassy, Dublin, to FCO.

43 TNA, PRO, CJ 4/56, 122658, July 30, 1971, John Peck, UK Embassy, Dublin, to FCO.

44 TNA, PRO, CJ 4/56, 122658, July 31, 1971, John Peck, UK Embassy, Dublin, to FCO.

45 NACP, RG 59, 1970–73, POL 12 IRE, 2/3/70, Box 2383, July 21, 1971, US Embassy, Dublin, to Department of State.

46 Craig, *Crisis of Confidence*, 94–95.

47 Hennessey, *Evolution of the Troubles*, 112–17.

48 Hennessey, *Evolution of the Troubles*, 120–21.

49 Craig, *Crisis of Confidence*, 95–99.

50 Bell, *The Irish Troubles*, 215–17.

51 English, *Armed Struggle*, 139–41; cain.ulst.ac.uk, CAIN Web Service, A Chronology of the Conflict, 1971, August 10, 1971.

52 NAI, DFA 2003/17/304, August 9, 1971, "Text of Message from Mr. Heath to Mr. Lynch."

53 NAI, DT 2002/8/481, August 9, 1971, Statement issued by the Government Information Bureau on behalf of the Taoiseach."

54 Hennessey, *Evolution of the Troubles*, 139–41.

55 NAI, DT 2002/8/481, August 10, 1971, Statement issued by the Government Information Bureau on behalf of the Taoiseach.

56 TNA, PRO, FCO 33/1610, 122676, August 12, 1971, "Northern Ireland: Dr. Hillery's Discussion with the Home Secretary—Note of a Meeting at the Home Office on Wednesday 11 August."

57 TNA, PRO 33/1610, 122676, August 11, 1971, Alec Douglas-Home, FCO, to UK Embassy, Dublin.

58 TNA, PRO, FCO 33/1607, 122676, August 12, 1971, John Peck, UK Embassy, Dublin, to Stewart Crawford, FCO.

59 NAI, DT 2002/8/481, August 12, 1971, Statement issued by the Government Information Bureau on behalf of the Taoiseach.

60 TNA, PRO, FCO 33/1606, 122676, August 13, 1971, John Peck, UK Embassy, Dublin, to FCO.

61 TNA, PRO, FCO 33/1606, 122676, August 13, 1971, John Peck, UK Embassy, Dublin, to FCO.

62 McKittrick and McVea, *Making Sense of the Troubles*, 72.

63 Cain.ulst.as.uk, CAIN Web Service, PRONI Records on Cain, Public Records, CAB 4/1607, August 19, 1971, "Note of a Meeting Held at Chequers, Thursday, August 19, 1971."

64 NAI, DFA 2001/43/1436, August 19, 1971, Statement issued by the Government Information Bureau on behalf of Jack Lynch.

65 NAI, DFA 2001/43/1436, August 19, 1971, Text of message from Edward Heath to Jack Lynch.

66 TNA, PRO, FCO 33/1607, 122676, August 19, 1971, Alec Douglas-Home, FCO, to UK Embassy, Dublin.

67 TNA, PRO, FCO 33/1607, 122676, August 20, 1971, John Peck, UK Embassy, Dublin, to FCO.

68 NAI, DT 2002/8/481, August 20, 1971, Statement issued by the Government Information Bureau on behalf of the Taoiseach.

69 TNA, PRO, FCO 33/1607, 122676, August 20, 1971, Alec Douglas-Home, FCO, to UK Embassy, Dublin.

70 TNA, PRO, FCO 33/1607, 122676, August 22, 1971, John Peck, UK Embassy, Dublin, to FCO.

71 Craig, *Crisis of Confidence*, 99–100.

72 NACP, RG 59, 1970–73, POL 23–9 UK, 1/1/71, Box 2654, August 10, 1971, John Moore, US Embassy, Dublin, to Secretary of State.

73 NACP, RG 59, 1970–73, POL 23–9 UK, 1/1/71, Box 2654, August 13, 1971, Department of State to US Embassies, Dublin and London.

74 NACP, RG 59, 1970–73, POL 23–9 UK, 1/1/71, Box 2654, August 20, 1971, Department of State to US Embassy, Dublin.

75 NACP, RG 59, 1970–73, POL 23–8 UK, 7/9/71, Box 2654, August 27, 1971, Department of State Intelligence Note, Bureau of Intelligence and Research, "UK: What Next for Northern Ireland."

76 NACP, RG 59, 1970–73, POL 23–9 UK, 9/1/71, Box 2654, September 3, 1971, "Noon Briefing on Northern Ireland … September 2."

77 NAI, DT 2002/8/417, August 31, 1971, Statement issued by the Government Information Bureau on behalf of the Taoiseach and NAI, DFA, August 29, 1971, "Note" by Hugh McCann.

78 NAI, DT 2002/8/417, August 31, 1971, Statement issued by the Government Information Bureau on behalf of the Taoiseach.

79 NAI, DFA 2003/17/345, September 2, 1971, "Note" by Hugh McCann.

80 NAI, DT 2002/8/481, August 19, 1971, Donal O'Sullivan, Irish Embassy, London, to Sean Ronan, DFA.

81 TNA, PRO, FCO 33/1610, 122676, August 19, 1971, Stewart Crawford, FCO, to P.J. Woodfield, Home Office.

82 NAI, DT 2002/8/481, August 25, 1971, Donal O'Sullivan, UK Embassy, London, to Sean Ronan, DFA.

83 Hennessey, *Evolution of the Troubles*, 160–63.

Chapter 5

1 NAI, DFA 2003/17/393, August 29, 1971, "Secret Memo" by Hugh McCann.

2 NAI, DT 2002/8/481, August 29, 1971, "Desiderata in regard to Taoiseach's meeting with Mr. Heath."

3   NAI, DT 2002/8/487, August 31, 1971, "Note."

4   Walsh, *Patrick Hillery*, 272.

5   TNA, PRO, FCO 33/1612, 122676, September 2, 1971, "Republic of Ireland: Draft Brief for Mr. Lynch's Visit."

6   TNA, PRO, PREM 15/488, 122751, September 3, 1971, Burke Trend, cabinet secretary to Edward Heath.

7   NAI, DT 2003/16/503, date unknown, "Material for Meeting."

8   O'Donnell, *Fianna Fáil, Irish Republicanism and the Northern Ireland Troubles*, 39–40.

9   NAI, DFA 2003/13/6, September 9, 1971, "Report of the Discussions on 6 and 7 September 1917 at Chequers between the Taoiseach and the British Prime Minister."

10 NAI, DT 2002/8/487, September 7, 1971, "Transcript of Press Conference given by the Taoiseach ... after his meeting with the British Prime Minister ... on 6 and 7 September 1971."

11 TNA, PRO, FCO 33/1612, September 7, 1971, "Guidelines. Mr. Lynch's Visit."

12 TNA, PRO, FCO 33/1602, September 8, 1917, John Peck, UK Embassy, Dublin, to FCO.

13 NAI, DFA 2002/19/500, September 8, 1971, "Statement issued by the Government Information Bureau on behalf of the Taoiseach."

14 TNA, PRO, FCO 33/1602, September 11, 1971, John Peck, UK Embassy, Dublin, to FCO.

15 NAI, DFA 2002/19/500, September 11, 1971, "Statement issued by the Government Information Bureau on behalf of the Taoiseach."

16 TNA, PRO, FCO 33/1602, September 12, 1971, Edward Heath to Jack Lynch.

17 Hennessey, *Evolution of the Troubles*, 185–86.

18 NACP, RG 59, 1970–73, POL 23–8 UK, 7/9/71, Box 2654, September 21, 1971, Department of State: Research Study. "UK: Heath Seeks way out of Northern Ireland Dilemma."

19 NAI, DFA 2003/17/394, September 23, 1971, "Chequers II—Our possible proposals."

20 NAI, DT 2002/8/488, September 26, 1971, Government Information Bureau, "Statement by ... Lynch at Dublin Airport."

21 TNA, PRO, CJ 4/48, September 24, 1971, "Record of a Meeting held in the Cabinet Office, Whitehall, on Friday 24 September, at 10 am."

22 TNA, PRO, CJ 4/48, September 24, 1971, "Visit of the Prime Ministers of the Irish Republic and Northern Ireland ... Steering Brief ... prepared by the Cabinet Office in consultation with Departments."

23 Cain.ulst.ac.uk, CAIN Web Service, PRONI Records on CAIN, n.a. 1971, "Tripartite Talks (September 1971) Memorandum for Brian Faulkner, then

Northern Ireland Prime Minister ... at Chequers, 27–28 September 1971," [PRONI Public Records, CAB/9/R/238/8].

24 TNA, PRO, CJ 4/48, 122658, INIPMV (71) "Visit of the Prime Ministers of the Irish Republic and of Northern Ireland: Record of Meetings Held at Chequers, 26–28 September 1971," subsection "Record of Discussion with Faulkner, 26 September 1971."

25 TNA, PRO, CJ 4/48, 122658, INIPMV (71) "Visit of the Prime Ministers of the Irish Republic and of Northern Ireland: Record of Meetings Held at Chequers, 26–28 September 1971," subsection "Record of a Discussion with the Prime Minister of the Irish Republic held at Chequers on Monday 27 September 1971."

26 TNA, PRO, CJ 4/48, 122658, INIPMV (71) "Visit of the Prime Ministers of the Irish Republic and of Northern Ireland: Record of Meetings Held at Chequers, 26–28 September 1971," subsection "Record of a Discussion with the Prime Ministers of the Irish Republic and Northern Ireland held at Chequers on Monday 27 September 1971 at 12 noon."

27 TNA, PRO, CJ 4/48, 122658, INIPMV (71) "Visit of the Prime Ministers of the Irish Republic and of Northern Ireland: Record of Meetings Held at Chequers, 26–28 September, 1971," subsection "Record of a Discussion with the Prime Ministers of the Irish Republic and Northern Ireland held at Chequers on Monday September 27, 1971 at 3:15 pm."

28 TNA, PRO, CJ 4/48, 122658, INIPMV (71) "Visit of the Prime Ministers of the Irish Republic and of Northern Ireland: Record of Meetings Held at Chequers, 26–28 September 1971," subsection "Record of a Discussion with the Prime Minister of the Irish Republic held at Chequers on Tuesday 28 September 1971 at 11:15 am."

29 TNA, PRO, CJ 4/48, 122658, INIPMV (71) "Visit of the Prime Ministers of the Irish Republic and of Northern Ireland: Record of Meetings Held at Chequers, 26–28 September 1971," subsection "Record of a Discussion with the Prime Ministers of the Irish Republic and Northern Ireland held at Chequers on Tuesday 28 September 1971 at 3 pm.," and NAI, DFA 2003/17/304, September 28, 1971, "Tripartite Talks on Northern Ireland: Chequers, 27 and 28 September 1971: Agreed Statement."

30 NAI, DFA 2003/17/336, September 28, 1971, "Transcript of Press Conference given by the Taoiseach."

31 TNA, FCO 33/1602, September 28, 1971, Alec Douglas-Home to "certain posts."

32 Hennessey, *Evolution of the Troubles*, 180, 185.

33 Walsh, *Patrick Hillery*, 272–73.

34 Kelly, *Fianna Fáil, Partition, and Northern Ireland*, 349.

35 Craig, *Crisis of Confidence*, 100–02.

36 Craig, *Crisis of Confidence*, 102–03.

37 Edward Heath, *The Course of My Life: The Autobiography of Edward Heath* (London, 1998), 430–31.

38 Peter Neumann, *Britain's Long War: British Strategy in Northern Ireland, 1969–1998* (New York, 2003), 63–64 .

39 TNA, PRO, FCO 33/1607, 122676, September 30, 1971, John Peck, UK Embassy, Dublin, to FCO.

40 TNA, FCO 33/1607, 122676, October 23, 1971, John Peck, UK Embassy, Dublin, to Denis Greenhill, FCO.

41 TNA, PRO, FCO 33/1607, 122676, October 1971 [exact date uncertain], "Memorandum on the situation in Ireland," by Ambassador John Peck.

42 Craig, *Crisis of Confidence*, 93–94.

43 Hennessy, *Evolution of the Troubles*, 197–98.

44 TNA, PRO, FCO 33/1607, 122676, October 7, 1971, Edward Heath to Jack Lynch.

45 Heath statement on October 6, 1971 quoted in Niall O Dochartaigh "Bloody Sunday: Error or Design," *Contemporary British History* (Volume 24, pp. 89–108, 2010), 96.

46 NAI, DFA 2003/17/304, October 9, 1971, "Message from the Taoiseach to the British Prime Minister."

47 NAI, DT 2002/8/205, October 12, 1971, Edward Heath to Jack Lynch.

48 TNA, PRO, FCO 33/1607, 122676, October 11, 1971, Stewart Crawford to Private Secretary, "Reply to Mr. Lynch's message to the Prime Minister."

49 NAI, DT 2002/8/483, October 7, 1971, "Statement by Dr. Patrick J. Hillery ... during the General Debate at the Twenty-sixth Session of the General Assembly of the United Nations."

50 NAI, DT 2002/8/205, September 28, 1971, Senator Trevor West to Jack Lynch.

51 Bell, *The Irish Troubles*, 254.

52 NACP, RG 59, 1970–73, POL 23–9 UK, 9/1/71, Box 2654, October 21, 1971, US Embassy, London to Secretary of State, "UK protests Senator Kennedy's Statement on Northern Ireland."

53 TNA, PRO, FCO 33/1475, December 28, 1971, Anthony Elliott, UK Embassy, Washington, to James Cable, Head of Planning Staff, FCO.

54 www.oireachtas.ie/parliament, Parliamentary Debates, Dáil Éireann, Volume 256, No. 1, October 20, 1971 "Adjournment Debate: Northern Ireland Situation."

55 www.oireachtas.ie/parliament, Parliamentary Debates, Dáil Éireann, Volume 256, No. 2, October 21, 1971, "Adjournment Debate: Northern Ireland Situation."

56 NAI, DT 2002/8/494, October 19, 1971, Hugh McCann, DFA, to John Peck.

57 NAI, DT 2002/8/493, October 20, 1971, John Peck, UK Embassy, Dublin, to Hugh McCann, DFA.

58 NAI, DT 2002/8/494, October 30, 1971, "Amnesty International: A Report on Allegations of Ill-treatment made by Persons Arrested under the Special Powers Act after 8 August 1971."

59 NACP, RG 59, 1970–73, POL 29 UK, Box 2656, November 9, 1971, John Moore, US Embassy, Dublin, to Secretary of State, "Subject: Deep Concern over Torture/Brutality Issue."

60 NACP, RG 59, 1970–73, POL 29 UK, Box 2656, November 5, 1971, John Moore, US Embassy, Dublin, to Secretary of State, "Subject: Brutality to Prisoners in Northern Ireland."

61 NAI, DT 2002/8/494, November 22, 1971, Hugh McCann, DFA, to the Department of the Taoiseach.

62 Cain.ulst.ac.uk, CAIN Web Service, Government Reports and Acts, "Report of the enquiry into allegations against the Security Forces of physical brutality in Northern Ireland arising out of the events of 9 August 1971."

63 NAI, DT 2002/8/495, November 18, 1971, Hugh McCann, DFA to Patrick Hillery, "Confidential."

64 TNA, PRO, CJ 4/198, 122658, November 25, 1971, Alec Douglas-Home, FCO, to "Certain Missions."

65 NAI, DFA 2003/17/304, November 29, 1971, Edward Heath to Jack Lynch.

66 NACP, RG 59, 1970–73, POL 23–9 UK, Box 2656, December 1, 1971, US Embassy, Dublin, to Secretary of State.

67 NAI, DT 2003/16/475, December 21, 1971, "Council of Europe: Press Communique—Ireland against the United Kingdom."

68 NACP, RG 59, 1970–73, POL 17 IRE, 4/19/73, Box 2383, December 2, 1971, US Embassy, Dublin, to Secretary of State, "Subject: Confrontation with British."

69 www.parliament.uk, Hansard, Commons Debates, HC DEB, November 25, 1971, Vol. 826, cc 1571–678.

70 www.parliament.uk, Hansard, Commons Debates, HC DEB, November 29, 1971, Vol. 827, cc 32–183.

71 NAI, DT 2002/8/484, December 6, 1971, "Address by the Taoiseach … at the Luncheon given by the Parliamentary Press Gallery Group, House of Commons … London."

72 NAI, DFA 2003/17/304, December 7, 1971, "Note of the Discussion between the Taoiseach and Mr. Heath on 6 December 1971," and TNA, PRO, PREM 15/486, 122751, December 6, 1917, "Note for the Record," Meeting of Jack Lynch and Donal O'Sullivan with Edward Heath.

73 TNA, PRO, FCO 87/7, 122751, January 10, 1972, John Peck, UK Embassy, Dublin, to Alec Douglas-Home, FCO, "Republic of Ireland: Annual Review for 1971."

74 NAI, DFA 2003/13/26, January 17, 1972, "Northern Ireland—the present situation."

75 Alvin Jackson, *Ireland, 1798–1998: Politics and War* (Malden, MA, 1999), 459.

76 TNA, PRO, FCO 49/340, 122719, December 23, 1971, James Cable, Head of the Planning Staff, FCO, to Michael Palliser, UK Delegation, EEC, Brussels.

77 TNA, PRO, PREM 15/1028, 122749, January 18, 1972, P.L. Gregson, 10 Downing Street, to J.A.N. Graham, FCO.

78 TNA, PRO, PREM 15/1710, January 23, 1972, "Note for the Record" Lynch and Heath meeting at Brussels.

79 NAI, DFA 2002/19/370, January 23, 1972, "Report in the Irish Times of 24 January 1972 on the press conference given by the Taoiseach in Brussels on 23 January 1972."

80 Cain.ulst.ac.uk, CAIN Web Service, Malcolm Sutton Chronological Lists of Deaths, 1971.

Chapter 6

1 Peter Pringle and Philip Jacobson, *Those are Real Bullets: Bloody Sunday, Derry, 1972* (New York, 2000) 1; English, *The Armed Struggle*, 148–49; Hennessy, *Evolution of the Troubles*, 270–71.

2 http://nationalarchives.gov.uk/20101103103930/http:/www.bloody-sunday-inquiry. org, Volume 1, Chapter 5, The Overall Assessment.

3 Niall Ó Dochartaigh, "Bloody Sunday, Error or Design?" *Contemporary British History* (Vol. 24, No. 1, pp. 89–108, March 2010) 91–92.

4 Ó Dochartaigh, "Bloody Sunday," 99–101.

5 Ó Dochartaigh, "Bloody Sunday," 105.

6 For example see Craig, *Crisis of Confidence*, 107–08; English, *Armed Struggle*, 150–51, 153–54; Hennessey *Evolution of the Troubles*, 313, 347–49.

7 NAI, DT 2003/16/503, 31 January 1972, "Derry Atrocity: Taoiseach's Special Broadcast."

8 NAI, DFA 2002/19/370, February 1, 1972, "Text of statement made in Dáil Éireann by the Taoiseach ... following the fatal shooting of thirteen civilians in Derry on January 31, 1972."

9 www.oireachtas.ie/parliament, Parliamentary Debates, Dáil Éireann, Volume 258, Number 6, February 1, 1972, "Statements on Northern Ireland Situation."

10 www.parliament.uk, Hansard, Commons Debates, HC Deb January 31, 1972, Volume 830, cc 32–43, "Northern Ireland."

11 www.parliament.uk, Hansard, Commons Debates, HC Deb February 1, 1972, Volume 830, cc 240–49, "Northern Ireland (Tribunal of Inquiry)."

12 www.parliament.uk, Hansard, Commons Debates, HC Deb February 1, 1972, Volume 830, cc 264–331, "Northern Ireland."

13 NAI, DT 2003/16/462, February 1, 1972, C.V. Whelan, Irish Embassy, London, to Hugh McCann, Department of Foreign Affairs, Dublin.

14 Hennessey, *Evolution of the Troubles*, 314; Keogh, *Jack Lynch*, 331–32; Craig, *Crisis of Confidence*, 109.

15 TNA, PRO, CJ 3/102, 122700, February 2, 1972, "Record of a Meeting between the Minister of State for Foreign and Commonwealth Affairs and the Irish Charge d'affaires."

16 TNA, PRO, CAB 128/50 (part 1) CM (72) 5th Conclusions, February 3, 1972.

17 TNA, PRO, FCO 87/26, 122751, February 3, 1972, John Peck, UK Embassy, Dublin, to FCO.

18 John Peck, *Dublin from Downing Street* (Dublin, 1978),12 .

19 Cain Website, New Years Releases 2003—Public Records of 1972, CAB 128/48, February 3, 1972, "Cabinet Minutes, Confidential Annex."

20 www.oireachtas.ie/parliament, Parliamentary Debates, Dáil Éireann, Volume 258, Number 7, February 3, 1972, "Committee on Finance—Adjournment Motion: Northern Ireland Situation."

21 Craig, *Crisis of Confidence*, 109–10.

22 TNA, PRO, CJ 3/102, 122700, February 2, 1972, "Record of a Meeting between the Minister of State for Foreign and Commonwealth Affairs and the Irish Charge d'affaires."

23 INA, DT 2003/16/462, February 3, 1972, Hugh McCann, DFA, to H.J. O'Dowd, Private Secretary to the Taoiseach, Department of the Taoiseach.

24 TNA, PRO, FCO 87/26, 122751, February 3, 1972, John Peck, UK Embassy, Dublin, to FCO.

25 www.oireachtas.ie/parliament, Parliamentary Debates, Dáil Éireann, Volume 258, Number 7, February 3, 1972, "Committee on Finance—Adjournment Motion: Northern Ireland Situation."

26 Alan F. Parkinson, *1972 and the Ulster Troubles: A Very Bad Year* (Dublin, 2010) 51.

27 TNA, PRO, FCO 87/100, 122700, February 2, 1972, UK Mission to UN to FCO, "Dr. Hillery's Press Conference."

28 NAI, DFA 2002/19/370, February 2, 1972, "Excerpts from transcript of interview given by Dr. P.J. Hillery ... on the Today Show on NBC-TV in New York."

29 NACP, RG 59, 1970–73, POL 7 IRE, 10/6/71, Box 2383, February 2, 1972, US Embassy, Dublin, to Secretary of State.

30 NACP, RG 59, 1970–73, POL 32 IRE, Box 2384, February 3, 1972, US Embassy, Dublin, to Secretary of State, "Ireland Crisis."

31 NACP, RG 59, 1970–73, POL IRE-US, 10/8/70, Box 2384, February 3, 1972, US Embassy, Dublin, to Secretary of State, "Hillery's call on Secretary Rodgers."

32 NACP, RG 59, 1970–73, POL 23–9 UK, 2/1/72, Box 2655, February 2, 1972, Walter Annenberg, US Embassy, London, to Secretary of State.

33 TNA, PRO, FCO 87/116, 122751, February 2, 1972, Alec Douglas-Home, FCO, to Washington and Ottawa Missions.

34 TNA, PRO, FCO 87/101, 122700, February 3, 1972, Lord Cromer, UK Embassy, Washington, to FCO; Bell, *The Irish Troubles*, 278.

35 NACP, RG 59, 1970–73, POL 23–9 UK, 2/1/72, Box 2655, February 3, 1972, Department of State to US Embassy, Dublin, "Hillery Call on Secretary."

36 NACP, RG 59, 1970–73, POL 23–9 UK, 2/1/72, Box 2655, February 3, 1972, Department of State to US Embassies, Dublin and London, William Rogers' Press Briefing.

37 TNA, PRO, FCO 87/116, 122751, February 3, 1972, Steward Crawford to Mr. White, "Dr. Hillery's Visit to Washington."

38 Walsh, *Patrick Hillery*, 278–80

39 Walsh, *Patrick Hillery*, 282–83.

40 NACP, RG 59, 1970–73, POL 23–9 UK, 2/1/72, Box 2655, February 5, 1972, US Embassy, Dublin, to Secretary of State, "Ireland Crisis: GOI Looking Beyond Friends."

41 A.J. Wilson, *Irish America and the Ulster Conflict* (Belfast, 1995), 57–59.

42 TNA, PRO, FCO 87/102, 122700, February 16, 1972, Donald Tebbitt, UK Embassy, Washington, to G. Reddaway, FCO.

43 TNA, PRO, FCO 87/102, 122700, March 2, 1972, HTA Overton, North American Department, FCO, to Mr. Hankey and Stewart Crawford, FCO, "Northern Ireland: US Attitude."

44 NACP, RG 59, 1970–73, POL 23–9 UK, 9/1/71, Box 2654, November 22, 1971, Memorandum of a Conversation.

45 Wilson, *Irish American and the Ulster Conflict*, 64–65; Joseph Thompson, *American Policy and Northern Ireland: A Saga of Peacebuilding* (Westport, CT, 2001), 36–38.

46 NACP, RG 59, 1970–73, POL 1 UK-US, Box 2658, March 6, 1972, "Public Information Series ... Statement on the situation in Northern Ireland, February 29, 1972 ... Hillenbrand to ... House Committee on Foreign Affairs."

47 TNA, PRO, FCO 87/102, 122700, March 2, 1972, HTA Overton, North American Department, FCO, to Mr. Hankey and Sir Stewart Crawford, FCO, "Northern Ireland: US Attitude."

48 TNA, PRO, FCO 87/102, 122700, March 3, 1972, Lord Cromer, UK Embassy, Washington, to FCO, "Northern Ireland: Senator Kennedy and Mr. Lynch."

49 NACP, RG 59, 1970–73, POL 7 10/6/71, IRE, Box 2383, March 6, 1972, US Embassy, Dublin, to Secretary of State.

50 www.oireachtas.ie/parliament, Parliamentary Debates, Dáil Éireann, Volume 259, No 7, March 7, 1972, "Ceisteanna—Questions. Oral Answers. Northern Ireland Situation."

51 NACP, RG 59 1970–73, POL 7 IRE Box 2383, March 8, 1972, John Moore, US Embassy, Dublin, to Secretary of State.

52 NACP, RG 59, 1970–73, POL 7 IRE, 10/6/71, Box 2383, March 9, 1972, Department of State to US Embassy, Dublin.

53 Keogh, *Jack Lynch*, 338.

54 TNA, PRO, CJ 3/102, 122700, February 15, 1972, Kenneth Whitaker to David James, MP, House of Commons, London, "Strictly Personal."

55 TNA, PRO, CJ 3/102, 122700, March 14, 1972, Kenneth Whitaker, Central Bank of Ireland, Dublin, to Sir Leslie O'Brien, Governor, Bank of England.

56 Bell, *The Irish Troubles*, 291–92.

57 Keogh, *Jack Lynch*, 334.

58 Cain.ulst.ac.uk, CAIN Web Service, Malcolm Sutton: An Index of Deaths for the Conflict in Ireland.

59 TNA, PRO, CJ 4/280, December 1971, no exact date, "Secret Perimeter—UK Eyes Only: The Probable Effects of Direct Rule in Northern Ireland."

60 Hennessey, *Evolution of the Troubles*, 323–26.

61 Hennessey, *Evolution of the Troubles*, 326–29.

62 Cain.ulst.ac.uk, CAIN Web Service, New Year Releases 2003, Public Records of 1972, PREM 15/1004, March 13, 1972, Sir Alec Douglas Home to Edward Heath.

63 Hennessey, *Evolution of the Troubles*, 329–30.

64 Hennessey, *Evolution of the Troubles*, 331–37, and cain.ulst.ac.uk, CAIN Web Service, PRONI Records, "Main Points made by Mr. Heath at Downing Street Meeting on March 22, 1972, about the Northern Ireland situation" (March 22, 1972), Public Records CAB/4/1647, and cain.ulst.ac.uk, CAIN Web Service, PRONI Records, "Later Statement by Mr. Heath in the Course of the Discussion in which he defined the United Kingdom Government's ideas" (March 22, 1972), Public Records CAB/4/1647.

65 www.parliament.uk, Hansard, Commons Debates, HC Deb March 24, 1972, Volume 833, cc 1859–74, "Northern Ireland."

66 TNA, PRO, FCO 87/71, 122700, March 24, 1972, FCO to UK Embassy, Dublin, "Text of Message from the Prime Minister to Mr. Lynch."

67 TNA, PRO, FCO 87/71, March 24, 1972, John Peck, UK Embassy, Dublin, to FCO.

68 TNA, PRO, FCO 87/71, March 24, 1972, John Peck, UK Embassy, Dublin, to FCO, "Statement issued ... by the Taoiseach."

69 TNA, PRO, FCO 87/71, March 25, 1972, John Peck, UK Embassy, Dublin, to FCO.

70 TNA, PRO, FCO 87/71, March 25, 1972, John Peck, UK Embassy, Dublin, to FCO, "Direct Rule: Irish Reactions."

71 TNA, PRO, FCO 87/71, March 29, 1972, "Message Received from ... Jack Lynch ... for Edward Heath."

72 NACP, RG 59, 1970–73, POL 23–9 UK, 3/1/72, Box 2655, March 24, 1972, Department of State: Intelligence Note.

73 NACP, RG 59, 1970–73, POL 23–9 UK, 3/1/72, Box 2655, March 25, 1972, Department of State: Press Guidance on Northern Ireland.

74 NACP, RG 59, 1970–73, POL 23–9 UK, 1/1/72, Box 2654, March 29, 1972, Richard Nixon to Edward Heath.

75 TNA, PRO, FCO 87/71, April 24, 1972, FCO to UK Embassy, Dublin, Message from Heath to Lynch.

76 INA, DFA, 2003/13/16, April 28, 1972, "Meeting between the Minister for Foreign Affairs and Sir Alec Douglas-Home, Secretary of State for Foreign and Commonwealth Affairs on 27/4/72."

77 Keogh, *Jack Lynch*, 335–37.

78 Craig, *Crisis of Confidence*, 114.

Conclusion

1 Ronan Fanning, "The Anglo-American Alliance and the Irish Question in the Twentieth Century" in Judith Develin and Howard B. Clarke (eds.) *European Encounters: Essays in Memory of Albert Lovett* (Dublin, 2003), 205–10.

2 McKittrick and McVea, *Making Sense of the Troubles*, 81–82.

3 McKittrick and McVea, *Making Sense of the Troubles*, 91, 95–96, 98–106.

4 McKittrick and McVea, *Making Sense of the Troubles*, 163–66.

5 McKittrick and McVea, *Making Sense of the Troubles*, 219–20.

Bibliography

Books and articles

Arthur, Paul, *Special Relationships: Britain, Ireland and the Northern Ireland Problem* (Belfast, Blackstaff Press, 2000).

Bell, J. Bowyer, *The Irish Troubles: A Generation of Violence, 1967–1992* (New York, St. Martin's Press, 1993).

Bell, J. Bowyer *The IRA 1968–2000: Analysis of a Secret Army* (New York, Frank Cass, 2000).

Bew, Paul, *Ireland: The Politics of Enmity, 1789–2006* (New York, Oxford University Press, 2006).

Cochrane, Feargal, *Northern Ireland: The Reluctant Peace* (New Haven, CT, Yale University Press, 2013).

Coogan, Tim Pat, *The IRA: A History* (Niwot, CO, Roberts Rinehart Publishers, 1994).

Coogan, Tim Pat, *The Troubles: Ireland's Ordeal and the Search for Peace* (New York, Palgrave, 1996).

Craig, Anthony, *Crisis of Confidence: Anglo-Irish Relations in the Early Troubles, 1966–1974* (Dublin, Irish Academic Press, 2010)

English, Richard, *Armed Struggle: The History of the IRA* (New York, Oxford University Press, 2003).

Fanning, Ronan, "Playing It Cool: The Response of the British and Irish Governments to the Crisis in Northern Ireland, 1968–9," *Irish Studies in International Affairs* (Volume 12, pp. 57–85, 2001).

Farren, Sean, *The SDLP: The Struggle for Agreement in Northern Ireland, 1970–2000* (Dublin, Four Courts Press, 2010).

Hamill, Desmond, *Pig in the Middle: The Army in Northern Ireland, 1969–1984* (London, Methuen, 1985).

Hennessey, Thomas, *A History of Northern Ireland, 1920–1996* (Dublin, Gill & Macmillan, 1997).

Hennessey, Thomas, *The Evolution of the Troubles, 1970–72* (Dublin, Irish Academic Press, 2007).

Jackson, Alvin, *Ireland, 1798–1998: Politics and War* (Malden, MA, Blackwell Publishing, 1999).

Kelly, Stephen, *Fianna Fail, Partition and Northern Ireland, 1926–1971* (Dublin, Irish Academic Press, 2013).

Kennedy, Michael, *Division and Consensus: The Politics of Cross Border Relations, 1925–69* (Dublin, Institute of Public Administration, 2000).

Kennedy, Michael, "'This Tragic and Most Intractable Problem': The Reaction of the Department of External Affairs to the Outbreak of the Troubles in Northern Ireland," *Irish Studies in International Affairs* (Volume 12, pp. 87–95, 2001).

Keogh, Dermont, *Jack Lynch: A Biography* (Dublin, Gill & Macmillan, 2008).

Moloney, Ed, *A Secret History of the IRA* (London, Allen Lane, 2002).

McKittrick, David and McVea, David, *Making Sense of the Troubles: The Story of the Conflict in Northern Ireland* (Chicago, New Amsterdam Books, 2002).

Mulholland, Marc, *The Longest War: Northern Ireland's Troubled History* (New York, Oxford University Press, 2002).

Neumann, Peter R., *Britain's Long War: British Strategy in Northern Ireland, 1969–1998* (Basingstoke, Palgrave Macmillan, 2003).

O'Brian, Justin, *The Arms Trial* (Dublin, Gill & Macmillan, 2000).

Ó Dochartaigh, Niall, *From Civil Rights to Armalites: Derry and the Birth of the Irish Troubles* (Cork, Cork University Press, 1997).

Ó Dochartaigh, Niall, "Bloody Sunday: Error or Design?," *Contemporary British History* (Volume 24, Number 1, pp. 89–108, 2010).

O'Donnell, Catherine, *Fianna Fail, Irish Republicanism and the Northern Ireland Troubles, 1968–2005* (Dublin, Irish Academic Press, 2007).

O'Duffy, Brendan, *British-Irish Relations and Northern Ireland: From Violent Politics to Conflict Regulation* (Dublin, Irish Academic Press, 2007).

O'Halpin, Eunan, *Defending Ireland: The Irish State and Its Enemies since 1922* (New York, Oxford University Press, 1999).

O'Kane, Eamonn, "The Republic of Ireland's Policy toward Northern Ireland: The International Dimension as Policy Tool," *Irish Studies in International Affairs* (Volume 13, pp. 121–33, 2002).

Parkinson, Alan F., *1972 and the Ulster Troubles: A Very Bad Year* (Dublin, Four Courts Press, 2010).

Patterson, Henry, *Ireland's Violent Frontier: The Border and Anglo-Irish Relations during the Troubles* (London, Palgrave Macmillan, 2013).

Patterson, Henry, *Ireland since 1939: The Persistence of Conflict* (New York, Penguin Books, 2006).

Prince, Simon, *Northern Ireland's' 68: Civil Rights, Global Revolts and the Origins of the Troubles* (Dublin, Irish Academic Press, 2007).

Pringle, Peter and Jacobson, Philip, *Those Are Real Bullets: Bloody Sunday, Derry, 1972* (New York, Grove Press, 2000).

Rose, Peter, *How the Troubles Came to Northern Ireland* (New York, Palgrave, 2001).

Smith, Jeremy, "'Walking a Real Tight-Rope of Difficulties': Edward Heath and the Search for Stability in Northern Ireland, June 1970–March 1971," *Twentieth-Century British History* (Volume 18, Number 2, pp. 219–53, 2007).

Thompson, Joseph, *American Policy and Northern Ireland: A Saga of Peacebuilding* (Westport, CT, Praeger, 2001).

Walsh, John, *Patrick Hillery: The Official Biography* (Dublin, New Island, 2008).

Warner, Geoffrey, "The Falls Road Curfew Revisited," *Irish Studies Review* (Volume 14, Number 3, pp. 325–42, 2006).

Wilson, A.J., *Irish America and the Ulster Conflict* (Belfast, Blackstaff Press, 1995).

Memoirs

Callaghan, James, *Time and Chance* (London, Collins, 1987).

Faulkner, Pádraig, *As I Saw It: Reviewing over 30 Years of Fianna Fáil and Irish Politics* (Dublin, Wolfhound Press/Merlin, 2005).

Heath, Edward, *The Course of My Life: The Autobiography of Edward Heath* (London, Hodder & Stoughton, 1998).

Peck, John, *Dublin From Downing Street* (Dublin, Gill & Macmillan, 1978).

Whitelaw, William, *The Whitelaw Memoirs* (London, Aurum, 1989).

Online sources

CAIN (Conflict Archive on the Internet) Web Service—Conflict and Politics in Northern Ireland, cain.ulst.ac.uk

Houses of the Oireachtas, Parliamentary Debates, Dáil Éireann, www.oireachtas. ie/parliament

United Kingdom Parliament, Hansard, Commons Debates, www.parliament.uk

Foreign Relations of the Unites States Series, history.state.gov

The National Archives, UK, webarchive.nationalarchives.gov.uk

Archival sources

National Archives of Ireland, Dublin—Department of the Taoiseach, Department of External Affairs, Department of Foreign Affairs, Papers of Jack Lynch.

The National Archives, Kew—Foreign and Commonwealth Office, Office of the Prime Minister, Cabinet Minutes.

National Archives, College Park Maryland—State Department Records.

Index